MAPPING THE GREAT IRISH FAMINE

MAPPING THE GREAT IRISH FAMINE

A Survey of the Famine Decades

LÍAM KENNEDY, PAUL S. ELL,
E.M. CRAWFORD & L.A. CLARKSON

FOUR COURTS PRESS

Set in 10.5 on 13.5 Bembo by
Carrigboy Typesetting Services for
FOUR COURTS PRESS LTD
Fumbally Court, Fumbally Lane, Dublin 8, Ireland
e-mail: info@four-courts-press.ie
website: www.four-courts-press.ie
and in North America for
FOUR COURTS PRESS
c/o ISBS, 5804 N.E. Hassalo Street, Portland, OR 97213.

A catalogue record for this title is available from the British Library.

ISBN 1–85182–353–0 hbk
ISBN 1–85182–357–3 pbk

Printed in Great Britain by
MPG Books Ltd, Bodmin, Cornwall.

David S. Johnson

1943–1998

In Memoriam

Gone.
From Bristol,
Oxford.
Leaving this, your home.

Bluff, firm, fair,
Earthy-wise,
'times sensitive and kind.
Rest well.

Dermot Feenan
16 June 1998

CONTENTS

LIST OF FIGURES, MAPS, TABLES & ILLUSTRATIONS   9

PREFACE   13

INTRODUCTION   15
  Famine 1845–1849: the great discontinuity?   15
  Counties, baronies and poor law unions   18

THE UNPEOPLING OF IRELAND   25
  Lost generations: population and the Great Famine   26
  Emptying the land   30
  Death and the Great Famine   36
  Shrinking Ireland: emigrants and exiles   40

SEX, MARRIAGE AND FAMILIES   43
  Adam and Aoife: gazing at gender ratios   44
  Before the altar: age at marriage for women and men   50
  Celibacy in Irish society: men without women, women without men   54
  Households and families   60

THE CONDITION OF THE PEOPLE   65
  The economy of the potato eaters   66
  The food of the people   68
  Cabin and castle: housing the people   76
  Catholics and Protestants   88
  The literate and the 'ignorant'   94
  An béal bocht: the decline of the Gaelic language   102
  The burden of disease   104
  The plight of the poor   125

TOIL IN COUNTRY AND TOWN   141
  Wages before the Famine   142
  Work in field, workshop and factory, 1841–71   144
  Gardens and farms: agricultural holdings, 1841–71   162
  Cultivating the soil   176
  Taking stock: herds, flocks, pigs and poultry   193

CONCLUSION   207

LIST OF CONTRIBUTORS   212

INDEX   213

LIST OF FIGURES, MAPS, TABLES
& ILLUSTRATIONS

FIGURES

1 Population change, 1687–1971 — 26

2 Population increase (in 000s) in towns containing at least 5,000 persons in either 1841 or 1871 — 27

3 Number and percentage of the population living in towns of 5,000 or
more and in the countryside in 1841 and 1871 — 27

4 Population per 100 acres, 1841 and 1871 — 30

5 Famine mortality, 1846–51 — 38

6 Gender ratios (males per 100 females) in 1841 and 1871 — 45

7 Male celibacy in 1841 and 1871 — 54

8 Female celibacy in 1841 and 1871 — 55

9 Potato and oat prices, Belfast market, 1841–61 — 66

10 Potato yields before, during and after the Famine — 67

11 The 'potato' wage, 1840–50 — 67

12 Oatmeal consumption, c.1836 — 71

13 Bread consumption, c.1836 — 72

14 Butter consumption, c.1836 — 72

15 Milk consumption, c.1836 — 73

16 Fish consumption, c.1836 — 75

17 Percentage of fourth-class housing related to the average, annual wage income
of rural labourers in each county in 1841 — 77

18 Percentage of fourth-class housing in 1841 and 1861 — 79

19 Percentage of illiterate males related to the proportion of male Gaelic speakers, 1851 — 95

20 Percentage of illiterate females related to the proportion of female Gaelic speakers, 1851 — 96

21 Percentage of females and males who were illiterate in 1841 and 1871 — 97

22 Deaths from selected diseases in Ireland, 1844–51 — 105

23 Deaths from starvation diseases, 1845–51 — 107

24 Average death rates from dropsy, 1847–9 — 109

25 Average death rates from marasmus, 1847–9 — 109

26 Deaths from infections in Ireland, 1844–51 — 113

27 Deaths from dysentery and diarrhoea in Ireland, 1843–50 — 120

28 Deaths from smallpox, 1835–50 — 122

29 Numbers of people receiving outdoor relief, 1848 — 137

30 Total occupied male population (adjusted figures) — 146

31 Total occupied female population (adjusted figures) — 147

32 Male urban occupations, Belfast, Cork, Dublin, Limerick, Waterford — 149

33 Female urban occupations, Belfast, Cork, Dublin, Limerick, Waterford — 149

34 Acreage under various crops, 1847–71 — 176

35 Percentage of cultivated land under various crops, 1847–71 — 177

36 Acreage under various grains, 1847–71 — 177

37 Acreage under flax, 1847–71 — 178

38 Livestock numbers in Ireland, 1847–71 — 194

39 County cattle numbers, arranged according to the ranking in 1841 — 194

40 County sheep numbers, arranged according to the ranking in 1841 — 195

41 County pig numbers, arranged according to the ranking in 1841 — 195

9

42 County poultry numbers, arranged according to the ranking in 1841   196
43 County cattle numbers per 100 acres, arranged according to the ranking in 1841   196
44 County sheep numbers per 100 acres, arranged according to the ranking in 1841   197
45 County pig numbers per 100 acres, arranged according to the ranking in 1841   197
46 County poultry numbers per 100 acres, arranged according to the ranking in 1841   198

MAPS

1   Index to counties   19
2   Index to poor law unions   21
3   Index to baronies, cities and towns   23
4   Towns with populations of 5,000 or more in 1841 and 1871   28
5   Percentage population decline at barony level   29
6   Population density: number of people per 100 acres at county level   32
7   Population density: number of people per 100 acres at poor law union level   33
8   Population related to adjusted land area at county level   34
9   Population of poor law unions related to poor law valuations for 1851   35
10 Average annual excess death rates, 1846–51   37
11 Excess mortality 1846–50 as a % of population at county level   39
12 Emigration after the Famine at county level   41
13 Gender ratios at county level   46
14 Gender ratios at poor law union level   47
15 Gender ratios for ages below 17 years at county level   48
16 Gender ratios for ages above 55 years at county level   49
17 Mean age at marriage for women at county level   52
18 Mean age at marriage for men at county level   53
19 Male non-marriage in Irish society at county level   58
20 Female non-marriage in Irish society at county level   59
21 Change in mean houseful size at barony level   61
22 Mean houseful size at county level   62
23 Mean houseful size at barony level   63
24 Potato consumption at county level, c.1836   70
25 Oatmeal consumption at county level, c.1836   71
26 Milk consumption at county level, c.1836   73
27 (a) Eggs and (b) bacon consumption at county level, c.1836   74
28 Fish consumption at county level, c.1836   75
29 Percentage first-class houses at county level   80
30 Percentage second-class houses at county level   81
31 Percentage third-class houses at county level   82
32 Percentage fourth-class houses at county level   83
33 Percentage first-class houses at barony level   84
34 Percentage second-class houses at barony level   85
35 Percentage third-class houses at barony level   86
36 Percentage fourth-class houses at barony level   87
37 Geography of religion in 1861 at county level   91
38 Geography of religion in 1861 at barony level (a and b)   92 & 93
39 Percentage of illiterate females at county level   98
40 Percentage of illiterate males at county level   99
41 Percentage of illiterate females at barony level   100
42 Percentage of illiterate males at barony level   101
43 Percentage of females who could speak Irish at county level   103
44 Death rates in 1847 at county level   108

45 Death rates from measles at county level (a) 1847 and (b) 1849 — 114
46 Death rates from scarlatina at county level, 1850 — 115
47 Death rates from consumption at county level, 1849 — 116
48 Death rates from fever at county level, 1847 — 117
49 Death rates from diarrhoeal diseases at county level, 1847 — 119
50 Death rates from smallpox at county level, 1849 — 121
51 Death rates from cholera at county level, 1849 — 123
52 Workhouse relief during year ending 29 September 1847 at poor law level (130 unions) — 127
53 Workhouse relief during year ending 29 September 1849 at poor law level (131 unions) — 127
54 Workhouse inmate mortality rates for week ending 3 April 1847 at poor law level (130 unions) — 129
55 Seed distribution of Society of Friends at county level — 130
56 Money granted by Society of Friends at county level — 131
57 Food relief granted by Society of Friends at county level — 131
58 Employment on public works for week ending 8 August 1846 at county level — 132
59 Employment on public works for week ending 13 March 1847 at county level — 133
60 Number of daily rations dispensed in each poor law union by Relief Committees as a % of the population on 3 July 1847 — 135
61 Persons receiving outdoor relief per 1,000 of the population in the week ending 1 July 1848 at poor law union level — 138
62 Income of a male labourer in 1835 at county level — 143
63 Percentage of occupied males engaged in agriculture at county level — 150
64 Percentage of occupied females engaged in agriculture at county level — 151
65 Percentage of occupied males engaged in dealing at county level — 152
66 Percentage of occupied females engaged in dealing at county level — 153
67 Percentage of occupied males engaged in domestic service at county level — 154
68 Percentage of occupied females engaged in domestic service at county level — 155
69 Percentage of occupied males engaged in manufacturing at county level — 156
70 Percentage of occupied females engaged in manufacturing at county level — 157
71 Percentage of occupied males engaged in professional services at county level — 158
72 Percentage of occupied females engaged in professional services at county level — 159
73 Occupational distribution of males in five towns and cities — 160
74 Occupational distribution of females in five towns and cities — 161
75 Number of holdings not exceeding 1 acre at county level, 1847 — 164
76 Number of holdings above 1 acre and not exceeding 5 acres at county level, 1847 — 165
77 Number of holdings not exceeding 1 acre at county level — 166
78 Number of holdings above 1 and not exceeding 15 acres at county level — 167
79 Number of holdings above 15 and not exceeding 50 acres at county level — 168
80 Number of holdings above 50 and not exceeding 200 acres at county level — 169
81 Number of holdings above 200 acres at county level — 170
82 Number of holdings not exceeding 1 acre at poor law union level — 171
83 Number of holdings above 1 and not exceeding 15 acres at poor law union level — 172
84 Number of holdings above 15 and not exceeding 50 acres at poor law union level — 173
85 Number of holdings above 50 and not exceeding 200 acres at poor law union level — 174
86 Number of holdings above 200 acres at poor law union level — 175
87 Wheat as a % of total acreage under cultivation at county level — 179
88 Oats as a % of total acreage under cultivation of county level — 180
89 Flax as a % of total acreage under cultivation at county level — 181
90 Barley, bere and rye as a % of total acreage under cultivation at county level — 182
91 Meadow as a % of total acreage under cultivation at county level — 183
92 Potatoes as a % of total acreage under cultivation at county level — 184
93 Other root, green crops, peas and beans as a % of total acreage under cultivation at county level — 185
94 Wheat as a % of total acreage under cultivation at poor law union level — 186

95 Oats as a % of total acreage under cultivation at poor law union level — 187

96 Flax as a % of total acreage under cultivation at poor law union level — 188

97 Barley, bere and rye as a % of total acreage under cultivation at poor law union level — 189

98 Meadow as a % of total acreage under cultivation at poor law union level — 190

99 Potatoes as a % of total acreage under cultivation at poor law union level — 191

100 Other root, green crops, peas and beans as a % of total acreage under cultivation at poor law union level — 192

101 Cattle population per 100 acres at county level — 199

102 Sheep population per 100 acres at county level — 200

103 Pig population per 100 acres at county level — 201

104 Cattle population per 100 acres at poor law union level — 202

105 Sheep population per 100 acres at poor law union level — 203

106 Pig population at per 100 acres poor law union level — 204

TABLES

1 Average county density of population, 1841–71 — 30

2 The population of poor law unions related to poor law valuations — 31

3 Marriage rates in various European countries, 1871 — 57

4 Percentage decline in population, inhabited houses and houseful size — 60

5 National share of adherents of various denominations 1834, 1861 and 1871 — 90

6 Number of so-called ophthalmia cases treated in Irish workhouses — 111

7 Statistics of blindness in Irish workhouses, 1849–51 — 112

8 Cases and deaths from cholera in major towns, 1849 — 124

9 Total numbers relieved in the workhouses, 1844–53 — 125

10 Deaths recorded from main killer diseases in workhouses, 1845–50 — 128

11 Total occupied male population of Ireland from the censuses — 145

12 Total occupied female population of Ireland from the censuses — 145

13 Total occupied male population of Ireland (adjusted figures) — 146

14 Total occupied female population of Ireland (adjusted figures) — 146

15 Number of persons holding land, 1845 — 162

16 Number and sizes of holdings in 1847 and 1851 — 163

17 Number and sizes of holdings in 1852, 1861 and 1871 — 163

18 The components of agricultural output — 193

ILLUSTRATIONS

1 'A Terrible Record' — 24

2 'The House of Pat Brennan' — 42

3 The Cork Society of Friends' Soup House — 64

4 'General view of the potato plant, its root, leaves, tubers, and apples (fruit)' — 68

5 A diseased potato stem — 69

6 'Boy and Girl at Cahera' — 139

7 'The Village of Tullig' — 205

PREFACE

For several years the Department of Economic and Social History in Queen's University, Belfast has been in the process of creating a Database of Irish Historical Statistics covering the years 1821 to 1971. This now contains most of the main longitudinal data drawn from the population censuses and similar sources, together with a certain amount of cross-sectional information. Other material is being added as resources allow.

The database was the brain-child of Líam Kennedy and Max Goldstrom. They persuaded the Economic and Social Research Council of the UK to finance the project with two grants, one in 1990 and the second in 1993. In addition, the Queen's University has supported the project generously. The authors are grateful to the ESRC and the University for their support.

Throughout its life the database has benefited from the devoted service of Margaret Crawford who was appointed as Research Officer in 1990 and who designed the first stage of the project covering the period 1821 to 1911. She also acted as consultant for the second stage that carried the database from 1911 to 1971. Martin Dowling joined the enterprise in 1993 as Research Officer to create the second stage and at the same time Paul Ell brought to the project his cartographic and computing skills. Elaine Yeates joined the team initially to input data, but quickly became an expert custodian and manager of the database. Anne Rodgers acted as part-time secretary for three years. Ann McVeigh investigated the possibilities of optical character recognition and, as a result, OCR largely replaced inputting data via the keyboard. A peripatetic army of students and others attended to a myriad of mundane tasks. Finally we have received unstinting help from the University Computer Centre in solving hardware and software problems. The full database, one of the largest of its kind, has been deposited in the ESRC Archive at the University of Essex.

It was always the intention of its creators that the database should be a platform for further scholarship relating to Irish economic and social history. Since much of its earlier contents cover the Famine and post-Famine decades, and because of the crucial importance of the Great Famine in Irish history, it seemed sensible to start there. The result is the present volume. Its purpose is to survey the impact of the Great Famine in the short and medium terms, by means of maps, graphs and text. The lengths of the periods investigated are dictated by the data: some are available for four or five decades; others only for a year or two. A second purpose is to present a picture of the regional effects of the Famine. Sometimes the focus is on the county; sometimes on the barony; at other times on the poor law union. We have suggested explanations where possible, although in a volume of this kind explanations of events at a regional level are necessarily tentative. But we hope that local historians will add their own expert knowledge to the patterns.

A database, like a library, contains the raw material for historians. This material has to be adapted – for example, numbers of deaths may have to be converted into death rates – and, in the present case, processed for mapping and graphing. In the production of this study the authors are indebted, once more, to Elaine Yeates. She has helped to extract statistical data required by the authors and generated the maps and graphs. We are grateful, too, to Janette Lee, lecturer in Geographical Information Systems, for her assistance with digitising map boundaries and imparting training to others. P. Ferguson, of the Trinity College Dublin Map Library, assisted in the compilation of a Poor Law Union map. Irene Boada and Lucia Pozzi helped to write the sections on gender ratios and marital behaviour. Frank Geary helped to untangle the occupational statistics. We have also received assistance from Ken Bartley and Humphry Southall.

Líam Kennedy, Margaret Crawford and Leslie Clarkson have written the bulk of the text. Paul Ell is responsible for the cartographic work and has written the section on religion. The volume is dedicated to Dave Johnson, colleague, friend, and head of department who died before the project was ready for the publishers.

INTRODUCTION
FAMINE 1845–1849: THE GREAT DISCONTINUITY?

The histories of all countries have their dramatic turning points. For Britain it is the industrial revolution (an English political historian might argue for the Glorious Revolution of 1688 or even, in the spirit of Sellars and Yeatman, 1066; and a Scotsman for 1707). In France, 1789 has pride of place; for America it is the revolution of 1776; for Russia, the revolution of 1917. But what is the great climacteric for Ireland? Is it 1169, or 1541, or 1801, or 1916, or 1922? Or is the hinge of Irish history 1845, the year that heralded the dreadful climax of what Cecil Woodham-Smith once described as 'the doom of Ireland'?[1] Few historians are prepared to employ the language of the literary critic, Terry Eagleton, who described the Famine as 'the most important episode of modern Irish history and the greatest social disaster of nineteenth-century Europe – an event with something of the characteristic of a low-level nuclear attack'.[2] Few, nevertheless, would dissent from the sentiment.

Although there is general agreement about the importance of the Famine in Irish historiography, there is less unanimity about the vulnerability of Irish society to famine. George O'Brien, writing in 1918, had no doubts: '... the country lived in a chronic state approaching famine, and ... the particular years which are mentioned by historians as famine years were simply the years in which the chronic symptoms became acute.'[3] Woodham-Smith's 'doom of Ireland' imagery is also laden with the burden of ineluctable disaster.

O'Brien has been the most influential exponent of Ireland as a land haunted by hunger. He was following an interpretation established in 1851 by William Wilde who prefaced the census of that year, of which he was principal author, with a monumental table chronicling famine, pestilence, frosts, flood and drought throughout Ireland's history. Wilde concluded, under the heading 'The Last General Potato Failure and the Great Famine and Pestilence of 1845–50', 'we now approach the eventful epoch, towards the consideration of which all the foregoing extracts form but the introduction.'[4]

There is, nevertheless, an alternative view. In 1950, K.H. Connell explicitly denied O'Brien's interpretation, writing that, 'it is remarkable, but apparently true, that during eighty years of increasing dependence on the potato, even the rumblings of disaster were seldom heard.'[5] (Connell's use of the word 'remarkable' hints that he had some doubts about departing from the thesis of impending disaster.) More recently, Professor Ó Gráda has suggested that Ireland was 'desperately unlucky in the mid-nineteenth century'. Too many people lived on potatoes at a time when the plant was struck by a hitherto unknown fungal infection. The Great Famine was utterly unpredictable.[6] The same interpretation is to be found in Peter Solar's essay, 'The Great Famine was no ordinary subsistence crisis'.[7]

There is common consent that the Famine adversely affected all social classes in Ireland, a

1 Cecil Woodham-Smith, *The great hunger: Ireland 1845–1849* (London, 1962), p. 32. **2** Terry Eagleton, *Heathcliff and the great hunger: studies in Irish culture* (London, 1995), p. 33. **3** George O'Brien, *The economic history of Ireland in the eighteenth century* (Dublin and London, 1918), p. 102. **4** [William Wilde], 'Table of Cosmical Phenomena, Epizootics, Epidemics, Famines, and Pestilences, in Ireland', *The census of Ireland for the year 1851*, part

V. *Tables of deaths*, vol. 1, BPP, 1856, xxix, pp. 41–235. See also E. Margaret Crawford, 'William Wilde's table of Irish famines 1900–1850', in E. Margaret Crawford (ed.), *Famine: the Irish experience 900–1900* (Edinburgh, 1989), pp. 1–30. **5** K.H. Connell, *The population of Ireland 1750–1845* (Oxford, 1950), p. 146. **6** Cormac Ó Gráda, *The Great Irish Famine* (London, 1989), p. 76. **7** In Crawford (ed.), *Famine: the Irish experience*, pp. 112–33.

feature that distinguishes it from many famines elsewhere. Among the landed elite, a minority of landlords was pushed over the edge into bankruptcy. The urban and rural middle classes were burdened by higher local taxation and, in some cases, fell victim to famine-related diseases. Industrial workers engaged in handicraft production faced a contraction of demand for their products. But it was the bottom third of society that was disproportionately ravaged by hunger, diseases and death. The impact of the Famine varied also by region, to an extent that is still insufficiently appreciated. Ulster, according to popular belief, escaped the worst ravages of hunger. There are signs, though, among the plethora of publications marking the one-hundred-and-fiftieth anniversary of the Great Famine, that some of the province's historians wish to claim for it a share of the country's suffering; and it is clear that parts of Ulster were badly afflicted. A similar claim might be made for the Irish capital, Dublin, which sometimes seems to fall outside the pale of national history.[8]

The impact of the Great Famine on long-term economic development is a matter for debate. Was it a watershed that set the economy flowing in a different direction? Or was it, as Raymond Crotty argued three decades ago, a catalyst speeding up changes already in train?[9] Maybe some synthesis of the two is in order? Mary Daly's observation must be borne in mind: 'The Famine cannot be seen in isolation from the changes taking place in Ireland and in western Europe in the preceding and succeeding decades.'[10] The present volume throws some light on these issues, and broadens the terms of the debate beyond the economic. The maps trace regional patterns and change. Where possible they have been drawn down to the smallest practicable unit: the 320 or so baronies, the ancient divisions of the counties, or the 163 poor law unions created in the wake of the act of 1838. The diagrams encompass, broadly, the years 1841–71; the precise periods being dictated by the data available.

It is a moot point whether the population would have turned down had the Great Famine never happened. After all, as some of the subsequent sections show, the demographic mechanisms that regulate the pace and direction of population change were already working to slow down population growth before the Famine. In the east of Ireland the age at first marriage – never unusually low by west European standards – was already shifting upwards and so was the incidence of celibacy. A smaller proportion of females therefore was moving into the child-breeding population, with an inevitable decline in general fertility. Emigration, likewise, was gathering momentum before 1845. The position on mortality is more obscure, but we can at least conjecture that the combined effects of industrialisation and urbanisation might push up death rates, at least in the short run. However, it is stretching the case to its limits to argue that these mechanisms would have tilted the population into decline rather than merely to retard its growth. This fundamental problem is discussed more fully in the conclusion.

The social impact of the Great Famine was immediate: the population fell by approximately 20% between 1841 and 1851. Poor cottiers and labourers endured most of the losses; as they disappeared so did their hovels and their garden plots. Since so many cottiers were Gaelic speakers, the use of Irish as a common channel of communication declined sharply also. There were implications for religious observance and, with a time lag, for nationalist politics as well. The economic consequences were equally complex. The Irish countryside before the Famine was overstocked with labour. This is not to say that population densities were excessively high by European standards, for they were not. But, relative to the requirements for production – the demand for labour emanated primarily from the agricultural sector – there was an abundant supply of labour. This was reflected in low earnings, high levels of under-employment and poor housing. The Great Famine reaped a grim harvest of men, women and children, changing radically conditions in the labour market, altering the scale and composition of demand for commodities and services, and affecting production patterns in the long run. Perversely for such a disruptive force, it helped draw isolated local communities into a national mainstream, though the distinctiveness of east Ulster always needs to be borne in mind.

8 Mary Daly, *Dublin, the deposed capital: a social and economic history, 1860–1914* (Cork, 1985); Cormac Ó Gráda, *Black '47 and beyond: the Great Irish Famine in history, economy and memory* (Princeton, N.J., 1999), pp. 157–93. 9 Raymond D. Crotty, *Irish agricultural production: its volumes, and structure* (Cork, 1966), pp. 46–51. 10 Mary Daly, *The Famine in Ireland* (Dublin, 1986), p. 124.

The Famine was a unique historical event. It was singular in its immediate cause: a failure of the principal food of one-third of the population, brought on by a hitherto unknown disease in the Ireland of the mid-1840s. The intellectual moment in time was one when ideas of *laissez-faire* economics and providentialism were in the ascendant, a malign combination that would have less force in later years. To exacerbate matters, the political entity within which the crisis unravelled – the United Kingdom – was not a political unity. The Great Famine was a tragedy played out against a backcloth of generations of suspicion and mistrust. Through its legacy, and through the medium of the Irish diaspora, the Famine reinforced, perpetuated and internationalised the problem of Anglo-Irish relations.

COUNTIES, BARONIES AND POOR LAW UNIONS

Over the centuries Ireland has been subdivided into a number of administrative units. The principal public boundaries used for civil purposes were those of townlands, parishes, baronies, counties and provinces. In the nineteenth century other networks of administrative units were added, called poor law unions and electoral divisions. In this atlas three units appear: counties, baronies and poor law unions.

Counties have proved the most enduring administrative unit in Ireland. The shiring commenced in the late twelfth century as part of the Anglo-Norman colonization. During the sixteenth century it was extended to form Westmeath, King's County (Offaly) and Queen's County (Laois), Galway, Leitrim, Mayo, Roscommon, Sligo, Clare, Antrim, Down and Longford. Early in the seventeenth century the shiring of Ulster was completed with the formation of Donegal, Tyrone, Armagh, Fermanagh, Monaghan, Cavan and Coleraine. Wicklow was the last county to be shired in 1606. The mosaic was now virtually complete; the only major modification was the demise of county Coleraine to be replaced by county Londonderry in 1613. County Londonderry was created from an amalgamation of county Coleraine along with the town and north-eastern Liberties of Coleraine, the barony of Loughinsholin from county Tyrone, and the town and north-western liberties of Derry. In all the country was divided into 32 counties, 12 in the province of Leinster, 6 in Munster, 9 in Ulster and 5 in Connacht.

Baronies are of great antiquity, and when constituted into public civic divisions by the English, they were frequently called after towns, villages or castles. By the time of the first completed official census in 1821 the principal county and barony boundaries were established, although there were minor changes during the course of the century. In 1841 the number of baronies was 313. They were sub-units of counties and were used by the census commissioners as administrative units until 1891.

When the Poor Law was introduced into Ireland by the Act 1 & 2 Vict. cap. 56 the Commissioners found the existing boundaries of parishes and counties inconvenient because of their unequal size, and so new divisions were formed to be known as poor law unions, which were further sub-divided into electoral divisions. Initially the country was divided into 130 unions, but shortly after the scheme was introduced it became evident that more unions were required and so in 1848 another one was added, to be followed by 32 more in 1850, making a total of 163.

For the purposes of the maps in this atlas the barony boundaries are shown as they appeared in 1841, and later data have been adjusted to fit within these boundaries. The poor law union maps are based on 163 unions as recorded in the 1851 census, except where indicated. To all intent, county boundaries remained constant throughout this period.

PROVINCE OF LEINSTER	PROVINCE OF MUNSTER	PROVINCE OF ULSTER	PROVINCE OF CONNACHT
Carlow	Clare	Antrim	Galway
Dublin	Cork	Armagh	Leitrim
Kildare	Kerry	Cavan	Mayo
Kilkenny	Limerick	Donegal	Roscommon
King's County (Offaly)	Tipperary	Down	Sligo
Longford	Waterford	Fermanagh	
Louth		Londonderry	
Meath		Monaghan	
Queen's County (Laois)		Tyrone	
Westmeath			
Wexford			
Wicklow			

Map 1: Index to counties

Antrim	1	Dublin	9	Limerick	17	Roscommon	25
Armagh	2	Fermanagh	10	Londonderry	18	Sligo	26
Carlow	3	Galway	11	Longford	19	Tipperary	27
Cavan	4	Kerry	12	Louth	20	Tyrone	28
Clare	5	Kildare	13	Mayo	21	Waterford	29
Cork	6	Kilkenny	14	Meath	22	Westmeath	30
Donegal	7	Laois	15	Monaghan	23	Wexford	31
Down	8	Leitrim	16	Offaly	24	Wicklow	32

Key to Poor Law Unions created between 1838 and 1850

Abbeyleix	1	Cavan	41	Gortin	82	Navan	123
Antrim	2	Celbridge	42	Granard	83	Nenagh	124
Ardee	3	Claremorris★	43	Inishowen	84	Newcastle	125
Armagh	4	Clifden	44	Kanturk	85	Newport★	126
Athlone	5	Clogheen	45	Kells	86	New Ross	127
Athy	6	Clogher	46	Kenmare	87	Newry	128
Bailieborough	7	Clonakilty★	47	Kilkeel	88	Newtownards	129
Ballina	8	Clones	48	Kilkenny	89	Newtownlimavdy	130
Ballinasloe	9	Clonmel	49	Killadysert★	90	Oldcastle	131
Ballinrobe	10	Coleraine	50	Killala★	91	Omagh	132
Ballycastle	11	Cookstown	51	Killarney	92	Oughterard★	133
Ballymahon★	12	Cootehill	52	Kilmacthomas★	93	Parsonstown	134
Ballymena	13	Cork	53	Kilmallock	94	Portumna★	135
Ballymoney	14	Corrofin★	54	Kilrush	95	Rathdown	136
Ballyshannon	15	Croom★	55	Kinsale	96	Rathdrum	137
Ballyvaghan★	16	Dingle†	56	Larne	97	Rathkeale	138
Balrothery	17	Donaghmore★	57	Letterkenny	98	Roscommon	139
Baltinglass	18	Donegal	58	Limerick	99	Roscrea	140
Banbridge	19	Downpatrick	59	Lisburn	100	Scarriff	141
Bandon	20	Drogheda	60	Lismore	101	Shillelagh	142
Bantry	21	Dromore West★	61	Lisnaskea	102	Skibbereen	143
Bawnboy★	22	Dublin North	62	Listowel	103	Skull★	144
Belfast	23	Dublin South	63	Londonderry	104	Sligo	145
Belmullet★	24	Dundalk	64	Longford	105	Strabane	146
Borrisokane★	25	Dunfanaghy	65	Loughrea	106	Stranorlar	147
Boyle	26	Dungannon	66	Lowtherstown	107	Strokestown★	148
Caherciveen	27	Dungarvan	67	Lurgan	108	Swineford	149
Callan	28	Dunmanway	68	Macroom	109	Thomastown★	150
Carlow	29	Dunshaughlin	69	Magherafelt	110	Thurles	151
Carrick on Shannon	30	Edenderry	70	Mallow	111	Tipperary	152
Carrick on Suir	31	Ennis	71	Manorhamilton	112	Tobercurry★	153
Carrickmacross	32	Enniscorthy	72	Middleton	113	Tralee	154
Cashel	33	Enniskillen	73	Milford	114	Trim	155
Castlebar	34	Ennistimon	74	Millstreet★	115	Tuam	156
Castleblayney	35	Fermoy	75	Mitchelstown★	116	Tulla★	157
Castlecomer★	36	Galway	76	Mohill	117	Tullamore	158
Castlederg	37	Glennamaddy★	77	Monaghan	118	Urlingford★	159
Castlereagh	38	Glenties	78	Mountbellew★	119	Waterford	160
Castletown★	39	Glin★	79	Mountmellick	120	Westport	161
Castletowndevlin★	40	Gorey	80	Mullingar	121	Wexford	162
		Gort	81	Naas	122	Youghal★	163

† created in 1848

★ created in 1850

Map 2: Index to poor law unions

Key to Baronies Cities and Towns, 1841

Aran 1
Athenry 2
Ballymoe
    (Co. Galway) 3
Ballynahinch 4
Clare 5
Clonmacnowen 6
Dunkellin 7
Dunmore 8
Galway 9
Kilconnell 10
Killian 11
Kiltartan 12
Leitrim
    (Co. Galway) 13
Longford
    (Co. Galway).... 14
Loughrea 15
Moycullen 16
Ross 17
Tiaquin 18
Galway Town 19
Carrigallen 20
Drumahaire 21
Leitrim
    (Co. Letrim) 22
Mohill 23
Rosclogher 24
Burrishoole 25
Carra 26
Clanmorris 27
Costello 28
Erris 29
Gallen 30
Kilmaine 31
Murrisk 32
Tirawley 33
Athlone (Co.
    Roscommon) ... 34
Ballintober North .. 35
Ballintober South .. 36
Ballymoe (Co.
    Roscommon) ... 37
Boyle 38
Castlereagh (Co.
    Roscommon) ... 39
Frenchpark 40
Moycarn 41
Roscommon 42
Carbury (Co. Sligo).. 43
Coolavin 44
Corran 45
Leyny 46
Tireragh 47
Tirerrill 48
Carlow 49
Forth (Co. Carlow) .. 50
Idrone East 51
Idrone West 52
Rathvilly 53
St Mullin's Lower .. 54
St Mullin's Upper .. 55
Balrothery East 56
Balrothery West ... 57
Castleknock 58
Coolock 59
Dublin 60
Nethercross 61
Newcastle
    (Co. Dublin) 62
Rathdown
    (Co. Dublin) 63

Uppercross 64
Dublin City 65
Carbury
    (Co. Kildare) 66
Clane 67
Connell 68
Ikeathy &
    Oughterany 69
Kilcullen 70
Kilkea & Moone .. 71
Naas North 72
Naas South 73
Narragh & Reban
    East 74
Narragh & Reban
    West 75
Offaly East 76
Offaly West 77
Salt North 78
Salt South 79
Callan 80
Crannagh 81
Fassadinin 82
Galmoy 83
Gowran 84
Ida 85
Iverk 86
Kells 87
Knocktopher 88
Shillelogher 89
Kilkenny City 90
Ballyboy 91
Ballybritt 92
Ballycowan 93
Clonlisk 94
Coolestown 95
Eglish 96
Garrycastle 97
Geashill 98
Kilcoursey 99
Philipstown Lower .. 100
Philipstown Upper.. 101
Warrenstown 102
Ardagh 103
Granard 104
Longford (Co.
    Longford) 105
Moydow 106
Rathcline 107
Strule 108
Ardee 109
Drogheda 110
Dundalk Lower .. 111
Dundalk Upper .. 112
Ferrard 113
Louth 114
Deece Lower 115
Deece Upper 116
Duleek Lower 117
Duleek Upper ... 118
Dunboyne 119
Fore (Co. Meath) .. 120
Kells Lower 121
Kells Upper 122
Lune 123
Morgallion 124
Moyfenrath Lower.. 125
Moyfenrath Upper.. 126
Navan Lower 127
Navan Upper 128
Ratoath 129
Skreen 130

Slane Lower 131
Slane Upper 132
Ballyadams 133
Clandonagh 134
Clarmallagh 135
Cullenagh 136
Maryborough East.. 137
Maryborough West.. 138
Portnahinch 139
Slievemargy 140
Stradbally 141
Tinnahinch 142
Upperwoods 143
Brawny 144
Clonlonan 145
Corkaree 146
Delvin 147
Farbill 148
Fartullagh 149
Fore (Co.
    Westmeath) 150
Kilkenny West 151
Moyashel &
    Magheradernon.. 152
Moycashel 153

Moygoish 154
Rathconrath 155
Ballaghkeen 156
Bantry (Co.
    Wexford) 157
Bargy 158
Forth (Co.
    Wexford) 159
Gorey 160
Scarawalsh 161
Shelburne 162
Shelmaliere East .. 163
Shelmaliere West .. 164
Arklow 165
Ballinacor North .. 166
Ballinacor South .. 167
Newcastle (Co.
    Wicklow) 168
Rathdown (Co.
    Wicklow) 169
Shillelagh 170
Talbotstown Lower.. 171
Talbotstown Upper.. 172
Bunratty Lower ... 173
Bunratty Upper .. 174
Burren 175
Clonderalaw 176
Corcomroe 177
Ibrickan 178
Inchquin 179
Islands 180
Moyarta 181
Tulla Lower 182
Tulla Upper 183
Bantry (Co. Cork).. 184
Barretts 185
Barrymore 186
Bear 187
Carbery East (East
    Division) 188
Carbery East (West
    Division) 189
Carbery West
    (East Division) .. 190
Carbery West (West
    Division) 191

Condons &
    Clangibbon ... 192
Cork 193
Courceys 194
Duhallow 195
Fermoy 196
Ibane & Barryroe.. 197
Imokilly 198
Kerrycurrihy 199
Kinalea 200
Kinalmeaky 201
Kinnatalloon 202
Kinsale 203
Muskerry East ... 204
Muskerry West ... 205
Orrery & Kilmore.. 206
Cork City 207
Clanmaurice 208
Corkaguiny 209
Dunkerron 210
Glenarought 211
Iraghticonnor 212
Iveragh 213
Magunihy 214
Trughanacmy 215
Clanwilliam (Co.
    Limerick) 216
Connello Lower.. 217
Connello Upper .. 218
Coonagh 219
Coshlea 220
Coshma 221
Glenquin 222
Kenry 223
Kilmallock
    Liberties 224
Owenybeg 225
Pubblebrien 226
Shanid 227
Smallcounty 228
Limerick City 229
Clanwilliam
    (Co. Tipperary).. 230
Eliogarty 231
Iffa & Offa East ... 232
Iffa & Offa West.. 233
Ikerrin 234
Kilnamanagh
    Lower 235
Kilnamanagh
    Upper 236
Middlethird (Co.
    Tipperary) 237
Ormond Lower ... 238
Ormond Upper .. 239
Owney & Arra ... 240
Slievardagh 241
Coshmore &
    Coshbride 242
Decies within
    Drum 243
Decies without
    Drum 244
Gaultiere 245
Glenahiry 246
Middlethird (Co.
    Waterford) 247
Upperthird 248
Waterford City ... 249
Antrim Lower 250
Antrim Upper ... 251
Belfast Lower 252

Belfast Upper 253
Cary 254
Dunluce Lower ... 255
Dunluce Upper ... 256
Glenarm Lower ... 257
Glenarm Upper... 258
Kilconway 259
Massereene Lower.. 260
Massereene Upper.. 261
Toome Lower 262
Toome Upper 263
Belfast (Town) ... 264
Carrickfergus
    Town 265
Armagh 266
Fews Lower 267
Fews Upper 268
Oneilland East ... 269
Oneilland West ... 270
Orion Lower 271
Orion Upper 272
Tiranny 273
Castlerahan 274
Clankee 275
Clanmahon 276
Loughtee Lower .. 277
Loughtee Upper .. 278
Tullygarvey 279
Tullyhaw 280
Tullyhunco 281
Banagh 282
Boylagh 283
Inishowen 284
Kilmacrenan 285
Raphoe 286
Tirhugh 287
Ards 288
Castlereagh Lower.. 289
Castlereagh Upper. 290
Dufferin 291
Iveagh Lower ... 292
Iveagh Upper ... 293
Kinelarty 294
Lecale 295
Lordship of
    Newry 296
Mourne 297
Clanawley 298
Clankelly 299
Coole 300
Knockninny 301
Lurg 302
Magheraboy 303
Magherastephana.. 304
Tirkennedy 305
Coleraine 306
Keenaght 307
Loughinsholin ... 308
NE Liberties of
    Coleraine 309
NW Liberties of
    L'derry 310
Tirkeeran 311
Cremorne 312
Dartree 313
Farney 314
Monaghan 315
Trough 316
Clogher 317
Dungannon 318
Omagh 319
Strabane 320

Map 3: Index to baronies, cities and towns

23

'A Terrible Record'

SOURCE: *Weekly Freeman*, 1881

THE UNPEOPLING OF IRELAND

The world may have witnessed worse famines than that which afflicted Ireland between 1845 and 1849. But the deaths of one million or more people through starvation or starvation-related diseases and the loss of another million as a result of emigration were blows of traumatic intensity. They reversed a century of rapid population growth and ushered in a century of chronic decline. The Great Famine robbed Ireland of many tens of thousands of her men, women and children, sending them to early deaths or scattering them around the world.

The loss of so many people and so much talent set up reverberations that echo still through Irish historiography. Such consequences cannot be captured in maps and diagrams. But what these can do is to indicate the widespread and enduring nature of the emptying of Ireland. The immediate falls in population were caused principally by excess mortality, which was higher in the west and south of the country than in the east and north. In the long run the loss of population was mainly the consequence of emigration. As with famine mortality, emigration rates were higher in the west than the east. Some part, too, was played by a reduction in the general fertility rate, the consequence of delayed marriage or no marriage at all.

Few parts of Ireland were unaffected by these changes. Substantial growth of population occurred only in and close to the eastern cities of Belfast and Dublin. Some of the smaller towns lost population more slowly than the surrounding countryside. The result was that, at the same time as Ireland was becoming an emptier land, it was also becoming a more urbanised society.

LOST GENERATIONS: POPULATION AND THE GREAT FAMINE

In the century before the Great Famine the population of Ireland grew faster than anywhere else in western Europe. Growth was particularly vigorous before 1820. It was already slowing down in the 1820s and 1830s as delayed marriage in the eastern part of the country lowered fertility and as emigration carried some of the natural increase to other parts of the United Kingdom and across the Atlantic Ocean. What the trend of population might have been in the absence of the disaster of the 1840s is a matter for speculation. But it a matter of fact that between 1841 and 1851 the population of Ireland declined by almost 20%. Between 1851 and 1861 the population fell by a further 11.5%; and in the decade 1861–71 by 6.7%. In all, Ireland lost one-third of its population in three decades; and the decline persisted until well into the twentieth century. Figure 1 illustrates the long-term trends in population change from the end of the seventeenth century. The totals before 1821 are estimates; those from 1821 onwards are based on census figures.

The maps (pp. 28–9) show the changes in population between 1841 and 1871 both at urban and barony levels. The fall in population during the 1840s, 1850s and 1860s was remarkably widespread. Between 1841 and 1851 only county Dublin gained population, principally because of the growth of the city. Even county Antrim, notwithstanding the pulling power of Belfast, lost people, albeit only 9,000 or 10,000. A wide swathe of counties lost more than 20% of their populations and a few – Longford, Laois, Cavan, Monaghan, Galway, Leitrim, Mayo, Roscommon, Sligo – lost close to 30%. Over the longer period of 1841–1871 county Antrim, including Belfast, as well as county Dublin, gained population, but all other counties lost at least 5% of their people and most lost 20% or more.

The barony maps reinforce the picture of widespread loss. Between 1841 and 1871 308 out of 320 baronies shed population. Sixty baronies suffered falls of at least 50% and only nine lost fewer than 5% of their inhabitants. Nevertheless, the inter-quartile range of the reductions was quite narrow (17.5%). This bunching around the median is reflected also in the low standard deviation (13.3). The smallest falls were normally experienced in baronies close to large cities. The largest losses, by contrast, were scattered widely throughout Ireland, although only one fall exceeding 50% (the barony of Coole in county Fermanagh) occurred in the province of Ulster.

If we examine population changes decade by decade, the picture does not alter dramatically. Between 1841 and 1851 population declined in 298 baronies. The average fall among the losers was 23%, although five baronies suffered losses in excess of 40%. Over the longer period 1841–61, the mean decline among the 308 baronies that shed population was 33.6%. This was offset in a small measure by 12 baronies that increased population, on average by 42%.

Figure 1: Population change, 1687–1971

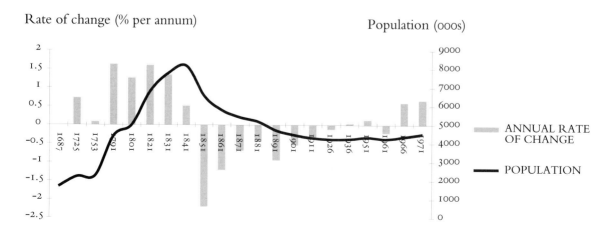

26

Figure 2: Population increase (in 000s) in towns containing at least 5,000 persons in either 1841 or 1871

Population change (000s)

[bar chart with vertical axis labeled 120, 100, 80, 60, 40, 20, 0 and horizontal axis labels: BELFAST, PEMBROKE, RATHMINES & RATHGAR, DUBLIN, DERRY, DUN LAOGHAIRE, BLACKROCK, LURGAN, PORTADOWN, NEW KILMAINHAM, COBH, BANBRIDGE, BRAY, ARKLOW, BALLYMENA, LISBURN, NEWRY, NEWTOWNARDS, ATHLONE, FERMOY, WEXFORD]

With one exception, the baronies gaining population were those covering the cities and their suburbs and the industrialising towns of Ulster. The exception was Offaly East in county Kildare containing the Curragh, where the growth of population was owing entirely to the soldiers and their dependants in the army camp. The two baronies encompassing Belfast – one on either side of the river Lagan – collectively increased their populations by 99,000 between 1841 and 1871. Baronies embracing Dublin, its suburbs and its dormitory towns, experienced gains ranging from 3,000 to 21,000. The population of Derry increased by almost a quarter and other Ulster towns gaining population included Ballymena, Lisburn, Lurgan, Portadown, Banbridge, Newry and Newtownards (see Figure 2). One or two 'old' cities such as Kilkenny and Limerick lost substantial chunks of their populations – Kilkenny 6,000 (33%) and

Limerick 9,000 (19%). Between 1841 and 1871 the numbers of people living in towns of 5,000 or more rose from 848,000 to 975,000.

In summary, the most dramatic decline in population occurred during the decade of the Great Famine. A few places *began* their declines before 1841 and a few lost population only after 1851. One or two baronies that appear to have suffered extreme declines in population were victims of boundary changes, but over the country at large the widespread and consistent losses were a reflection of the collapse of the rural economy that had rested on a potato culture. As Ireland lost over 2.7 million of her people between 1841 and 1871, so the proportion of the surviving population living in towns increased. The 21 towns that gained population (see Figure 2) were mostly on the eastern side of Ireland. In 1841 they contained 10.4% of the population. In 1871 they accounted for 18%.

Figure 3: Number and percentage of the population living in towns of 5,000 or more and in the countryside in 1841 and 1871

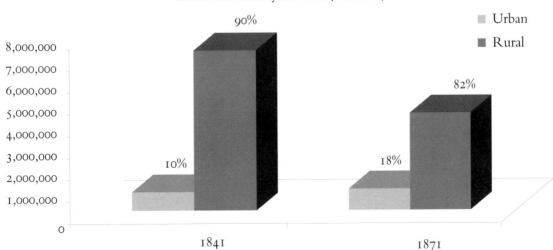

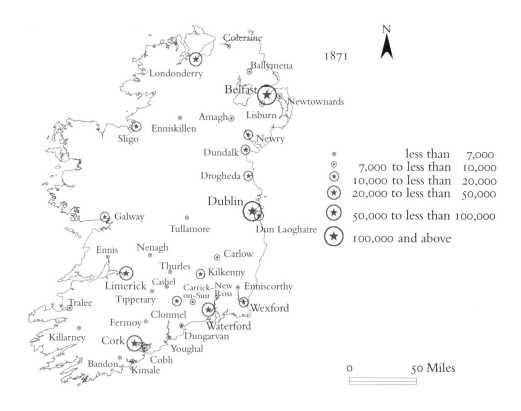

Map 4: Towns with populations of 5,000 or more in 1841 and 1871

1841 to 1851

1841 to 1861

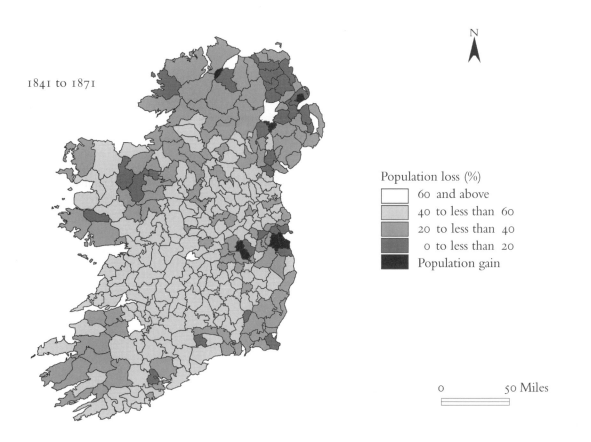

1841 to 1871

N

Population loss (%)

☐ 60 and above
▨ 40 to less than 60
▨ 20 to less than 40
▨ 0 to less than 20
■ Population gain

0   50 Miles

Map 5: Percentage population decline at barony level

EMPTYING THE LAND

There are various ways of measuring population densities. The simplest is to relate population to land area, regardless of its quality. This is done in the first series of maps that follow; they show population per 100 acres by poor law union in 1841, 1851, 1861, and 1871. The maps demonstrate, broadly, an east-west gradient, with the highest population densities in the east of the country and close to the towns, and also in a cluster of poor law unions in south-east Ulster associated with the major linen-producing regions.

passage of time was Antrim (from seventh to second), reflecting the pulling power of Belfast. Antrim and Dublin were the only two where the density of population was greater in 1871 than it had been in 1841.

Although the geographical distribution of population densities changed little, the densities themselves altered a good deal. County densities in 1871 were, on average, only 69% of their levels in 1841, and the variance was greater, indicating an ever-growing contrast between the more densely populated

Figure 4: Population per 100 acres, 1841 and 1871

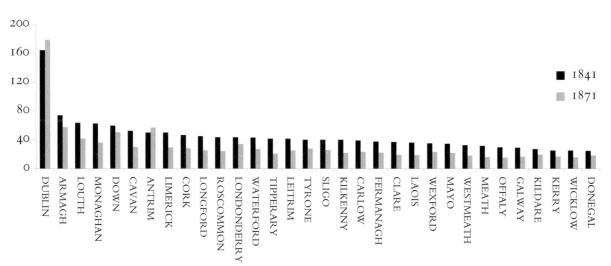

The geographical pattern hardly changed over time, notwithstanding the loss of population between 1841 and 1871. This can be seen from Figure 4 which arranges the population of the counties per 100 acres according to their rank order in 1841. The only county that significantly broke rank with the

counties such as Dublin and Antrim, together with the eastern cities and towns that sucked population into themselves, and the western and rural counties that shed population more heavily than the east (see Table 1).

Table 1: Average county density of population, 1841–71

YEAR	MEAN POPULATION PER 100 ACRES	STANDARD DEVIATION	COEFFICIENT OF VARIATION
1841	45.2	24.7	0.55
1851	37.1	27.8	0.75
1861	33.5	28.9	0.86
1871	31.4	29.1	0.93

A simple population/land ratio conceals more than it reveals. It is more instructive to relate the population to the quality of the land. A straightforward method of doing that is to divide the population, not by land area, but by the area of useful land. This is possible only at county level and the next set of maps relates population to land area (per 100 acres) excluding waste and water (map 8). As the maps show, densities then shift westwards, except for two important clusters in 1841 in south Ulster and Dublin. In other words, there was a tendency for the highest densities to be in areas where much land was of limited agricultural use. With the passing of time, the tide ebbed away from the west to a limited extent. By 1871 there was a pronounced concentration of population in the north-east, reflecting industrial development and urbanisation in the Lagan and Bann valleys. And there remained a concentration in Dublin and its hinterland.

An even more revealing measure is to associate population with poor law valuations. This can be done by dividing the population of a poor law union by its rateable value. The reasoning behind this approach is that the valuation was a proxy for the economic worth of the union. In predominantly rural unions the rate was levied principally on landed property. In unions centring on large towns the rate fell on urban property as well as on agricultural land.[1] For any given union population the greater the valuation the lower the density and *vice versa*. The final result might hinge on a high base population or a low valuation. The highest union valuations were generally found in the east of Ireland. The valuations for 1851 have been used for 1841, 1851, 1861 and 1871. Any changes over the period, therefore, were the result of changes in the population of the union.

The results of controlling for economic worth in this way are shown in the final set of maps (map 9).

The pattern produced by relating population to land values is the reverse of that produced by using the acreage of the county or union. Densities were highest on the poorest land in the west. Throughout the whole period 1841–71 the most heavily populated unions were almost all on the western fringes. By 1861 and 1871 the picture had altered somewhat from that in 1841, although it was still evident. The population of Ireland in 1841 had been concentrated on the poor potato land of the west. The Great Famine and subsequent emigration dislodged three million people from the country by 1871, but many of those remaining still clung to their potato patches on the poorest land.

The means of the country-wide ratios of population related to poor law valuations are shown in Table 2. Between 1841 and 1871 the means declined by 38%. There were just four gainers: Belfast where the ratio doubled, Rathdown where it increased by 21%, Dublin South where it went up by 11%, and Dublin North where the increase was 10%.

Two points are worthy of note. The first was the decline in density by more than one-third between 1841 and 1871; much of this decline occurred during the Famine decade. The second was the increase in the coefficient of variation (a measure of dispersion), noticeable after 1851.

In conclusion, the density of population during the pre-Famine and immediate post-Famine decades present a paradox. Conventional economic theory, from Ricardo onwards, predicts that the best land will be occupied first and that therefore is where we should expect to find the greatest densities of population. But in mid-nineteenth-century Ireland, it was the worst land that was most densely populated, testimony to the powerful distorting power of the potato on the iron laws of economics.

Table 2: The population of poor law unions related to poor law valuations

YEAR	MEAN	STANDARD DEVIATION	COEFFICIENT OF VARIATION
1841	0.95	0.51	0.54
1851	0.73	0.38	0.52
1861	0.64	0.38	0.59
1871	0.59	0.37	0.63

1 The act of 1838 establishing a poor law in Ireland empowered the poor law guardians 'to make and levy such rates as may be necessary on every occupier of rateable hereditaments within the union'. The rate was a poundage rate made upon an estimate of the net annual valuation of the hereditaments. See George Nicholls, *A history of the Irish Poor Law* (London, 1856), pp. 227–8.

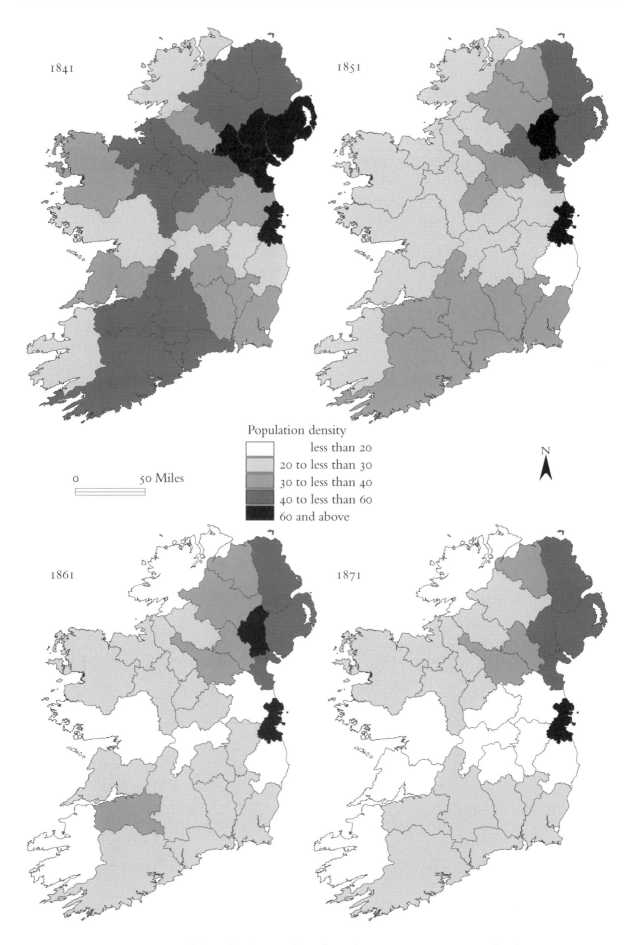

Population density

less than 20
20 to less than 30
30 to less than 40
40 to less than 60
60 and above

0   50 Miles

N

Map 6: Population density: number of people per 100 acres at county level

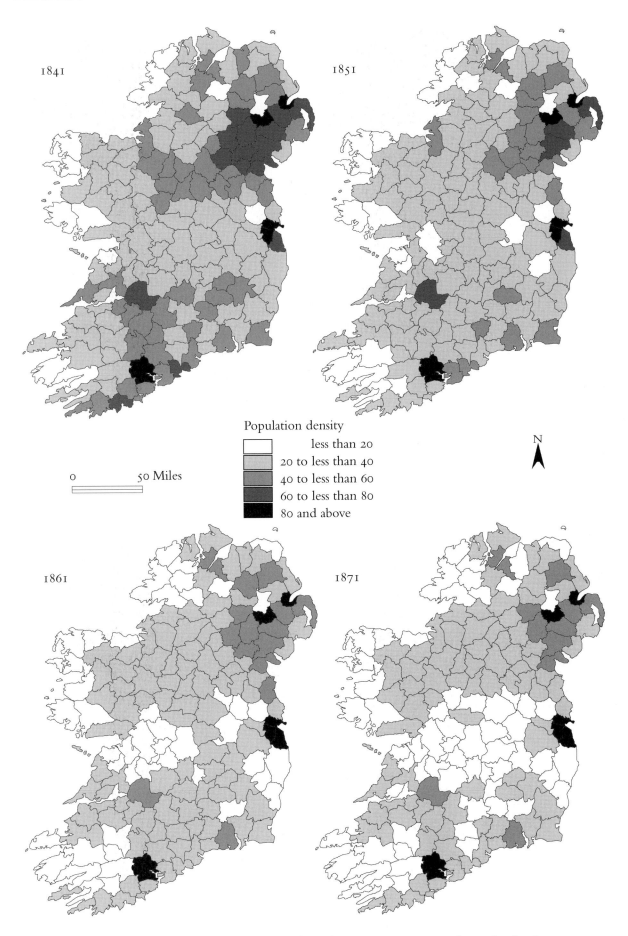

1841

1851

Population density

less than 20

20 to less than 40

40 to less than 60

60 to less than 80

80 and above

0   50 Miles

N

1861

1871

Map 7: Population density: number of people per 100 acres at poor law union level

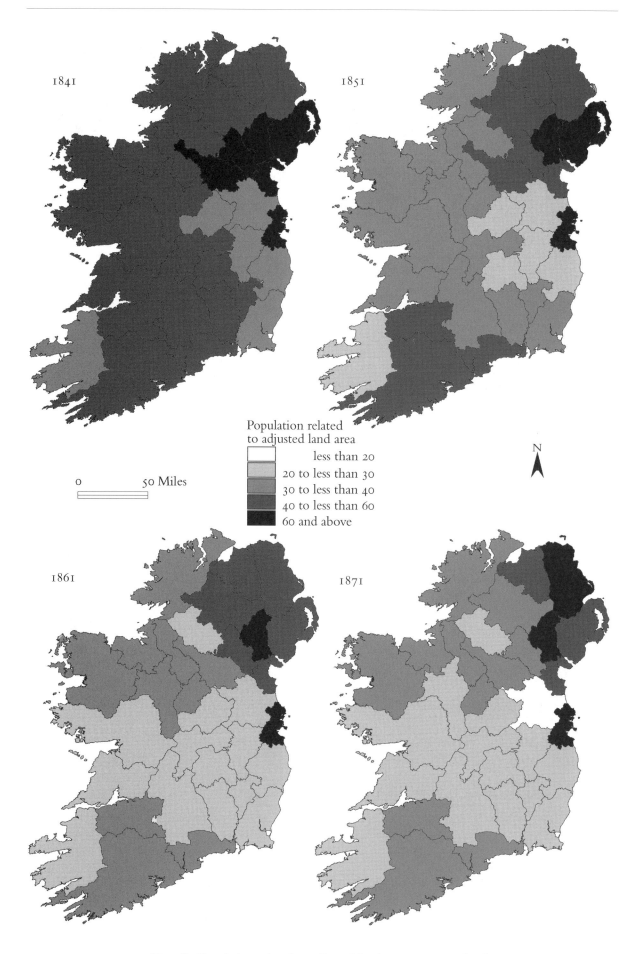

Map 8: Population related to adjusted land area at county level

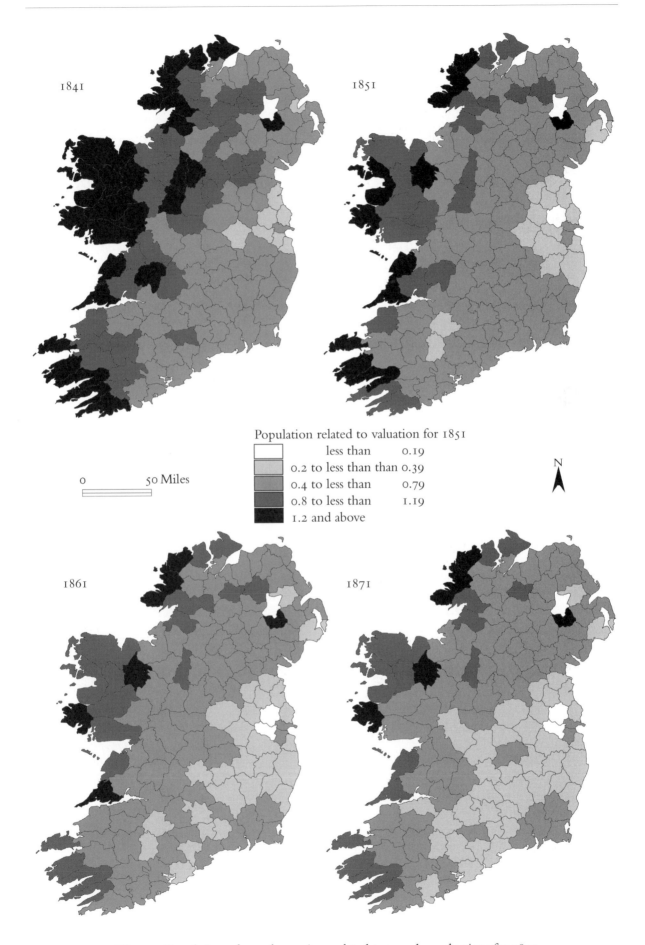

Map 9: Population of poor law unions related to poor law valuations for 1851

DEATH AND THE GREAT FAMINE

Over a million Irish people – men, women and children – died as a result of the Great Famine. Without doubt, this was the greatest calamity in modern Irish history. The severity of the Famine can be measured in a variety of ways. But the most telling indicator is the extent of death.

Some died directly as a result of the Famine, due to outright starvation. More usually, malnourished people were ravaged by famine-related diseases, resulting in massive mortality. When calculating numbers of fatalities caused by the Famine, or mortality rates (deaths per thousand of the population), it is important to exclude those who, in the normal course of events, would have died anyway during the second half of the 1840s. Thus, the notion of famine mortality, as used by historians and demographers, refers to these excess or abnormal deaths only.

Needless to say, the calculation of Famine deaths is a hazardous enterprise. There are no comprehensive data on the numbers who died in the various parishes, baronies or poor law unions of Ireland, though attempts were made to count those who died in the workhouses, hospitals, sanitary institutions, prisons and prison hospitals. The general registration of deaths by the civil authorities lay in the future, only coming into being in 1864. Even had a system of official registration existed, the likelihood is that it would have been overwhelmed by the sheer scale of the tragedy. We are obliged, therefore, to resort to *estimating* the death toll on the basis of certain assumptions. The conclusions reached are of course sensitive to these assumptions, this being particularly true of attempts to understand the extent of Famine deaths at a level of analysis below that of Ireland as a whole.

With these reservations in mind, we may begin to look at the available evidence on the regional incidence of the Great Famine. Perhaps the best-known estimates of deaths at a county level are those by Joel Mokyr.[1] Two versions of Mokyr's county data are mapped here. The set of lower-bound estimates relates to deaths due to the Famine. These are averaged over the course of the Famine (1846–51) and expressed as an annual rate per thousand of the population. By using rates rather than totals, it becomes possible to compare the intensity of the tragedy across the different counties. The set of upper-bound estimates differ in that they include, not only those who died because of the Famine, but also those who *would have been born* had fertility not been checked as a result of the catastrophe. These averted births, or what might be called the 'unborn dead', are viewed by some demographers as part of the Famine death toll. Others would demur, believing the second approach serves artificially to inflate the numbers of deaths. One might argue for instance that marriage was postponed during the Famine (see pages 50–51) as a deliberate choice in the circumstances, resulting in a predictable fall in fertility. The likelihood is that this occurred during earlier, less virulent subsistence crises also, or even following a poor harvest year.

So, depending on which measurement is adopted – the upper-bound or the lower-bound estimate – the choice makes a big difference to the national death toll. The range of Mokyr's mortality figures goes from 1.1 million to 1.5 million Famine deaths in Ireland between 1846 and 1851. But, interestingly, there is not that much difference, in terms of regional patterns, between the two versions. In each, the west of Ireland is shown to be particularly badly affected, with Mayo, Sligo, Roscommon and Galway suffering most. The Munster counties, especially Cork, also appear to have been badly affected. Noteworthy also is the severe impact in the north midlands. By contrast, Dublin, the south Leinster counties and east Ulster emerge relatively unscathed. The finding that Dublin had virtually no Famine mortality is, however, hard to believe, in view of the influx of disease-carrying refugees to the capital city and the wretched state of many of the city's poor. Similarly, one might wonder if the impact on Wexford for instance, could have been so limited. While this county ranked as one of the more prosperous regions of Ireland, it nonetheless had large numbers of vulnerable agricultural labourers.

1 Joel Mokyr, *Why Ireland starved: A quantitative and analytical history of the Irish economy, 1800–1850* (London, 1983), pp. 266–7.

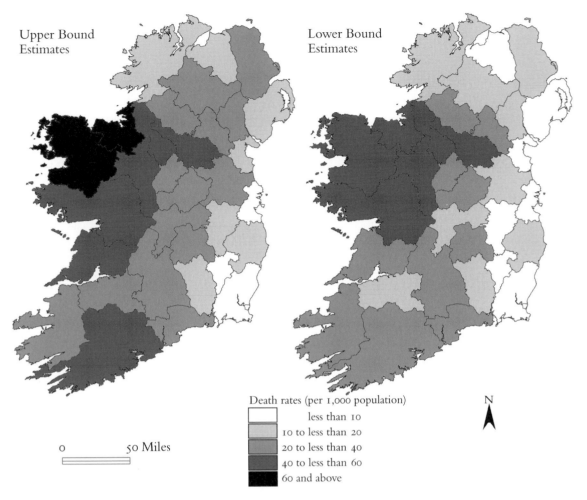

Upper Bound
Estimates

Lower Bound
Estimates

Death rates (per 1,000 population)

less than 10
10 to less than 20
20 to less than 40
40 to less than 60
60 and above

N

0   50 Miles

Map 10: Average annual excess death rates, 1846–51
SOURCE: Mokyr (1983)

Anomalies such as these have led Ó Gráda to revisit a pioneering set of estimates of Famine mortality generated by the historical geographer S.H. Cousens, and published as far back as 1960.[2] Cousens' estimates of mortality during the Famine are computed on a different basis to those of Mokyr, relying heavily on retrospective information on deaths contained in the 1851 census of Ireland. While these death tables have been rightly criticised as under-estimating the true extent of mortality – Cousens' conclusion of an aggregate (excess) mortality of 801,000 for Ireland is now regarded as much too low – the regional patterns he detects seem plausible enough. In other words, while the overall total is probably well under the mark, the *share* of each county in the national death toll may be tolerably accurate.

Why the difference? The first and most important point to be made is that the regional pictures

painted by Mokyr and by Cousens are not so very different. Cousens' map of the regional incidence of Famine mortality, which relates to the period 1846–50, shows that Connacht suffered heavily, as did the south-west. But Clare was affected more severely than Mokyr suggests, while virtually all of Ulster escaped lightly. The anomaly of Dublin disappears. The basis of the calculations is different, which helps explain why the patterns are not the same. In particular, Mokyr's death rates are highly sensitive to assumptions about the regional incidence of emigration, which was the other great source of 'disappearance' from Irish society between 1841 and 1851. Cousens' approach to estimating Famine deaths, based on the death tables in the 1851 census, is independent of the elusive issue of the regional distribution of emigration. It may be noted also that Mokyr expresses his death rate in terms of the average *annual* number of deaths per thousand of

2 Cormac Ó Gráda, *Ireland before and after the Famine: explorations in economic history, 1800–1925* (Manchester, 1993), pp. 138–44; S.H.

Cousens, 'Regional death rates in Ireland during the Great Famine, from 1846 to 1851', *Population Studies*, 14 (1960), 55–74.

the population during the years 1846–51, while Cousens presents his data in terms of the proportion (%) of people who died over the *whole* period 1846–50. These differing modes of presentation, and the differing class breaks used in the two sets of maps, have some effect on the regional patterns revealed. Finally, it is important to emphasise that both rates refer to excess rather than total mortality.

Whichever version, that of Mokyr or that of Cousens, is preferred, there is no doubt that the Famine had a highly uneven impact when viewed spatially. In part this was a matter of geography – see Figure 5 below which also brings out the regional dimension[3] – but was primarily due to differences in economic and social structure. The western counties were characterised by tiny landholdings, low levels of income, low levels of urbanisation and industrialisation, and heavy dependence on the potato crop. The result was vulnerability to famine, under the stress of repeated crop failures. The role of landlords, as a bulwark against disaster, also seems to have varied regionally, being at its most efficacious in Ulster and at its most malign in parts of the West. Mass evictions, which were put into effect on some estates, added to the sum of human suffering and

further exposed families to the ravages of disease. Kilrush in County Clare is an extreme example.[4]

> While hundreds are being turned out houseless and helpless daily on one small property in Killard division, no less than 23 houses, containing probably 100 souls, were tumbled in one day, 27th March [1846]. I believe the extent of land, occupied with these 23 houses did not exceed 50 acres. The suffering and misery attendant upon these wholesale evictions is indescribable … The number of houseless paupers in this Union is beyond my calculation; those evicted crowd neighbouring cabins' villages, and disease is necessarily generated.

For more than a million people it was the ability to get out of Ireland, to Britain and North America, which offered the best chance of survival. But these opportunities were in turn structured by social and economic circumstances, again biasing outcomes against communities in the west of the island. Life in the New World, rather than the next, was a more likely outcome, if one came from Meath rather than Mayo, Kildare rather than Clare.

Figure 5: Famine mortality, 1846–51

Death rates (per 1,000)

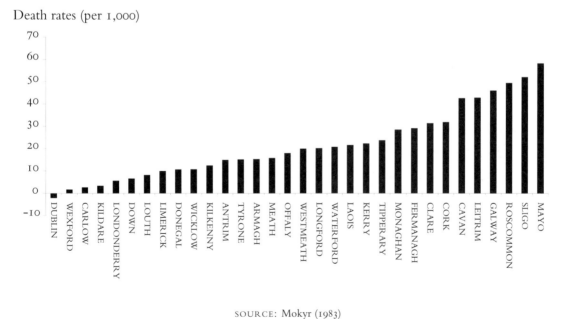

SOURCE: Mokyr (1983)

3 Based on Mokyr's lower-bound estimates of annual excess death rates, for each county during the period 1846–51.   **4** *Reports and returns relating to evictions in the Kilrush union,* BPP, 1849, xlix, p. 319.

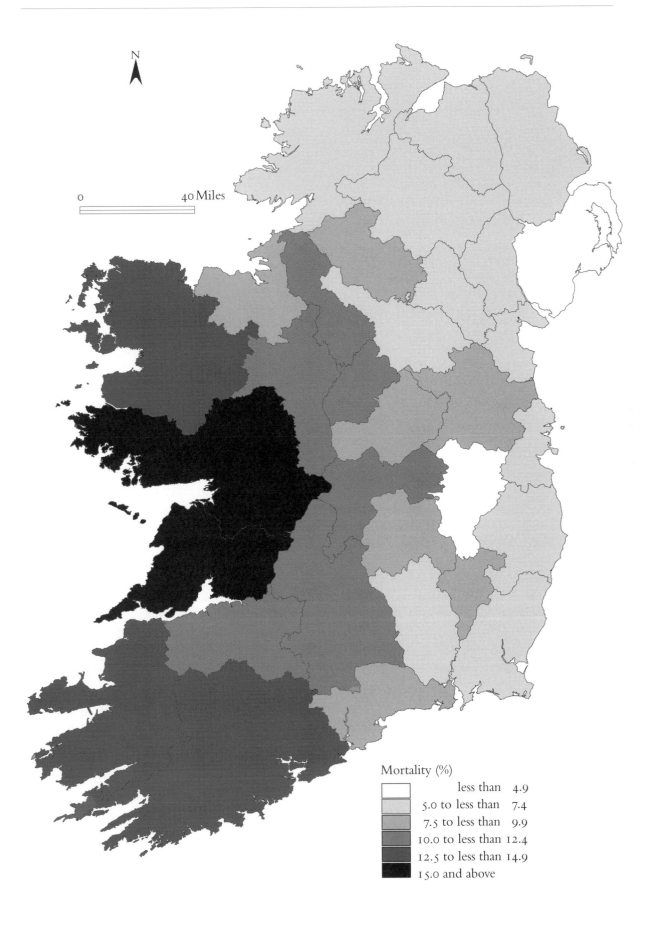

N

0   40 Miles

Mortality (%)

	less than 4.9
	5.0 to less than 7.4
	7.5 to less than 9.9
	10.0 to less than 12.4
	12.5 to less than 14.9
	15.0 and above

Map 11: Excess mortality 1846–50 as a % of population at county level
SOURCE: Cousens (1960)

SHRINKING IRELAND: EMIGRANTS AND EXILES

Emigration was a well-established feature of Irish social life before the Famine, though its regional incidence is less well understood. The presumption is that counties in the east of Ireland and in Ulster were disproportionately represented in this outflow. Official sources estimated the flow of migrants from Ireland to destinations *outside* the United Kingdom from 1825 onwards, but it was not until 1851 that the systematic enumeration of emigration from Irish ports began.[1] Even then, there were problems with the statistics leading to considerable under-reporting and geographical bias. The latter is particularly serious as our interest here is the regional pattern to emigration.

An alternative approach is to use age-cohort analysis of census data to derive indirect measures of emigration. In essence, one looks at the extent to which the younger age groups (those people most prone to emigrate), were depleted in numbers as between one census date and the next. The method is explained in Ó Gráda.[2] The principal complication is that it does not separate out internal migration from emigration. While this is a problem – population loss, other than through death, is assumed to be due to emigration – it is not a severe one for most Irish counties. The rivulets of internal migration were as nothing compared to the flood of people out of the country. The exercise can be conducted only for the post-Famine decades as comparisons between the censuses of 1841 and 1851 are vitiated by the huge death toll.[3]

Looking first at women, the most striking fact perhaps is that the practice of emigration was firmly entrenched in all parts of the island, and with above average intensity in the west after 1851. Thus Clare, Galway, Kerry, and Roscommon were at, or close to the top of the hierarchy in terms of emigration losses. At one time it was thought that counties in the west of Ireland were under-represented, proportionately speaking, in the emigrant traffic before the agricultural depression and land war of the late 1870s and 1880s. It is now clear that neither poverty, gender constraints nor social barriers in the form of

Gaelic culture were sufficient to prevent a strong western participation in the outflow. The women of the west were awake long before 1879.

The importance of female emigration to the band of countryside between Dublin and the Shannon (counties Meath, Westmeath and Offaly) is also noteworthy. It would seem here that the first decade of post-Famine adjustment offered poor opportunities for female livelihoods, relative to the perceived opportunities abroad. This region, it may be added, was experiencing a shift towards labour-extensive pastoral farming, which probably forms part of the explanation. By contrast, Antrim experienced a net inflow of women in the 1860s, on the back of the rapid expansion of Belfast, the Linenopolis of the North. Unlike the Irish countryside, where the demand for female labour was contracting, the linen lords of Ulster were creating new openings for female labour power, albeit at low rates of remuneration. More generally, one can say that by 1871 there was a broad regional pattern to female emigration from Ireland, with a great exodus of women from the less-urbanised midlands and west of Ireland and a more limited outflow from the eastern coastal regions.

As in the case of women, there was a heavy emigration of men during the decade after the Famine. The spatial traces left by male and female emigrants were broadly comparable, though by no means identical. Male migration from the mid-west, for example, was more pronounced during the 1850s. During the 1860s the regional focus was still on the west, the leading emigrant-producing regions being west of a line drawn from Malin Head, in north Donegal, to the Shannon estuary. The lowest level of out-migration, hardly surprisingly, was from the county of Antrim which contained the rapidly expanding town of Belfast. It is important, finally, to underline a point of major significance: unusually in the context of European migrations, there was a rough equality of the sexes in terms of the outflow of people from the shrinking society of later-nineteenth-century Ireland.

1 *Commission on emigration and other population problems, 1948–1951* (Dublin, 1956), pp. 314–19. 2 Cormac Ó Gráda, 'Some aspects of nineteenth-century Irish emigration' in L.M. Cullen & T.C. Smout (eds), *Comparative aspects of Scottish and Irish economic and social history, 1600–1900* (Edinburgh, 1977), pp. 65–73.

See also Ó Gráda, 'A note on nineteenth-century Irish emigration statistics', *Population Studies*, 29 (1975), pp. 143–9. 3 The data are from Líam Kennedy, *An historical database of Irish county statistics* (Belfast, 1996).

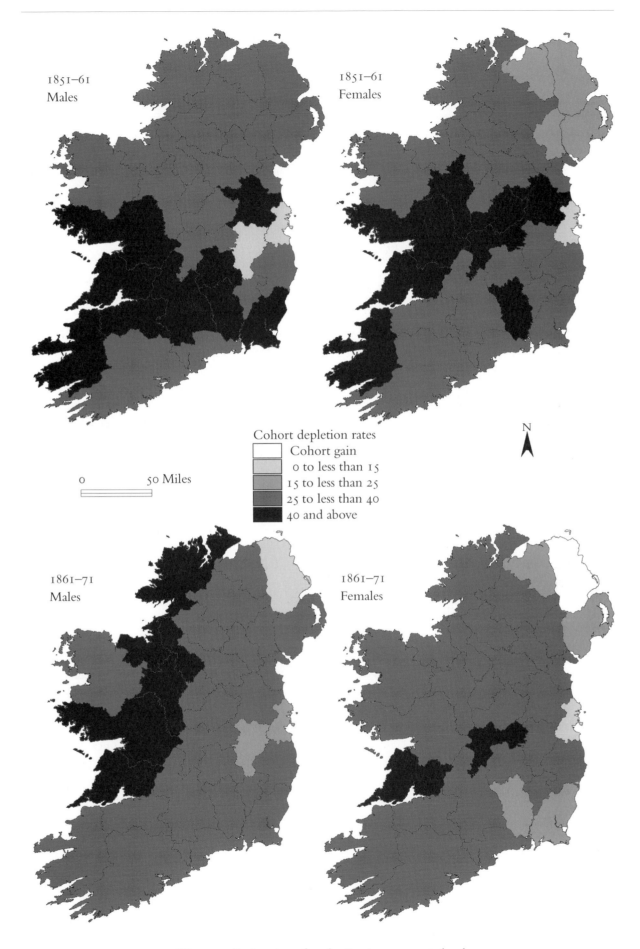

1851–61
Males

1851–61
Females

Cohort depletion rates

	Cohort gain
	0 to less than 15
	15 to less than 25
	25 to less than 40
	40 and above

0   50 Miles

N

1861–71
Males

1861–71
Females

Map 12: Emigration after the Famine at county level

'The House of Pat Brennan'

SOURCE: *Pictorial Times*, 7 February 1846

SEX, MARRIAGE AND FAMILIES

During the second half of the nineteenth century Irish society became characterised by a late age of first marriage and high rates of permanent celibacy. There was also a growing gender imbalance in town and country, with an excess of females in the more industrialised and urbanised regions of the east and a surplus of males within some age cohorts and in parts of rural Ireland. These features are sometimes contrasted with those of pre-Famine Ireland, which is portrayed as a society of youthful and widespread marriage. To what extent, though, did the Great Famine alter marital behaviour and gender ratios?

The simple answer that emerges from the following section is that the Great Famine had only a limited impact on patterns of marriage and family formation. Change from a mean age at marriage close to the west European norm (not, it should be noted, from an unusually low marriage age) to a higher mean age, and a shift away from marriage to permanent celibacy, were already in train before 1841. On the whole, the eastern side of the country was in the van of such adjustments, although there were many differences at local level. As for gender imbalances, these were likewise slow in emerging and were influenced by different opportunities for employment and emigration.

Accompanying the gradual shifts in the pattern of family formation were changes in the number and composition of households. Once more, changes were gradual after the immediate impact of the Famine. Not only did the number of households decline, the size of households also fell. As marriage became the less preferred – or the less obtainable – option so the structure of households changed, with relatively fewer composed of husbands, wives and young children and relatively more of unmarried siblings or a married couple and co-resident kin. Changes in the composition of households cannot be mapped, but they were an integral part of social and cultural change in post-Famine Ireland.

The balance between men and women in different parts of Ireland may not seem like the most interesting of social statistics. Yet it can offer clues to some of the most fundamental features of social life: inward and outward migration, the availability of marriage partners, gender preference and the sexual division of labour. The gender ratio, defined here as the number of men per 100 women, also offers an oblique view of the impact of the Great Famine, as experienced in gender terms. Thus, comparing the county maps for the years 1841 and 1851, we see that the regional patterns apparent before the Famine – a balanced gender ratio in the western half of the island, with female surpluses in the north-east, in Dublin, and in the south-east – is very similar to that after the Famine. This indicates remarkable stability, which lends *indirect* support to the view that the impact of the Famine was largely neutral in gender terms. This, it is worth noting, would conflict with some contemporary accounts which suggest that as the crisis facing Irish society deepened, women were the first to go hungry. Still, there may be a danger of statistical dilution through focusing on general patterns only.

The Famine had its greatest impact in the far west of the island. Perhaps gender ratios, indicating differential survival or differential migration during the Famine decade, showed greater change there? Exploring this possibility through the medium of the more detailed poor law union maps suggests that shifts over time at a local level could be pronounced during the Famine decade. The wild and impoverished district of Connemara, for example, moved from being a male-surplus to a female-surplus district. More generally, the movement in the gender ratio in Connacht and in the north and the south-west was in the direction of relatively more women. It is still possible that women suffered disproportionately during the Famine years, and that the changing balance was due to greater male outmigration during the 1840s. We cannot be sure, as we cannot easily distinguish between the impact of the Famine in terms of mortality and in terms of migration. But, on the face of it, the pattern of

change between 1841 and 1851 is not immediately consistent with the view that the mortality impact of the Famine was concentrated disproportionately on women.[1]

Taking the whole period, 1841–71, what is perhaps most striking is how slowly changes in the male-female ratio evolved. True enough, the ratio of men to women for Ireland as a whole declined. In 1841 there were 97 males for every 100 females. Thirty years later the equivalent male figure was down to 95. But set against the economic and demographic upheavals of the period, the pace of change was moderate enough. This consistency over time was largely true of the county pattern also. In 1871, just as in 1841, the counties in which the numbers of women exceeded men were in the north-east, the south-east, Dublin and Limerick (see Figure 6). The greater availability of female employment in the more urbanised east of the country would seem to be the main explanation. The industrialisation of east Ulster generated thousands of jobs in factories and mills, as well as giving a boost to forms of home industry such as sprigging, embroidery and shirt-making. In Dublin the demand for shop assistants and domestic servants favoured young women. In other areas, such as south-west Donegal or Belmullet in county Mayo, an excess of women over men was apparent by 1871. The reasons for the imbalance were different to those in the east, however. The lack of employment in these local, peripheral economies generated outflows of men, either on a permanent or on a seasonal basis.

The primary contrast with these patterns was the broad band of male-surplus districts, in process of consolidation since the Famine, which stretched across the middle of Ireland. In this midland region, where dry cattle production dominated and the development of towns was limited, the best opportunities for women lay in migration to the urban centres of the eastern seaboard or in seeking livelihoods outside of Ireland. This surplus of males was at its most extreme in the case of county Kildare, but special circumstances were at play here. The large military encampment at the Curragh, despite attracting a

---

1 A greater biological capacity on the part of women to survive famine has also been suggested. See Robert Dirks, 'Social responses during severe food shortages and famine', *Current Anthropology*, 21 (1980), 24.

following of poor women and prostitutes, distorted the gender ratio in the direction of a preponderance of males. More generally, in areas characterised by surplus males, one suspects that an urge to enhance their marriage as well as their economic prospects had been a vital force motivating female outmigration.

So far we have looked at the gender structure of the population as a whole. The population can in turn be subdivided into any number of age categories and a gender ratio for each age group can be calculated. For example, the sex ratio at birth for males and females is typically in the ratio of 105 males to 100 females. A much higher ratio, as in countries like India today, suggests a strong preference for male children and the prevalence of selective abortion and infanticide directed against female births. Where such practices were not current, as in nineteenth-century Irish society, one might still find wide differences in gender ratios within particular age categories. Mortality and migration are two processes which tend to be gender-specific and hence can profoundly alter gender ratios. For the purposes of illustration, we have chosen two age categories: the youthful segment of the population (those less than 17 years of age) and the elderly (those exceeding 55 years of age). Before discussing the results, a word of caution is in order. Age reporting in the early Irish censuses was by no means precise, and this will introduce some bias into any analysis which uses age in the construction of its categories.

It is apparent that the gender ratio linking young males and females does not vary greatly over time or space, though it is noteworthy that the ratio shifts temporarily in favour of young males during the Famine decade in the mid-western counties of Galway, Clare and Tipperary. More intriguing are

the findings in relation to the elderly in Irish society. The map of Ireland in 1841 suggests that in Connacht and in the north midlands the ratio of males to females was considerably higher than elsewhere on the island. This is an intriguing finding, and it is by no means obvious why this might have been so. One line of interpretation might be that it indicates a lower life expectancy for women in these regions, possibly reflecting a lower status for women in western peasant society. This is by no means inconceivable. Contemporary accounts suggest that women experienced considerable physical hardships as a result of poor housing, prolonged childbearing, and heavy farmwork (which included the haulage of seaweed on the Atlantic seaboard). Primitive technologies, both of transport and farming technique, may have meant that western women were excessively burdened relative to their counterparts in the east. Selective migration along gender lines, in earlier years, could also of course account for the dominance of older males in the population. This seems more plausible in relation to an eastern county like Kilkenny, where the ratio was the highest for all the Irish counties, and less so in relation to western counties.

In view of this varied backdrop, the changed distribution by the end of the Famine is striking. The pattern across Ireland had become much more even, and in no county did elderly males outnumber elderly females. Again the question arises: does this suggest an equal, or ever greater survival capacity on the part of women, in this instance older women, during the ordeal of the Famine? The question becomes even more pointed if one recalls that the elderly are a segment of the population with a low propensity to migrate or emigrate.

Figure 6: Gender ratios (males per 100 females) in 1841 and 1871

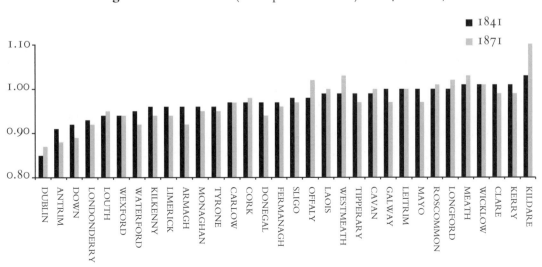

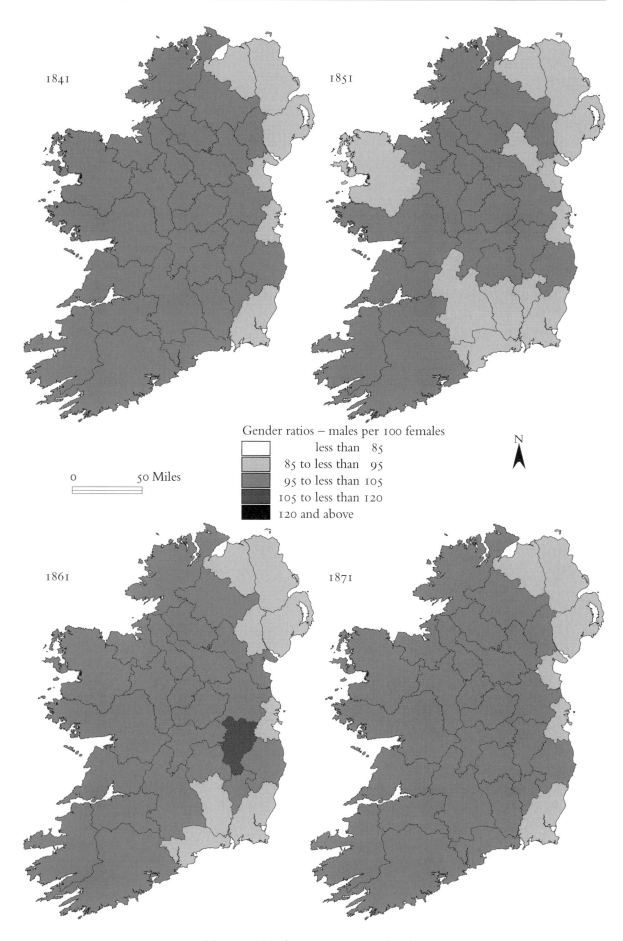

Map 13: Gender ratios at county level

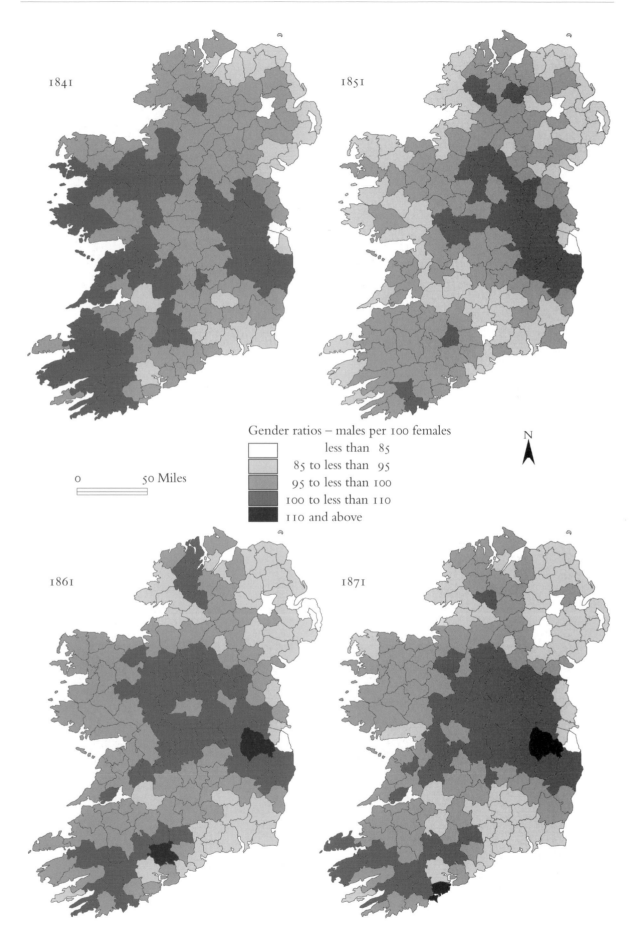

Map 14: Gender ratios at poor law union level

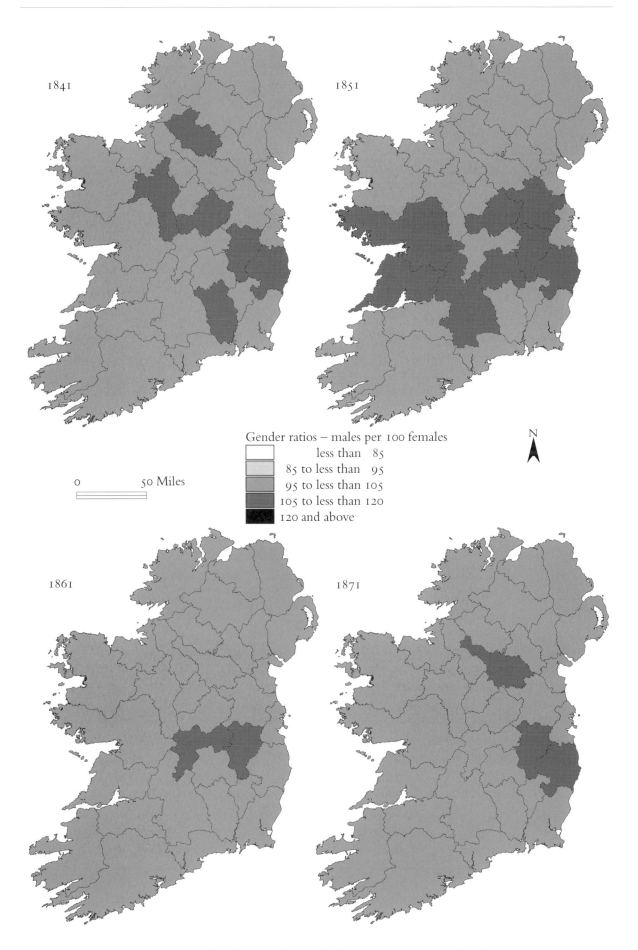

Map 15: Gender ratios for ages below 17 years at county level

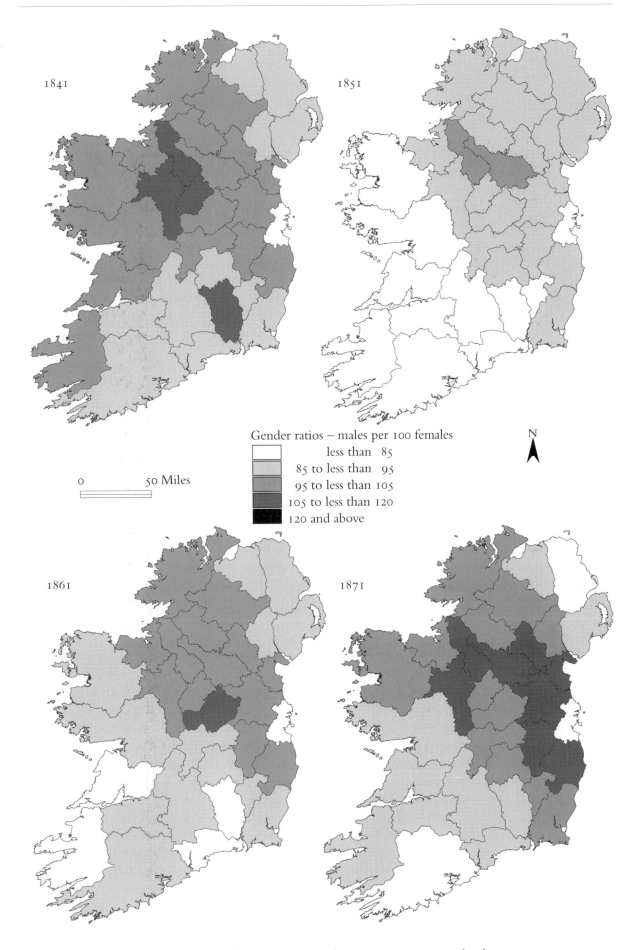

1841

1851

Gender ratios – males per 100 females

	less than 85
	85 to less than 95
	95 to less than 105
	105 to less than 120
	120 and above

0   50 Miles

N

1861

1871

Map 16: Gender ratios for ages above 55 years at county level

BEFORE THE ALTAR: AGE AT MARRIAGE FOR WOMEN AND MEN

Contrary to some of the stereotypical accounts of life in Ireland on the eve of the Famine, the Irish did not marry at a very young age, recklessly and without forethought. More usually, Irish women married in their mid-twenties while Irish men married in their late-twenties. This was in line with patterns elsewhere in western Europe where a mature age at marriage tended to be the norm.

Official source materials for the period 1841–71 do not provide information on age at marriage, though the census of Ireland does indicate the marital status of males and females for different age categories. From the proportions single in these different age groups we can derive an indirect estimate of marriage age. The measure used here is the singulate mean age at marriage (SMAM). Though widely used, it is an approximation and is likely to be less accurate in the context of an emigration-prone society (such as Ireland after the Famine).[1] The misreporting of ages in the census would also adversely affect the accuracy of the measure.

These reservations should not be pressed too far, and the problems are by no means unique to Ireland and the Irish data. The broad patterns, as distinct from the detailed representation of variations in age at marriage, seem robust enough. Beginning with women: on the eve of the Famine, and somewhat surprisingly in view of the diverse economic conditions found on the island, it emerges there was not that much variation in age at marriage in different parts of the country. Still, some regional contrasts do become apparent. The women seemingly most impatient for marriage in 1841 were to be found in the west. In Mayo and Kerry the mean age at marriage for women was under 25 years, whereas in south Leinster, in counties Carlow and Wexford, for example, it was almost 28 years. Still, most counties clustered close to the national average of 26 years, the coefficient of variation for marriage ages across the counties being only 0.03.

During the Famine marriages were postponed, an understandable reaction to the chaos into which society was plunged. Between 1841 and 1851, roughly a year and a half on average was added to the waiting time. Notice, for instance, how the 'white' counties of Mayo and Kerry become 'coloured' in the map for 1851, signifying a marrying age of 25 years or older (on average). This upward shift was not maintained, though. The mean age at marriage for women nationally seems to have been much the same two decades later in 1871. If the data can be relied upon – note the earlier reservations – then it is not easy to see how the Famine might have decisively refashioned marriage behaviour.

There was some increase in regional differentiation over time. In 1851 the mean age at marriage for women across the different counties varied between 26 and 29 years. Two decades later there was a little more variety: the range extended from 25 to 30 years. Or, viewed through the medium of another measure of dispersion, the coefficient of variation had increased from 0.03 to 0.05. In plain language, though, there was not that much change in marriage behaviour across space or over time immediately after the Famine, at least as revealed at the level of county averages. These averages could of course be concealing variations in behaviour at a sub-county level. Even the coarse-grained picture, however, reveals that the age at marriage in the far western counties of Mayo and Kerry remained persistently low by standards elsewhere. This is one of a number of indicators suggesting resistance to the 'modernisation' of mentalities in the west.

Continuity also marked the east of the country. In 1871, as in the pre-Famine period, a later age at marriage was to be found in Leinster and east Ulster. This was particularly true of county Offaly, and the south Leinster counties of Kilkenny and Wexford. In Offaly, for example, the typical woman married in her thirtieth year, the highest mean age at marriage for any of the Irish counties. An obvious link to delayed marriage stemmed from practices of inheritance and dowries within the farming community. The necessity for women of having a dowry, either by dint of personal accumulation or by virtue of a transfer from other members of the family (or a combination of the two), meant that marriages among farming families tended to be delayed, some-

---

1 The SMAM values are taken from Liam Kennedy, *An historical database of Irish county statistics* (Belfast, 1996).

times indefinitely. Among the smallholders of the west, such financial frictions in the marriage market seem to have been less of a problem. But other forces may have been equally or more relevant in producing a late age at marriage. These included the extent of outmigration, changing norms of what was an acceptable standard of living for a couple, and variations over space in the steepness of the socio-economic hierarchy. At the level of individual experience, though sentiment was by no means irrelevant to the bride's progress to the altar, material considerations took precedence over the romantic.

The age at which men typically married is of less interest, at least from the viewpoint of studying population change. Age at marriage for women in a society not practising contraception had immediate and direct implications for fertility. Nonetheless, the issue has its own intrinsic interest, and presumably was of concern to the men who made up our historic population. In 1841 men married on average some three years later than women: men at 29–30 years as compared to 26 or so years for women.

There is clear evidence of late-marrying regimes in parts of Ireland before the Famine. A regional zone which included the counties of south Leinster and extended westwards to Tipperary, and northwards to Laois, Offaly, Westmeath and Meath, roughly encompassed the areas of late marriage. Over much of the rest of the country men married at somewhat earlier ages. Within this larger zone, regional contrasts were much more muted. Age at marriage tended to be lower in the west of Ireland but the point is easily overstated. In the west marriage ages were not much below the average for the country as a whole. Or, to take specific examples, men married at much the same age, on average, in Sligo or Mayo in the west as in Armagh or Down in the north-east.

There is also an urban–rural contrast, which cannot be illustrated in the maps. In 1841 male marriage ages tended to be lower in Dublin city and in Belfast than in the country generally, and this difference persisted through the succeeding decades. A difference between the two major urban centres may also be noted: Belfast had a somewhat younger age at marriage than was the case in Dublin. This was not just a chance occurrence in 1841: a differential in Belfast's favour still existed in 1851, 1861 and 1871. It applied to women as well as men. One may surmise that this reflected better economic opportunities in the north.

During the Famine decade the waiting period for marriage lengthened by about one and a half years,

the same as for women, and presumably for the same reasons. In some famine-ravaged regions the switch to later marriage was especially marked. County Clare is a good example, where the mean age at marriage jumped by almost three years. But the general rise in marriage age was reversed in the next decade, and there appears to have been little change during the 1860s. Clare, it may be added, conformed to the national pattern. Thus it is the stability in the mean age at marriage for men, when set against the vast upheaval in Irish society, which impresses.

Regional patterns persisted over time. A later age at marriage for men was still visible in north Munster and upwards through the midlands after the Famine. Laois topped the late-marrying league of menfolk in 1851, Kildare in the following decade, while Meath held this dubious distinction in 1871. Why these midland and eastern counties should have established themselves as the locus for late marrying is not immediately obvious. The contrast is not only with urban centres like Dublin and Belfast, but also with other agricultural regions, especially those west of the Shannon. The gender imbalance in the midland counties is likely to carry some of the explanatory load. The role of inheritance in rural areas seems more relevant: farmers' sons served an apprenticeship to their fathers, sometimes a long and irksome one, before they got their hands on the family farm. Farm inheritance, or at the very least its promise, was a prerequisite to creating a new family unit. But this was true of the west also. Perhaps the wait was longer in the cattle-farming regions of the midlands where farms were worth waiting for, and patriarchal power was based firmly on control of the primary means of production and subsistence. A less elaborate class structure west of the Shannon may have been more conducive to marriage alliances than was the case in the socially-stratified society of the midlands and the south east where the search and negotiation costs associated with marriage transactions were higher. Possibly also, a degree of social emulation was at work. The strong farmers and other property holders such as shopkeepers, publicans and merchants, who were committed to careful marriage strategies long before the Famine, may well have influenced the marriage behaviour of lower social groups. Finally, one might surmise that local communities in the commercialised regions of the east were more receptive to social change which emphasised higher material expectations as the basis of a 'proper' marriage.

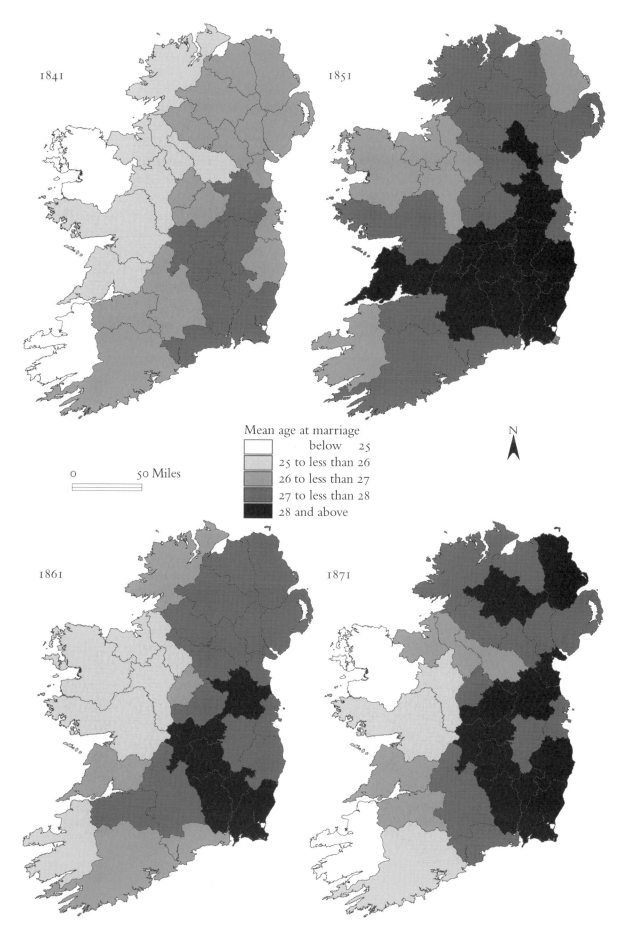

Map 17: Mean age at marriage for women at county level

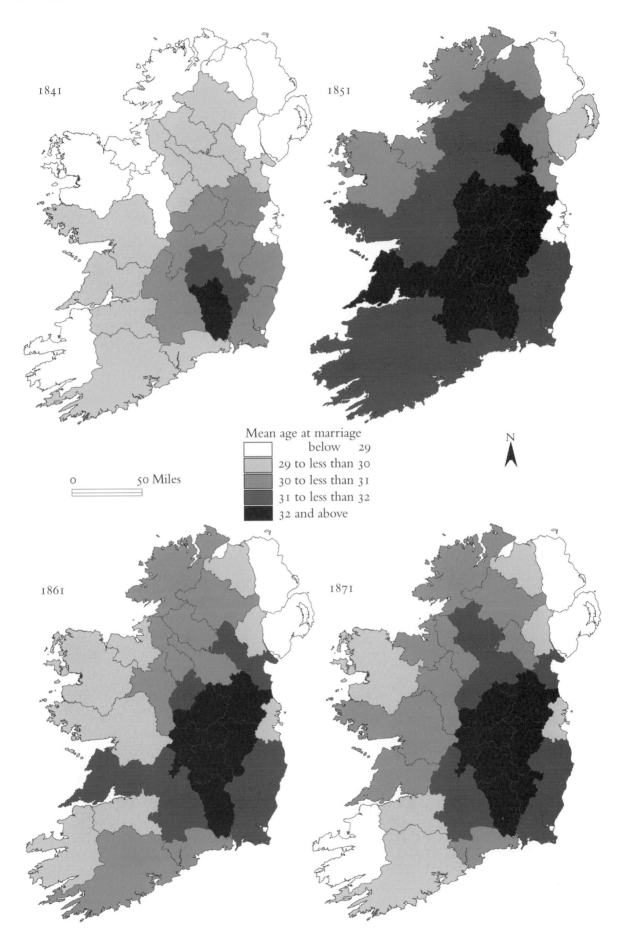

Map 18: Mean age at marriage for men at county level

CELIBACY IN IRISH SOCIETY: MEN WITHOUT WOMEN, WOMEN WITHOUT MEN

A distinctive feature of late nineteenth-century Irish society, and one which placed Ireland at the extreme of the West European marriage system, was an apparent reluctance to marry. This was not always so. While it would be an exaggeration to say marriage was universal before the Famine, typically nine out of every ten adults did marry. This was in line with behaviour in Britain and elsewhere in western Europe. Yet by 1871 some 17% of Irish men and 16% of women never married, and these proportions continued their upward course for the remainder of the century, and beyond. Did these trends originate with the Famine and the dislocation and 'psychic trauma' which accompanied the calamity, as some have argued?

The spatial distribution of non-marriage or permanent celibacy – conventionally measured as the proportion of the population aged 45–54 years still single – casts some doubt on this easy assumption. In 1841 some counties had already embraced a lower frequency of marriage. This is evident in the south-east of the island and also in parts of the midlands. In county Laois, to take the most extreme example, 17% of men in the age group 46–55 were unmarried, and likely to remain so. At the other end of the spectrum lay Gaelic-speaking, impoverished Mayo, where 95% of the same age group were married. Some women were finding it even more difficult to find partners. The celibacy rate for women was generally higher than for men, and was at its highest (18%) in the relatively prosperous county

of Down, and at its lowest once again in county Mayo where it stood at a mere seven percent. More generally, there is a contrast in terms of the frequency of marriage between the counties of eastern Ireland and east Ulster, on the one hand, and those of the west and south-west of the island on the other. Paradoxically, the barriers to marriage were higher in the more prosperous regions. This spatially-differentiated pattern points to different marriage regimes in pre-Famine Ireland, a point reinforced by the earlier discussion of regional variations in marriage age (see pages 50–51). It also indicates that some communities had come to accept that significant numbers among them would never marry. A high incidence of celibacy was well-established, even before the shock of the Great Famine.

Does it make sense to look for a 'Famine effect' in the celibacy rates for 1851? The incidence of celibacy in that year, one presumes, reflected decisions regarding marriage made a decade or more earlier. Typically decisions to marry, or not marry, were made by men and women during the age interval of 25 to 35 years, though of course there were always instances of late-marrying men and women. Thus the spatial patterns at the end of the Famine were likely to reflect longer-run social and economic forces making for change in Irish society. While this seems true enough, there remains the possibility that married persons might have been more likely to survive the crisis, as compared to single persons. Whether this was a significant factor in shaping the

Figure 7: Male celibacy in 1841 and 1871

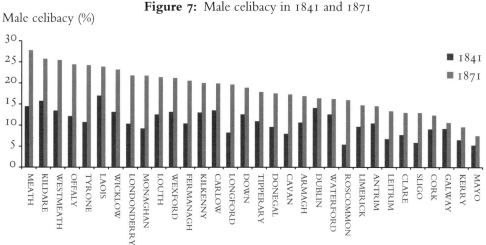

celibacy rates apparent at the end of the Famine must remain the subject of further investigation, though there are hints of this in the data.

The extent of change between 1841 and 1851 was, in fact, limited. Celibacy rates among men moved upwards in the counties close to Dublin, and also in parts of west Ulster, but in the west generally there was little change. In the urban centres of Dublin city and Belfast (not shown on the maps) the proportion of married men in the age group 45–54 years was little changed. The regional pattern to marriage and non-marriage among women in 1851 broadly conformed to the pattern of a decade earlier, though in Dublin city there was some rise in female celibacy. In Belfast there was only a marginal rise, which could be spurious (due to age mis-reporting and the small change in age categories between the censuses of 1841 and 1851).

A perceptible drift away from marriage was apparent in the decades after 1851. In Laois, by 1871, a quarter of all adult males would never marry. Among older women, the fraction was almost a fifth. A high incidence of non-marriage for men was particularly noticeable in the Leinster counties, and northwards into Monaghan, Tyrone and Londonderry. The picture for women was much the same, though the extent of non-marriage tended to be less than for men. The highest incidence of female celibacy was to be found in the counties of Dublin, Down and Londonderry. As with the case of men, marriage and modernity seemed to mix badly in the eastern half of the island.

The pace of change towards less frequent marriage was by no means uniform. Some counties showed a remarkable turnaround in marriage behaviour. In the pastoral county of Roscommon, for instance, men enjoyed very high levels of marriage in 1841. Yet by 1871 the proportion single had trebled in size. By contrast, a county like Carlow, where male and female celibacy levels were already high before the Famine, at 14% and 15% respectively, experienced only modest growth in celibacy over the three succeeding decades. Change was even more muted in the western counties of Mayo and Kerry. Levels of celibacy below 10%, for both men and women, were being recorded as late as 1871.

Still there was no mistaking the direction of change. Whatever way one looked, be it north or south, east or west, towards urban or rural Ireland, the trend was towards less frequent marriage. The only exceptions were the counties of Mayo and Kerry. The reasons for the widespread adoption of celibacy are still shrouded in controversy, though the explanations discussed elsewhere in relation to postponed marriage seem relevant here also. Among the more compelling but by no means complete explanations are those which stress the importance of living standards. People expected high and rising standards of living in post-Famine society and were not prepared to compromise these expectations for the pleasures and penalties of an improvident match. While average incomes undoubtedly rose during the second half of the century, it seems that notions of an acceptable standard of living outpaced these gains. Irish society was peculiarly open to outside influences. As a result of mass emigration to higher-wage economies in North America and Britain, and the contacts maintained between those who remained and those who left, gaps between living conditions in Ireland and elsewhere were keenly appreciated.

Figure 8: Female celibacy in 1841 and 1871

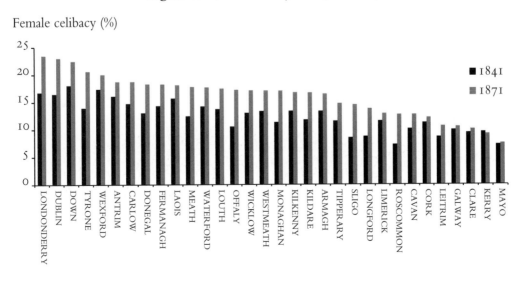

The historian R.E. Kennedy goes further in his analysis of the emigration-celibacy nexus.[1] For him, the decision to emigrate and the decision to remain permanently celibate were competing choices. Irish men and Irish women usually emigrated in their teens and twenties, while still unmarried. Marriage before emigration would have been an encumbrance, particularly as there was no guarantee in advance of a secure livelihood abroad. Those who remained were prepared to run the risk of not being able to marry, as became the fate of increasing minorities of men and women during the second half of the nineteenth century (see diagrams). Why did so many young people acquiesce in a social order 'so unnatural', to use K.H. Connell's phrase?[2] Extra-marital relationships were clearly not the answer. Prostitution was confined to the large towns and the vicinity of army barracks, while the low rates of illegitimacy characteristic of Irish rural society point to a high degree of sexual restraint. In farming communities loyalty to the family, and the shared belief in the importance of passing on the farm intact from one generation to the next, meant that non-inheriting sons, if they remained in Ireland, were prepared to submerge their personal interests and submit to a lifetime of celibacy. Women without dowries had similarly limited options. But, in the view of Connell (p. 121), 'the most pervasive, the most persuasive, of the agencies reconciling the young' to postponed marriage or non-marriage was Irish catholicism. If this was indeed the case, then one may presume that protestantism must have performed a similar function for its adherents. Postponed marriage and permanent celibacy were not just phenomena associated with Irish catholics; these were also features of protestant communities in Ireland.

It seems reasonable to assume some link between postponed marriage and permanent celibacy. But what kind of relationship? One could argue, for instance, that areas with high rates of non-marriage would be those where age at marriage was late. The same kinds of structural conditions and calculating attitudes which produced late ages of marriage might also be responsible for large numbers of people remaining unmarried. But equally one might hypothesise that delayed marriage and permanent celibacy were alternative strategies for handling pressure on

living standards arising from marriage. We can explore the issue, at least in a preliminary way, by correlating the mean age at marriage at a county level with the incidence of non-marriage or celibacy. It makes sense to do this separately for males and females, in case there was a gender-specific dimension to the question. The number of cases used was 34, that is, the 32 counties with Dublin city and Belfast entered as separate observations.

The results for women supported the first of the two hypotheses outlined above. High rates of celibacy were found to be positively associated with late ages of marriage. The correlation coefficient for female celibacy in 1871 and age at marriage in the same year was 0.62. A time lead might be appropriate, so female celibacy in 1871 was also related to age at marriage a decade earlier. The results were virtually identical. These findings suggest that, for women, late age at marriage and celibacy were not substitutes for each other; rather they appear to have been the joint product of similar historical circumstances. The outcome for men was similar. The correlation co-efficient linking celibacy in 1871 with age at marriage in that year turned out to be 0.68, while if marriage ages for the preceding decade are used the coefficient was a little higher at 0.70.

Being unmarried in mid-Victorian Ireland did mean abstinence from sexual relations in most cases. Permanent celibacy did not, however, imply living alone. The title of this commentary should not be read too literally. A variety of living arrangements was possible. An unmarried brother or sister might live with a married brother, or with another married relative. On farms their labour could be valuable, though their social and occupational status within the household would have been the subordinate one of 'relatives assisting'. The extended family household was common in Ireland during phases of the family life cycle and proved flexible, where resources permitted, in absorbing surplus relatives. Bachelors with some property and income might have the company of a niece or a nephew, and, in some cases, a living-in servant, thereby maintaining multiple-person households. An unmarried brother and sister, sometimes with other unmarried siblings, might form a non-family household. This could permit a division of labour along gender lines and economies of scale in household production and

1 R.E. Kennedy, *The Irish: emigration, marriage and fertility* (London, 1973), pp. 163–7.

2 K.H. Connell, *Irish peasant society: four historical essays* (Oxford, 1968), p. 118.

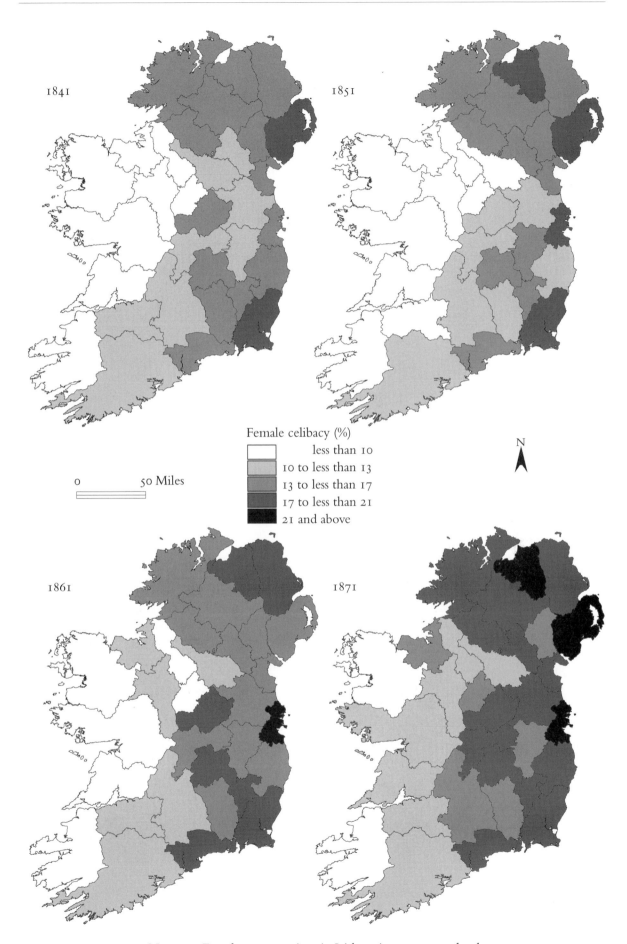

Map 20: Female non-marriage in Irish society at county level

HOUSEHOLDS AND FAMILIES

Domestic social groups are conventionally defined as families, households and housefuls. The statistics presented here relate to housefuls. Mean houseful size (MHFS) is calculated by dividing the population of a county or barony by the number of inhabited houses in the county or barony. A houseful is simply a collection of people living in a house. Complications may arise from the presence of hotels or institutions such as workhouses, hospitals, prisons or army camps, but, taking the country as a whole, they are not serious.

The persons comprising a houseful may or may not be related and they may or may not enjoy some functional relationship. The defining characteristic is that they occupy the same premises. The concept of the houseful becomes clearer when we consider another concept – the household. A typical household is a group of people living together consisting of a conjugal family unit – that is a married couple or the surviving widow or widower, together with their resident children (if any) – plus other kin, servants, apprentices and lodgers living in the house. In addition to sharing the same premises, the individuals forming a household are bound together by ties of consanguinity and economic function.

Finally, families. At the core of the typical household is the conjugal family formed by a married couple or a surviving widow or widower and those children who have not left home. In the usual case, therefore, families and households and housefuls fit together like a nest of Russian dolls. In many cases they will be identical; but families with servants, apprentices or lodgers become households; and a tenement block, for example, housing two or more families or households, becomes a houseful.[1]

The present analysis is pursued at the level of the barony and therefore covers the period 1841–61 (1861 was the last year for which the relevant data were gathered for baronies). Between 1841 and 1851 the population of Ireland fell by almost two million. In the next decade the population declined by a further 700,000. What happened to the number and size of housefuls during these two decades? In simple terms, both the number of inhabited houses declined and also the MHFS. In reality, the picture was more complex.

During the 1840s the number of inhabited houses throughout Ireland declined by 282,000 and the MHFS in the baronies increased fractionally from 6.13 to 6.14. During the 1850s the number of inhabited houses in Ireland fell by 51,000 and MHFS fell to 5.69. It was as though, during the Famine decade, one-fifth of all houses and their inhabitants disappeared, leaving the remaining four-fifths unscathed, whereas in the following decades the loss of population involved both a decline in the number of houses and in the MHFS (see Table 4).

The more detailed pattern during the 1840s revealed by the barony statistics shows that the MHFS in 190 baronies declined by an average of 0.25 persons. On the other hand, there were 130 baronies where MHFS increased by an average of 0.43 persons. The increases occurred mainly in towns and in the south-west of the country. By contrast, during the decade 1851–61 MHFS fell in 309 out of the 320 baronies in Ireland, on average by almost 0.5 persons. In just 11 baronies did MHFS increase, on average by less than one person (0.63). The increases were mostly in towns and their scale was unremarkable, except for the large increase (4.02) in Offaly East, county Kildare, the location of the Curragh army camp.

Table 4: Percentage decline in population, inhabited houses and houseful size

DECADE	POPULATION DECLINE (%)	DECLINE IN THE NO. OF INHABITED HOUSES (%)	CHANGE IN MHFS (%)
1841–51	22	21	0
1851–61	11	4.9	−7.3

1 Peter Laslett, 'Introduction: the history of the family', in Peter Laslett and Richard Wall (eds), *Household and family in past time* (Cambridge, 1972), pp. 23–44.

1841 to 1851

1851 to 1861

Change in houseful size

less than –1.50

–1.50 to less than –0.50

–0.50 to less than –0.01

No change

0.01 to less than 1.50

1.50 and above

0   50 Miles

N

Map 21: Change in mean houseful size at barony level

An inspection of the maps shows that, on the whole, the larger domestic units were to be found in the south-west of the country, with some clusters in the towns and cities. The picture is clear from the county maps where the southern and western counties of Tipperary, Waterford, Cork, Kerry, Limerick and Clare, together with the eastern county of Dublin had the largest housefuls. This pattern persisted throughout the period, although it was less pronounced by 1861.

The barony maps show the same pattern, although inevitably in a more spotty fashion. In particular they reflect the increase in the MHFS between 1841 and 1851 in the southern and western baronies. The most likely explanation for the increase in these regions was that evictions cleared away many of the smaller cabins, leaving the occupants to crowd in with kin. The large social units found in some towns is explained by tenement dwellings and lodgers. The 1861 map clearly demonstrates the widespread decline in the mean size of the houseful as continuing emigration carried away tens of thousands of men, women and children that had once populated the countryside.

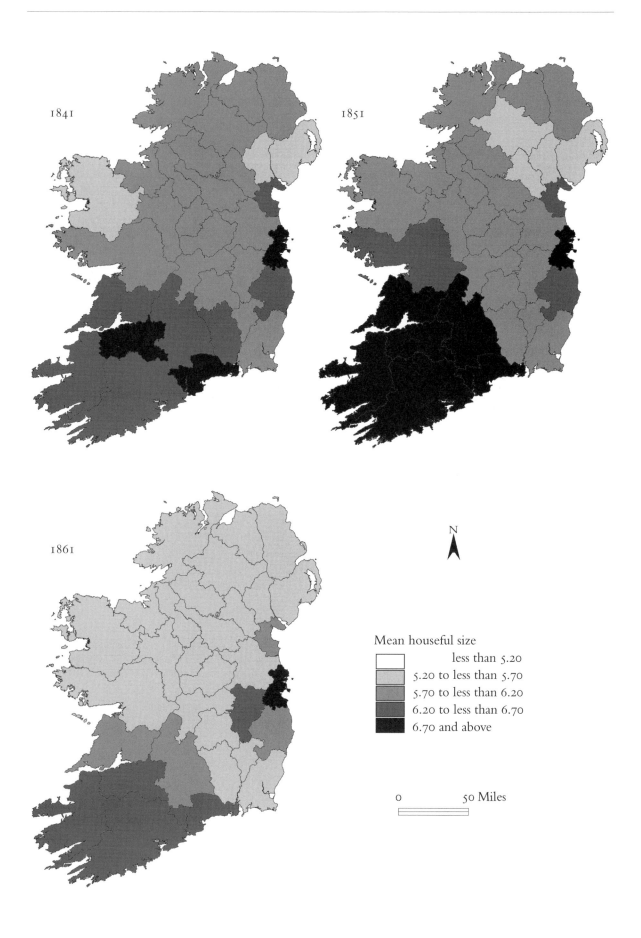

Map 22: Mean houseful size at county level

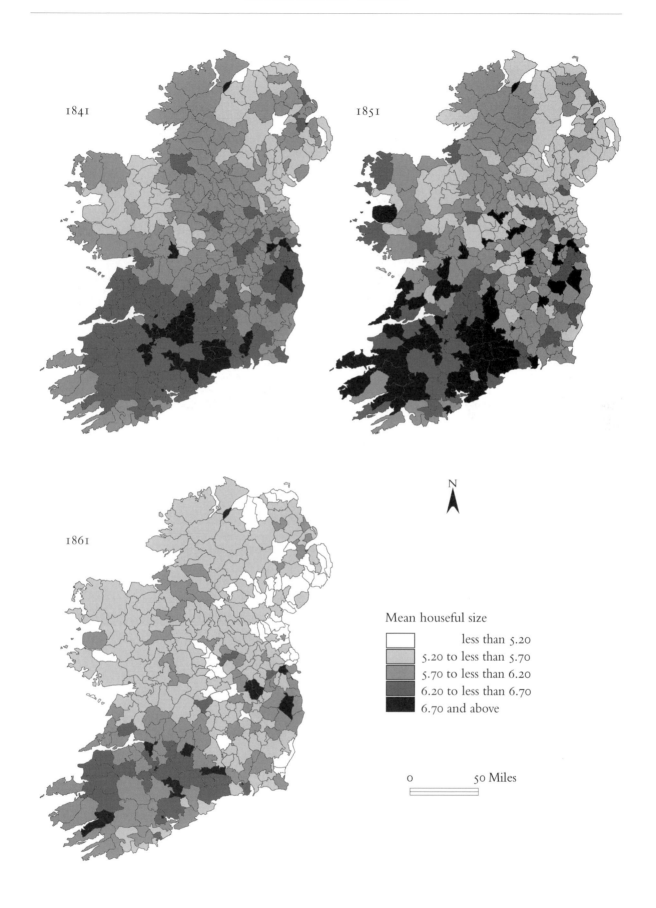

1841

1851

1861

N

Mean houseful size

less than 5.20

5.20 to less than 5.70

5.70 to less than 6.20

6.20 to less than 6.70

6.70 and above

0   50 Miles

Map 23: Mean houseful size at barony level

The Cork Society of Friends' Soup House

SOURCE: *Illustrated London News*, 16 January 1847.

THE CONDITION OF THE PEOPLE

Since this volume concentrates on the decades embracing the Great Famine, the emphasis is on the condition of the labouring classes. Some of the measures of welfare can be mapped; others are available only for a point in time or can be used to indicate trends over time.

Shelter is a basic requirement of existence and the Irish census commissioners gave close attention to the condition of houses. They classified housing into four categories, from the best (first class) to the worst (fourth class). Before the Famine very many impoverished families lived in the lowest class of housing. In Kerry and Mayo fourth class houses accounted for close to 60% of all dwellings, and in counties Galway, Cork, Sligo and Limerick the proportion was near to 50%. The Famine cleared away many tens of thousands of poor cottiers and, with them, their wretched dwellings. Better-off people lived in well-constructed houses. Not surprisingly, the highest proportions of the better houses in 1841 were located on the eastern side of the country. The distribution of good and bad houses changed little over the next two decades, except that the tide of first and second class houses spread westward. In large part this was because the Famine swept away the worst houses and their occupants, leaving the survivors living in relative comfort.

Food is even more fundamental to human existence than shelter. Before the Famine the bottom third of the population lived on a diet dominated by potatoes and supplemented from time to time by oatmeal, milk or skimmed milk, fish, cabbage or other vegetables. Potatoes were consumed in very large quantities and with their supplements provided a nutritionally rich diet. Measured by the standards of the nutritionist rather than the economist, Ireland was not poor in the 1830s. With the successive failures of the potato crop between 1845 and 1849, Ireland entered into a period of heavy mortality arising from starvation, nutritional deficiency diseases, but mainly from infections. Starving to death takes a long time and the victim is more likely to be overcome by fever or some other infection. Similarly, vitamin-deficiency diseases also worked insidiously by debilitating victims and softening them up for attacks by infections. The connection between infections and malnutrition was complicated. The major killers – typhus,

relapsing fever, diarrhoea, dysentery – were not caused directly by low levels of nutrition. They were social diseases, passed from person to person by vectors such as lice or fleas, which found it easier to operate when human populations were crowded together in search of food. Furthermore, they found easier pickings among the famished than among the well-fed. Soup kitchens, public works, workhouses: all were attempts by charitable organizations or government to soften the blow of the potato failure. All have been criticised in terms of scale and timing. Less often have they been viewed as foci of disease and death. Yet that is what they were.

There are less tangible indicators of well-being. For example, virtually everybody in mid-nineteenth century Ireland claimed to be a Christian, the great majority of them Roman Catholic. There was little change in denominational allegiance across the Famine decades, although it was the Roman Catholic population that suffered most. And then there is language and literacy. An ability to read and write is usually taken to be an indicator of welfare. The census commissioners were interested in such matters. Three points emerge from their findings. The first was that illiteracy was greater in the west of Ireland than in the east; it was lowest of all in the north-east. This accords well with other measures of welfare. Secondly, levels of literacy increased between 1841 and 1871 throughout Ireland. Thirdly, females were less literate than males although the gap narrowed with time. The Famine had some part to play in these trends, but the survivors were demanding more education and church and state were supplying greater opportunities to learn to read and write.

For the census commissioners literacy meant a proficiency in English. We can only guess at the proportion of Gaelic speakers before the Famine. It may have been more than a third, concentrated among the poorer sections of society. By 1851 the proportion was down to a quarter and it continued to fall over the next twenty years. The highest concentration of Gaelic speakers was in the west of Ireland, economically the least developed parts of the country. The Great Famine killed many Irish speakers and compelled many others to emigrate. Subsequent economic development further squeezed Gaelic from the lexicon of economically useful skills.

THE ECONOMY OF THE POTATO EATERS

Irish history without the potato in unthinkable. It is inextricably linked with the population explosion of the later eighteenth and early nineteenth centuries. It has been held responsible for the strong physique and height of Irish people as compared to most other Europeans in this period. It set Irish diet apart from that of other societies, though it can hardly be said to have lent itself to a sophisticated cuisine. Above all, it was a cheap source of food for the mass of the people.

Dependence on this miracle tuber did, however, have its disadvantages. Potatoes, as compared to oatmeal for example, had a high volume-to-value ratio, implying high transport costs and limits to the area over which it might be traded in times of dearth. Unlike cereals, potatoes could not be carried over from one harvest to the next. Thus buffer stocks could not be maintained with a view to smoothing fluctuations in production. This was an important source of vulnerability in the economy of the poor. Indeed potatoes would not last a full year, which meant that hunger haunted the cabins of the poor as the remaining stocks of potatoes rotted in the late spring and early summer. This seasonality is reflected in the course of prices during the year. Typically, they were at their lowest in the autumn

when the maincrop was harvested and at their highest during the 'hungry' months of June, July and August. It would be mistaken to think in terms of gentle rises in prices through the seasons. In fact the price rises between, say, October and June, were often of the order of 40 per cent or more. During the harvest year of 1841–42, for instance, the rise between these months was 47 per cent.[1] For households largely dependent on potatoes for sustenance and forced to enter the market to buy them, these surges in food prices meant, not just acute diminutions in their standard of living, but actual hunger. During the harvest year 1845–46, panic gripped the countryside and seasonal price rises reached astronomical proportions. The link between prices and starvation was a close one.

Figure 9 provides a window on the course of potato and oat prices before, during and after the Famine. The price in each case is in pence per hundredweight (112 pounds) and the observations are bi-monthly. Of the two major food crops, it is noticeable that potatoes were on a much lower price plane before the Famine, of the order of one third or so. Both sets of prices soared to terrifying heights in Black '47, before being moderated by a rising tide of imported substitutes, maize in particular. The

Figure 9: Potato and oat prices, Belfast market, 1841–61

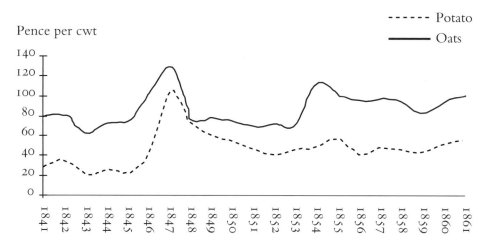

---

1 The data are from Líam Kennedy, 'The welfare of the poor: seasonality in food prices in Ireland, 1770–1925' (Discussion Paper, Economic & Social Research Institute, Dublin, 1998). On wages see Líam Kennedy & Martin Dowling, 'Prices and wages in Ireland, 1700–1850', *Irish Economic & Social History*, 24 (1997), 98–103.

Figure 10: Potato yields before, during and after the Famine

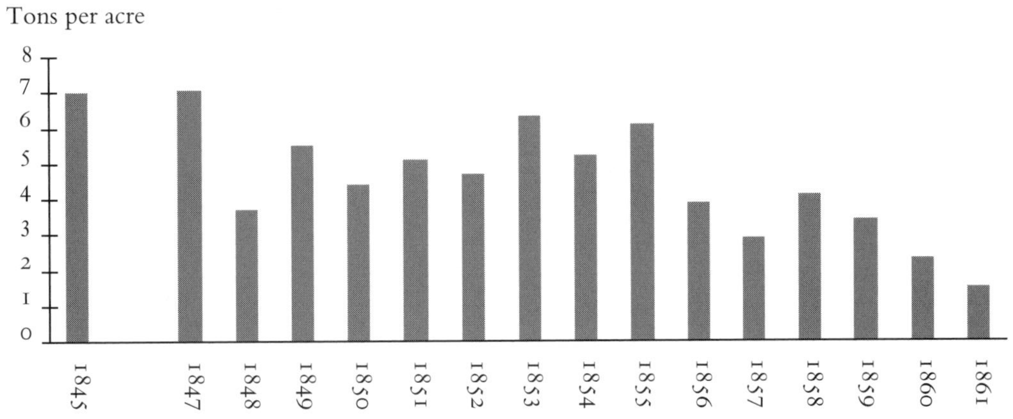

Tons per acre

more pronounced rise in the price of 'praties' reflects their humble status as an inferior good, as well as the devastation of potato supplies due to blight. Thus, as real incomes were crushed during the Famine due to rising food prices, especially rising potato prices, the demand for the commodity actually intensified. Sadly, it was not possible to substitute a cheaper foodstuff. The potato (in the Ireland of the 1840s) was an extreme case of an inferior good, possibly even an example of the elusive Giffen good.

Viewed in the longer run, it can be seen that potato prices moved onto a higher plane after the Famine, in the process narrowing the price differential that had existed between potatoes and oats. The real significance of this upward shift in potato prices was that it pushed up permanently the cost of subsistence in post-Famine society. This was linked to falling potato yields, part of the continuing

and malign legacy of *Phythophthora infestans*. The produce of potatoes averaged in the region of seven tons per acre before the Famine, whereas in its aftermath three and four tons were not uncommon (see Figure 10).

Using potatoes as the 'wage good', one can form the roughest of impressions of the impact of food failure on living standards. In Figure 11 money wages, relating to unskilled labour on the Parkanaur estate in county Tyrone, are deflated using a potato price series from the Belfast market. The results are expressed in index number form, and suggest a dramatic collapse in the purchasing power of wages with the onset of the Famine. If 'real' wages before the catastrophe were bumping along close to subsistence, this exercise indicates that the purchasing power of the poor fell disastrously in 1846–8. The ordeal of the poor was not simply a matter of economics, but economics certainly mattered.

Figure 11: The 'potato' wage, 1840–50

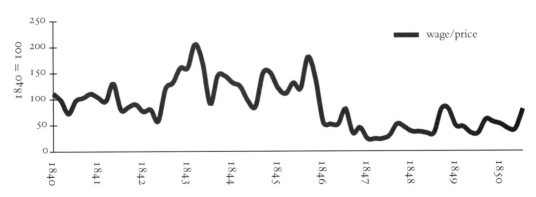

THE FOOD OF THE PEOPLE

Throughout the eighteenth and early nineteenth centuries the dietary pattern of the Irish poor became progressively simpler. The varied diet of pastoral products, grains and vegetables enjoyed by all early in the eighteenth century was progressively eroded by the dominance of one food, the potato. On the eve of the Famine there were three million 'potato people', constituting 40% of the population.

Accompaniments to potatoes fell into five groups. First, there were the more or less regular additions such as milk, skimmed milk and buttermilk. Secondly, there were seasonal substitutes, such as herrings, which were eaten when potatoes were scarce. Thirdly, certain foods had a regional bias; a notable example of this was the high consumption of oatmeal in the north-east of the country. Fourthly, in times of famine, all sorts of things were used in attempts to keep starvation at bay. Beaches were stripped bare of shell fish and seaweed, and cabbages, turnips, swedes as well as charlock and nettles were consumed. Finally, there were the luxury foods of meat, eggs, bread, butter, and very occasionally tea, enjoyed at festivals, weddings and wakes. These categories overlapped, and before the Great Famine they contrived to relieve the tedium of potatoes, potatoes and potatoes and provided those few essentials to good health that were absent from the principal staple. Diet in Ireland on the eve of the Great Famine was

therefore a simple one; the potato as the mainstay, with other items of food relegated to the seasonal, occasional, peripheral and celebratory.

This pattern was clearly revealed by the *Poor Inquiry (Ireland)*, published in 1836. The purpose of the *Poor Inquiry* was to assess the state of the labouring classes and one of the methods used was to circulate a questionnaire requesting information on a wide variety of aspects of labourers' lives. The questionnaire was sent to prominent residents, such as local gentry, justices of the peace, magistrates, catholic priests, and protestant clergy, in over two thousand parishes in Ireland, covering every county. The responses provide valuable information about how such people perceived the poor to have conducted their lives, including the food they ate. Hence we have a snapshot of the diet consumed by the labouring poor in Ireland on the eve of the Great Famine. Of the 2,500 or so parishes surveyed 1,569 useable answers about diet were returned. These responses provide a detailed pattern of the pre-Famine food consumption of the poor, and are illustrated by maps presented below. Six of the most commonly referred to foods – potatoes, oatmeal, milk, fish (including herrings), bacon, and eggs – have been selected for mapping. The maps show the percentage of responses that refer to the consumption of particular foods in each county. To demonstrate the seasonality of three foods – milk, oatmeal and fish – diagrams showing regular and occasional consumption have been included.

Potatoes dominated the Irish labourers' diet on the eve of the Great Famine and for several decades before. The arrival of the potato, however, is obscure, though a Spanish connection is hinted at by its the early Irish name of *an spáinneach*. The chronology of potato diffusion into the diet has generated much debate. Salaman has argued that potatoes were a basic food on the Irish menu by 1630. William Wilde suggested a later date of between the end of the seventeenth century and beginning of the eighteenth century. K.H. Connell proposed a later date still of 1730.[1]

'General view of the potato plant, its root, leaves, tubers, and apples (fruit)', *Illustrated London News*, 29 August 1846

1 Census of Ireland for the year 1851, Part V, Table of deaths, vol. 1, BPP 1856, xxix, p. 237; K.H. Connell, 'The potato in Ireland', *Past and Present*, 23 (1962), 60.

Among the labouring classes potatoes were consumed sometimes at two meals, at other times three, depending on the season. Consumption was high. Estimates range between eight and fifteen pounds daily. Potatoes were sometimes accompanied by milk or herrings and this menu was rich in all the nutrients required for human existence, assuring the poor of a highly nutritious, if monotonous diet. During hard times, however, this potato diet was accompanied by no more than salt or water flavoured with pepper.

Potato cultivation flourished in the wet, dull and cool climatic conditions of Ireland. Originally they were grown as a garden crop. Because of their soil enriching properties they proved an excellent clearing crop on newly tilled soil, as well as a valuable rotation crop to restore the fertility of ground used for cereal cultivation. As the demand for Irish cereals increased under the stimulus of rising prices, potatoes increasingly entered field cultivation regimes. Additional advantages of the potato for the poor were the ease of cultivation in 'lazy-beds', the lack of processing required to make them available for food, and the simple cooking method of boiling. Several potato varieties were grown. 'Black', 'cup' and 'apple' were prized, but it was the high yielding though watery 'lumper' which was cultivated by the poor. The attraction of the potato was its ability to yield enough food to feed a family on a small piece of land. On less than one acre a labourer could grow sufficient potatoes for his family for nine months of the year. Potatoes provided a higher food yield per acre than any grain crop. By the early nineteenth century over two million acres were under potatoes, yielding from 6 to 8 tons per acre.

The potato map demonstrates the dominance of the food throughout the entire country. Only a tiny minority of valid responses to the dietary question in the *Poor Enquiry* questionnaire failed to record potato consumption. These were in counties Antrim, Armagh, Down, Dublin, Louth and Cork. The oat eating habits of the north-east and the availability of cheap food in the cities of Dublin and Cork are likely explanations for the lesser prevalence of the potato in those areas.

Between 1845 and 1849 the potato crop was ruined three times by *Phytophthora infestans*, commonly called potato blight. In 1845 one-third of the crop was destroyed. The following year three-quarters of the harvest was lost. Yields were average in 1847, but little had been sown as seed potatoes were scarce. In 1848, yields were only two-thirds of normal. Since over 3 million people were totally dependent upon potatoes for food, famine was inevitable, hunger increasing with each failure. The nation-wide dominance of the potato in the Irish diet was never fully restored after the Great Famine.

Oatmeal plugged the gap between the old and new potato crop. Prior to 1750 oatmeal had fulfilled a more prominent role, but by the 1820s its importance had been displaced by potatoes as the chief food of the poor. A return to its former prominence occurred only during June, July and August; hence their name of 'meal months'. If the potato harvest was poor the summer gap was prolonged. Early in the nineteenth century protracted lean periods occurred with increasing regularity. Oatmeal, therefore, was resorted to earlier but supplies then ran out before the new potato crop matured. Oats required milling which incurred expenditure. Also, oatmeal provided less nourishment, pound for pound, than potatoes. The most convenient way to cook oatmeal was by boiling it in water to make porridge, referred to by the Irish as 'stirabout'. The one cooking utensil the poor possessed, the potato pot, was suitable also for this purpose. Some households used oatmeal to make bread but baking required greater culinary skills. Though all counties cultivated oats to a greater or lesser extent, there was a concentration of cultivation in the north-east, extending down through Cavan and Longford. Around this core was a fringe extending to a line roughly from Donegal Bay in the north-west to Wexford in the south-east. Consumption patterns followed cultivation concentrations. Thus consumption was high in Ulster and along the eastern seaboard counties. The preference for oatmeal in Ulster has been attributed to its Scottish connection.

A diseased potato stem, *Illustrated London News*, 29 August 1846

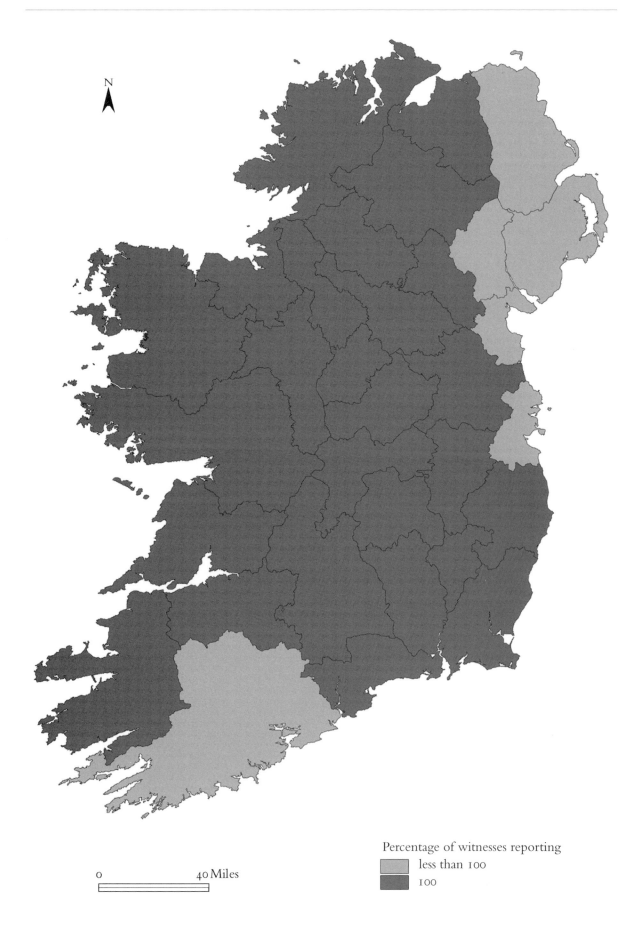

N

Percentage of witnesses reporting
less than 100
100

0   40 Miles

Map 24: Potato consumption at county level, *c.*1836

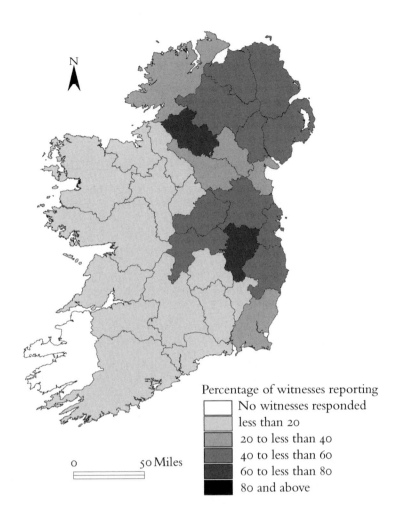

Map 25: Oatmeal consumption at county level, *c.*1836

Figure 12: Oatmeal consumption, *c.*1836

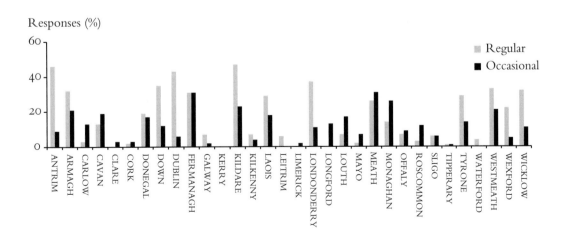

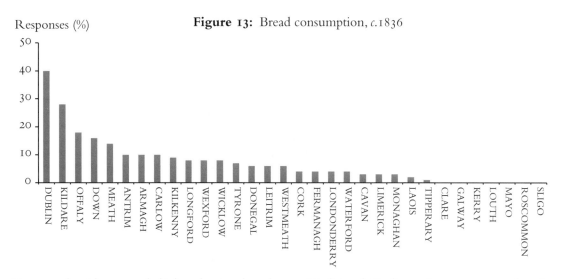

Figure 13: Bread consumption, *c.*1836

Responses (%)

Compared with oatmeal, little wheaten bread was eaten. Bread usually had to be purchased and was beyond the purse of most labourers: only a few of the better-off households had cooking equiment and skill for baking bread. Most bread was made of coarse wheaten flour, except in the north and in the Pale region where oatmeal was also used. The highest consumption was in county Dublin. The numerous bakeries in and around Dublin city gave labourers easy access to bread. In Kildare we learn that in 1836 'the demand for wheaten bread has greatly increased within the last three years'.[2]

By the end of the nineteenth century bread was often spread with butter. This had not been the case in the immediate pre-Famine decades. Butter had become too precious a product for home use and although Ireland produced great quantities much of it was exported. Consequently few counties in 1836 displayed a high level of consumption (see Figure 14).

Milk and other milk products had been the mainstay of the Irish diet for many centuries.

Traditional Gaelic society was pastoral and consequently diets were strongly shaped by milk products. This dietary inheritance was upheld through to the nineteenth century. Milk was consumed in a wide variety of forms, some liquid, others solid and semi-solid. In its liquid form whole milk, buttermilk, and skimmed milk were drunk in large quantities. As the dietary pattern of the poor eroded to potatoes, milk was an ideal complement. It provided a liquid accompaniment and was very nutritious, supplying those nutrients deficient in the potato. Buttermilk was a cheap alternative to milk and consequently became the poor man's drink. Buttermilk and skimmed milk are low in fat, the former being the residual liquid left when butter making was completed. As large quantities of butter were made for both the domestic and export markets, large amounts of buttermilk were available. Since the respondents to the *Poor Inquiry* may have been unaware of the differences in milk drinks, the map represents consumption of all types as a single item. The pattern displayed by the map

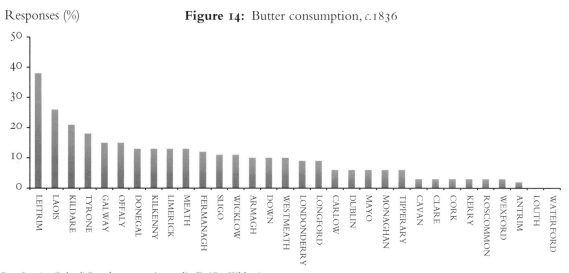

Figure 14: Butter consumption, *c.*1836

Responses (%)

2 *Poor Inquiry (Ireland)* Supplement to Appendix D (Co. Kildare), BPP, 1836, xxxi, p. 62. Evidence of James White, Esq.

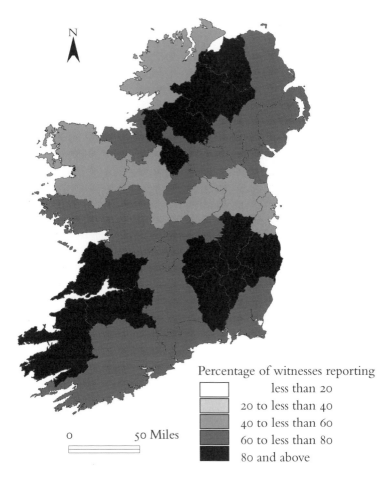

Map 26: Milk consumption at county level, *c.*1836

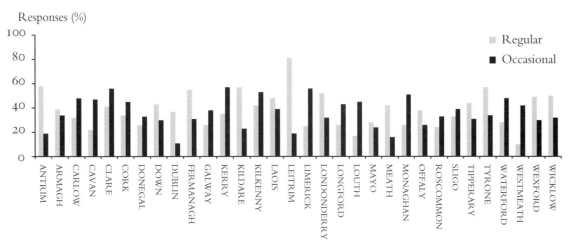

Figure 15: Milk consumption, *c.*1836

shows the lowest consumption in Donegal, Mayo Roscommon and eastwards along a narrow corridor to Dublin. Highest consumption was in three distinct pockets: the west of Ulster down to Leitrim; the south-west counties of Clare, Limerick and Kerry; and Laois, Carlow, Kildare, Kilkenny and Wicklow.

Turning to eggs and meat, labourers ate very few eggs, which were used principally for barter. The counties of Kildare and Mayo recorded the highest egg consumption. In Kildare labourers enjoyed the most varied diet of the entire country and eggs were one of several foods eaten there to relieve the

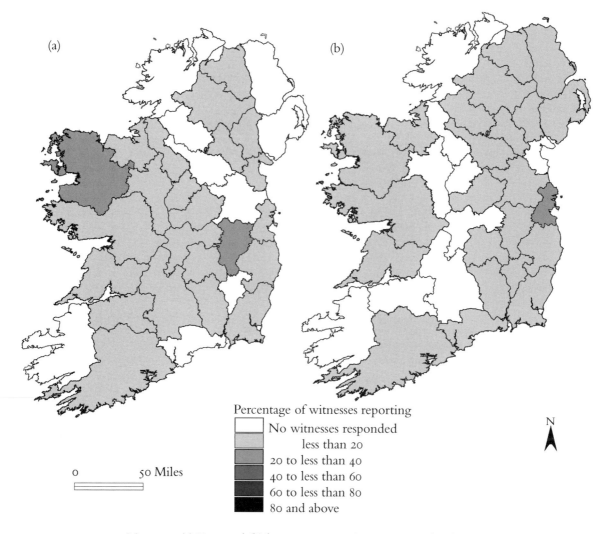

Map 27: (a) Eggs and (b) bacon consumption at county level, c.1836

tedium of potatoes and milk.[3] In the western counties of Galway and Mayo eggs fulfilled several roles. They added occasional variety to the menu, though they were used more as a medium of exchange. Even labourers in the interior of Mayo, well away from the coast, exchanged eggs for salt herrings.[4] Salt and pepper were also acquired in this way. Eggs were also commonly exchanged for goods such as soap and tobacco.

Although references to meat outnumbered those to bacon in the *Poor Inquiry*, respondents' comments suggest that the meat eaten by the poor was generally bacon. For instance, a county Kildare respondent recorded that 'the only flesh meat made use of [was] bacon, and that only on Sundays or holidays.'[5] Highest consumption was in the east and north, in counties Antrim, Down and Dublin. Even here meat, either

beef, pork or bacon, was a luxury confined to high days and holidays. Towns and cities such as Dublin, Waterford and Belfast, with their abundance of butchers' shops, gave the poor access to cheap cuts of meat, and consumption was therefore relatively high.

Fish was an important seasonal food in the diet of the poor. Like oatmeal, it filled the summer gap between the old and new potato crops. The perishable nature of fresh fish meant that the season for eating it was short. Two methods of preservation, drying and salting, lengthened the period of consumption and also facilitated transportation of fish inland.

The most popular fish among the poor was herrings. They were harvested from late July to the end of August, were cheaper than other fish, and very tasty. Herrings were often referred to as 'kitchen' by the Irish, a term reserved for tasty morsels.

3 L.A. Clarkson and E. Margaret Crawford, 'Dietary directions: A topographical survey of Irish diet, 1836' in Rosalind Mitchison and Peter Roebuck (eds), *Economy and society in Scotland and Ireland 1500–1939* (Edinburgh, 1988), p. 178. **4** The Poor Inquiry

(Ireland) Appendix E, Evidence of Revd Mr Dwyer, P.P., BPP, 1836, xxxii, p. 5. **5** The Poor Inquiry (Ireland) Supplement to Appendix D, Evidence of Revd Wm. Josiah Aylmer, BPP, 1836, xxxi, p. 60.

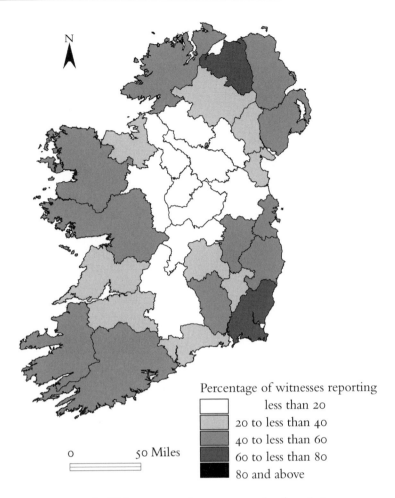

N

0   50 Miles

Percentage of witnesses reporting

less than 20
20 to less than 40
40 to less than 60
60 to less than 80
80 and above

Map 28: Fish consumption at county level, *c*.1836

So common were herrings in the labourer's diet that it is likely many of the references to fish in the *Poor Inquiry*, meant herrings rather than other species. For this reason herrings and fish data have been amalgamated to construct the map. As the map demonstrates, and not unexpectedly, the highest consumption of fish was in coastal counties, almost forming a complete circular fringe around the country. Londonderry and Wexford followed by Donegal, Down and Cork

were at the top of the league, with the midland counties at the bottom. In county Londonderry where almost 70 per cent of respondents recorded fish as part of labourers' diets their importance is reinforced by the *Ordnance Survey Memoirs* of the county. Parish after parish reported herrings along with potatoes as the food of the poor. For example, the memoir for the inland parish of Errigal, written in 1836, noted that 'salted herrings [were] much used.'[6]

Figure 16: Fish consumption *c*.1836

Regular
Occasional

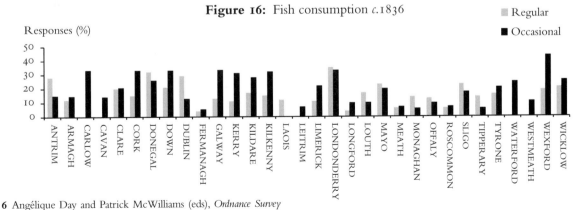

Responses (%)

6 Angélique Day and Patrick McWilliams (eds), *Ordnance Survey memoirs of Ireland. Parishes of Co. Londonderry*, vol. VIII (Belfast, 1994), p. 46.

CABIN AND CASTLE: HOUSING THE PEOPLE

Housing and shelter are basic human needs. How these needs have been met has varied through time. Before 1600, the commonalty lived in crude structures built from perishable natural materials. By the nineteenth century, with the exception of itinerants and vagrants, virtually everyone inhabited dwellings, however primitive, of a more enduring kind. The styles of vernacular architecture varied regionally, shaped by local conditions and the availability of different kinds of building materials. Students of material culture have devoted much energy to identifying and classifying different house types and relating these to their ecological setting.[1] The concern here, however, is with housing within the context of the socio-economic environment. The Irish census commissioners distinguished four classes of housing. The lowest, or fourth class, comprised 'all mud cabins having only one room' while the third class consisted of 'a better description of cottage, still built of mud, but varying from 2 to 4 rooms and windows'.[2] One may wonder if, in practice, the distinction between these two kinds of poor housing was observed consistently: certainly in 1871, by the admission of the census commissioners themselves, many houses which in previous censuses would have been classified as third class were relegated to the fourth-class category. Moreover, it is not clear how one-room buildings, but constructed of stone, would have been dealt with.[3] Moving up the scale, a house of the second class was typically 'a good farm house, or in towns, a house in a small street, having from 5 to 9 rooms and windows'. Finally, by a process of elimination, first-class houses were 'all those houses of a better description than the preceding classes'. The vague formulation of the last may not inspire confidence. The various classifications were, however, the outcome of a system of points which had been allocated on the basis of house size (number of rooms), quality (number of windows) and durability (whether its walls were constructed of mud, sods, stone or brick, and whether it was roofed by slate or thatch). No doubt there were anomalies and inconsistencies in the results generated by this scheme, but the broad patterns revealed seem plausible enough.

The extent of fourth-class housing before the Famine is striking. One might wonder why there was recourse to cheap housing on such a scale. The weight of the explanation must lie on the demand side. Ireland experienced possibly the most rapid expansion of population of any society in Europe in the century before the Famine.[4] At the middle of the eighteenth century Ireland was still thinly peopled, containing in the region of two-and-a-half million souls, or less than one-half the combined population of the Irish Republic and Northern Ireland today. But, by the eve of the Famine, the numbers had expanded to 8.5 millions, representing a growth of 240% in a century. This population explosion necessitated a huge increase in the provision of shelter. Because the growth in numbers was concentrated in the lower strata of Irish society, the demand was for low-cost, primitive forms of housing, using as inputs mud, turf, sods, straws and timber. Such plentifully available materials could be plundered from the local habitat, at relatively little expense to the cottiers and labourers who inhabited these dwellings. The spread of wretched living quarters was, therefore, a response to population pressure and chronic poverty.

While examples of fourth-class housing were to be found in plenty throughout the island, a regional dimension was strongly to the fore. In the west and the south-west the poorer sort of cabin, with earthen floor and no windows, proliferated. To take the extremes of the distribution, in the coastal baronies of Ross in west Galway, and Courceys and Bear in west Cork, more than 80% of the habitations were classified as fourth class. At the other end of the spectrum, away from the Atlantic seaboard, lay the major urban centres of Belfast, Dublin, Cork and Waterford, where less than three percent of dwellings fell into the lowest category.

---

1 For example, Alan Gailey, *Rural houses of the north of Ireland* (Edinburgh, 1984). See also F.H.A. Aalen, Kevin Whelan and Matthew Stout (eds), *Atlas of the Irish rural landscape* (Cork, 1997). 2 *Report of the Commissioners appointed to take the Census of Ireland for the year 1841* (BPP, 1843, xxiv), p. xiv. 3 Alan Gailey (private communication) suggests that the category of fourth-class housing may have included, not only the tiny, one-roomed dwellings of the labourers and cottiers, but also the larger one-roomed, internally undivided byre-dwellings of small farmers. Such a lack of discrimination would mean the category was more heterogeneous than is usually believed. 4 Joel Mokyr and Cormac Ó Gráda, 'New developments in Irish population history, 1700–1845', *Economic History Review*, 37 (1984) 473–88.

Figure 17: Percentage of fourth-class housing related to the average, annual wage income of rural labourers in each county, 1841

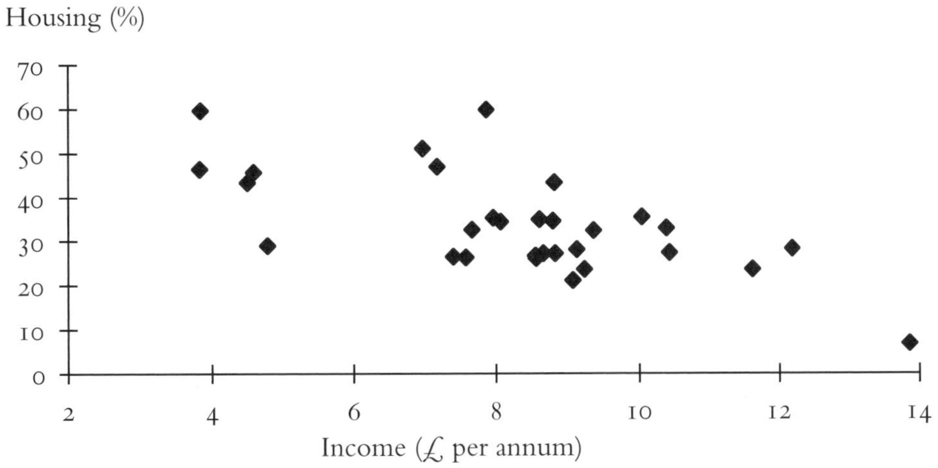

Housing (%)

Income (£ per annum)

The quality of housing is not just a measure of living conditions, important as this is. It may also be viewed as an imperfect indicator of wealth. One might well expect superior wealth to be embodied, to varying degrees in superior housing. Some contemporary observers warned, though, that there was no necessary connection between the two. Stories are told of households living in apparent squalor, yet who found large sums of capital to dower their daughters or to establish sons in farming or some other business. One partial test of this proposition is to relate the proportion of bad housing to some economic measure. If there was little or no connection between wealth on the one hand, and housing on the other, then this should show up in a weak, or non-existent relationship between the two variables. There are no good estimates of wealth, but as wealth is a function of income, we can, as a crude approximation, substitute income for wealth. The income estimates used here refer to the average wage income of the rural poor in the different counties of Ireland (see the discussion of these data in the section on wages before the Famine). The outcome of the test is illustrated in Figure 17. An inverse relationship between housing and income is apparent (the Pearson product-moment correlation coefficient is −0.67). Housing, it appears, is a normal good after all. As income rises, people in general demand more or better quality housing, individual cases to the contrary notwithstanding.

Viewed in regional perspective, these spatial distributions suggest a high degree of economic inequality between the east of Ireland and the west, whether measured in terms of income or housing quality. Both the former and the latter raise the spectre of vulnerability to famine. Income is relevant in the obvious sense of ensuring command over food resources, and housing conditions have a direct bearing on health and disease. Poor shelters – damp, draughty and dirty – offered good conditions for the propagation of disease which inevitably accompanied subsistence crises. Within a few short years this lethal combination would become manifest in the land.

The east-west divide is less sharply defined in 1841 in relation to the distribution of third-class housing but is strongly evident in the maps on second- and first-class housing. Second-class houses were only weakly represented within the housing stock in the west and the south-west, though the coastal baronies of Donegal fared better than one might have guessed. The importance of this class of housing in the hinterland of Belfast and also in the south-east is noticeable, betokening a widespread degree of comfort not encountered along the Atlantic seaboard. Broadly speaking, to the east of a line drawn from Derry to Cork there was a goodly presence of good-quality housing. This was especially true of the towns and cities. The barony of Belfast had 80% of its housing classified as second-class (the highest in Ireland), the corresponding figures for Cork and Waterford being 56% and 53% respectively. In other words, a majority of houses in these towns were reasonably spacious and of durable construction (though not necessarily in a good state of repair). But, as is evident from the maps, the phenomenon was by no means confined to urban Ireland: within the commercialised farming and linen producing regions of the east large minorities of householders also enjoyed access to more substantial and durable dwellings.

What of the very best class of housing? As one might expect, first-class housing was associated more with towns than the countryside. In 1841 Dublin had half its buildings in the first-class category. Its magnificent Georgian heritage, however, was under pressure as town houses were converted to tenement flats. Thus, the proportion of first-class houses (unlike the case of fourth-class housing) can give a very misleading picture of the living standards of individuals and households. One or more families crowded into a single room represented gross overcrowding, however grand the building might once have been. The case of Belfast is interesting. With 70,000 inhabitants in 1841, it was on the threshold of sustained expansion, challenging Dublin for economic and commercial supremacy by the later nineteenth century. Still, in each of the two baronies of Belfast Upper and Belfast Lower in 1841, fewer than five per cent of houses were of the first-class category.

In terms of the countryside, differences in the distribution of first-class housing are also apparent. Landlords, land agents, the business class, and professional people, that is, those most likely to inhabit first-class houses, showed a preference for living in the more fertile districts of Ireland. Hence the geographical spread of imposing residences showed a visible association with eastern Ireland. More precisely, the higher densities occurred south and east of an imaginary boundary drawn between Larne, north of Belfast, and Limerick, close to the mouth of the Shannon. The relative paucity of first-class dwellings in west Donegal, Mayo, Leitrim, Galway and west Clare is striking. The most extreme example was the Burren countryside of north Clare, closely followed by the baronies of Ross and the Aran Islands, where there were virtually no substantial residences whatsoever.

The housing patterns characteristic of pre-Famine Ireland, and their relationships to geography and social class, were to undergo transformation during the Famine decade. More than most measures of discontinuity, the decline of fourth-class housing shows the profound nature of the changes wrought on the Irish social structure. These habitations, which were one-roomed cabins in the main, faded from the face of Ireland within the space of a decade. Abandoned by hunger-stricken families, or levelled by landlords during the course of the mass evictions of the late 1840s, only in remote areas of the west did they survive in any numbers. (Even there, some of the apparent survivals may have been of the more substantial type of byre-dwelling rather

than the archetypal mud hut.) The Erris peninsula is an instructive case. In 1851 it held the highest proportion of fourth-class housing on the island. But even in Erris there had been a significant diminution, from 67% of the total in 1841 to 45% a decade later. Interestingly there was no further decline worth speaking of during the 1850s, the proportion in 1861 being 44%. Thus, in some remote parts of the west of Ireland, once the initial shock had been borne, it seems there was a stubborn resistance to economic and cultural forces making for change. But this was not the typical response. In the barony of Ross, for example, the proportion of fourth-class housing had shrunken to one in three by 1851 and one in five a decade later (though one suspects the dramatic decline from 85 per hundred before the Famine owes more than a little to shifting classifications).

Still the direction of change is not in dispute. Figure 18 based on baronial data, encapsulates the revolution in housing which was transforming rural society and, to a degree, the Irish landscape from the mid-nineteenth century onwards. The worst excesses of bad housing were being cleared away, with the rise to numerical dominance of the intermediate categories of housing (second and third class). Third-class housing was strongly associated with the west and the north-west in both 1851 and 1861. It was a significant presence only in exceptional parts of the east, notably in the remote and beautiful Glens of Antrim and the Cooley peninsula on the southern shores of Carlingford Lough. In time this form of inferior habitation would give way to higher standards of housing, aided by the continuing disappearance of rural labourers from the social structure. Indeed this process was in train during the 1850s and the 1860s. Between 1851 and 1861 the mean figure for the share of second-class housing in a barony, estimated across the 320 units (baronies, cities and towns), rose from 29% to 34%. The proportion of first-class housing also rose, though the elimination of fourth-class housing, would in any case have tended to boost the share of first-class housing within a shrinking housing stock. In terms of ranking, at all three census points in time Dublin, Cork, Waterford and Limerick were among the top five, out of a total of 320 units (baronies, cities and towns), in terms of proportionate holdings of first-class houses. At the other extreme, the Burren in north Clare and the Aran Islands featured consistently in the bottom five, attracting few first-class residences, or residents. A shift in the aesthetic sensibilities of the age, noticeable across Europe, in favour of wild and desolate landscapes was insufficient to compensate for the isolation and physical remoteness from the centres of commerce and culture. The burgeoning romantic movement had its limits as far as residence, as distinct from touring, was concerned.

The changing face of Ireland, in terms of housing standards and as represented on the maps, was due to a variety of forces. The Famine swept away one million souls and more than a million others fled the country during the course of the calamity. Cottiers and labourers bore the brunt of the crisis. With the devastation of these social elements went the destruction of their housing, which was generally the poorest available, either in the rural areas or on the edges of the towns and villages. For those who survived, both the social structure and the housing stock had been purged of the poorest strata. Thus the change in housing during the Famine was essentially a by-product of the class-specific nature of the Famine. In the post-Famine period, the winds of social change continued to affect housing as well as other sectors of the society. Rising incomes and a concern with respectability fuelled a demand for better housing, particularly in the more commercialised farming regions of the east. The continuing diminution of the rural poor through emigration reduced the demand for the poorest type of housing. The progress of industrialisation in Ireland, evident in east Ulster from the 1830s and accelerating in the later nineteenth century, exerted its own impact, taking the distinctive form of the red-bricked terraced houses of Belfast, Lisburn and Derry, and the mill villages of Sion Mills, Bessbrook, Gilford, Darkley and Drumaness.

Political change mattered also, though not until late in the nineteenth century. Municipal councils had concerned themselves with some of the worst town dwellings, particularly where these constituted a safety hazard, but such intervention was both limited and episodic. An era of more radical policy dawned when the British government inaugurated a scheme of building cottages, as they were commonly known, for labourers from 1883 onwards. However, the major fruits of this policy did not materialise until after 1900, when the responsibility for housing labourers was devolved to local councils, following the Local Government Act of 1898. The Congested Districts Board, it may be added, also financed housing improvements for smallholders in the West of Ireland.

Post-Famine society was the product of many forms of social transformation, of which changes in housing were among the most remarkable (and the least remarked upon). For demographic reasons the demand for housing units fell, but the structure of demand changed under conditions of greater prosperity. Moreover, rising expectations of material comfort, fuelled by comparisons within and without Irish society, informed the demand for improvement. Still, it may be as well to remind ourselves that the pace of change could be slow in some of the more remote corners of the countryside. Reporting on living conditions in the Rosses district of west Donegal in the 1890s, W.L. Micks, the first secretary of the Congested Districts Board, noted that 'cattle in many instances are housed at night at one end of the day room, and the poultry often perch overhead'.[5] While this heart-warming scene may have represented a mutually satisfactory accommodation between the human and animal kingdoms in the past, it is also clear that such practices were in terminal decline.

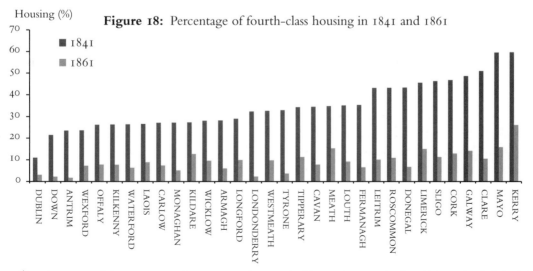

Housing (%)

Figure 18: Percentage of fourth-class housing in 1841 and 1861

■ 1841
■ 1861

5 W.L. Micks, *An account of the constitution, administration and dissolution of the Congested Districts Board for Ireland from 1891 to 1923* (Dublin, 1925), p. 253. But he adds immediately: 'The building of detached houses for cattle and fowl is increasing largely.'

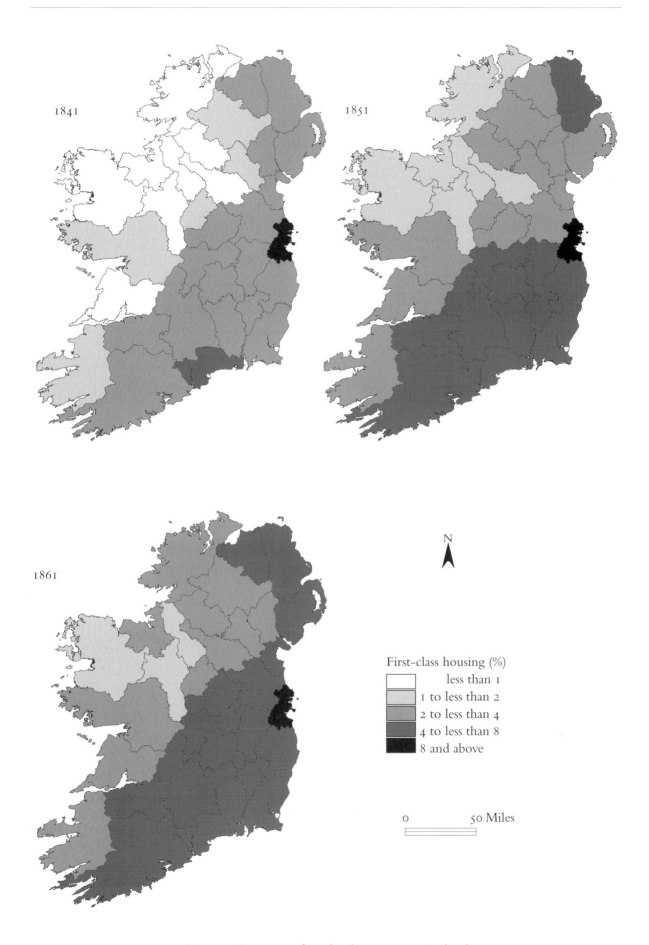

Map 29: Percentage first-class houses at county level

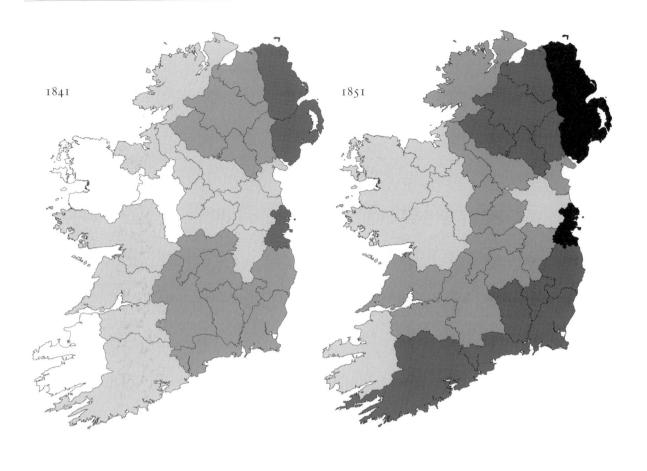

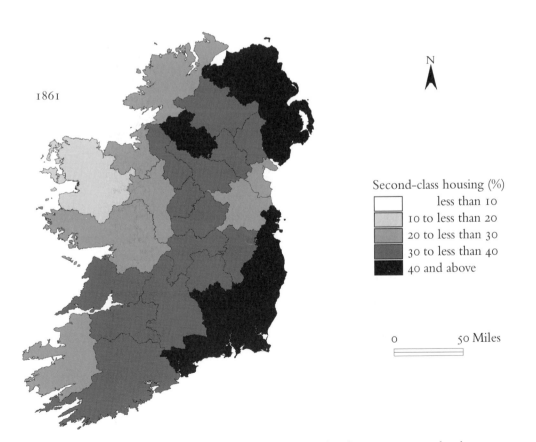

1841

1851

1861

N

Second-class housing (%)
less than 10
10 to less than 20
20 to less than 30
30 to less than 40
40 and above

0   50 Miles

Map 30: Percentage second-class houses at county level

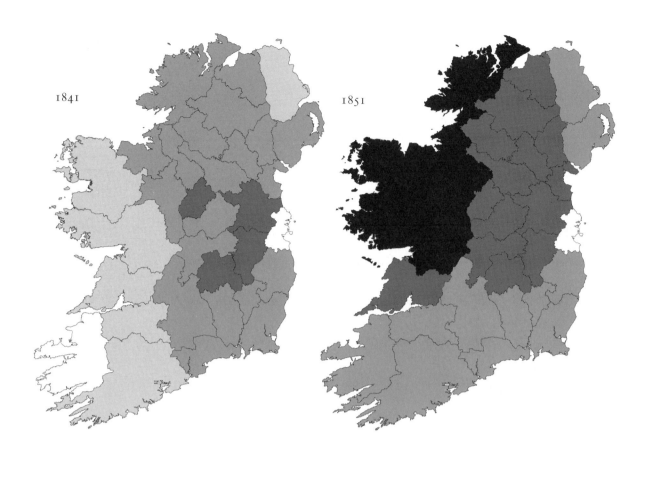

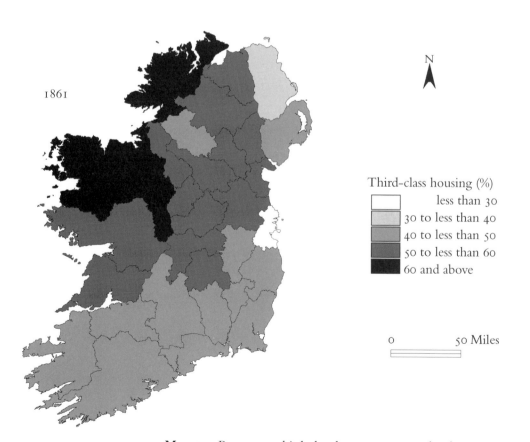

Map 31: Percentage third-class houses at county level

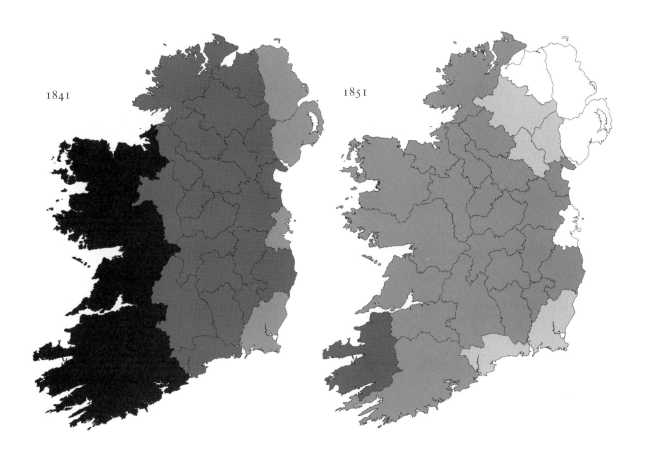

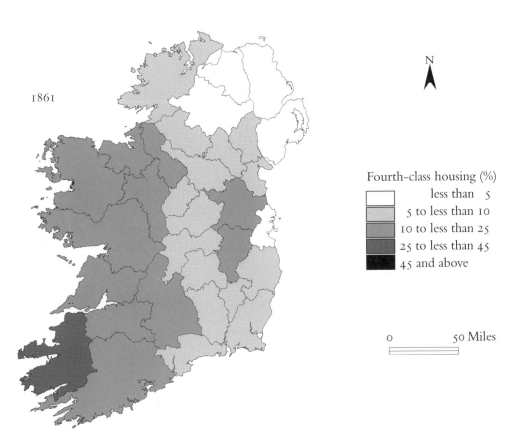

Map 32: Percentage fourth-class houses at county level

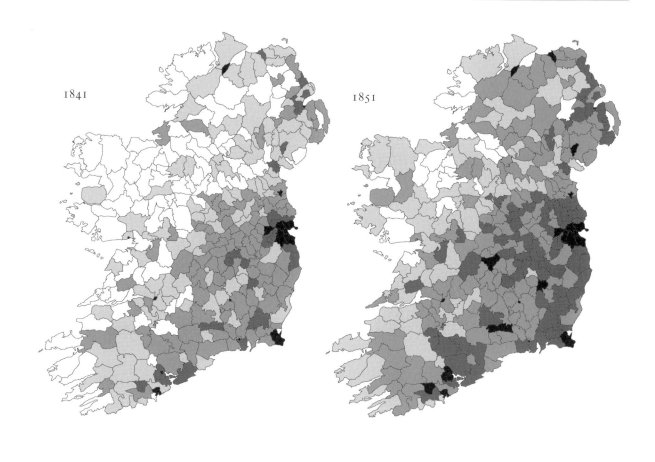

First-class housing (%)

less than 1

1 to less than 2

2 to less than 4

4 to less than 8

8 and above

0   50 Miles

Map 33: Percentage first-class houses at barony level

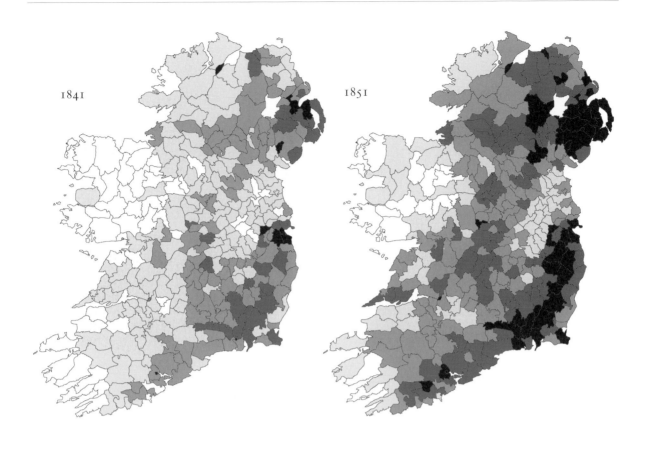

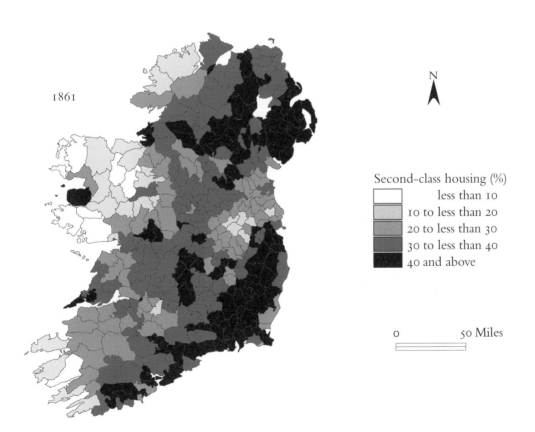

Second-class housing (%)

less than 10

10 to less than 20

20 to less than 30

30 to less than 40

40 and above

0   50 Miles

Map 34: Percentage second-class houses at barony level

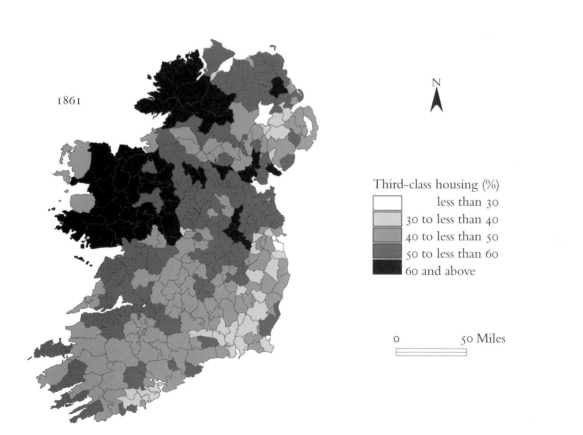

Map 35: Percentage third-class houses at barony level

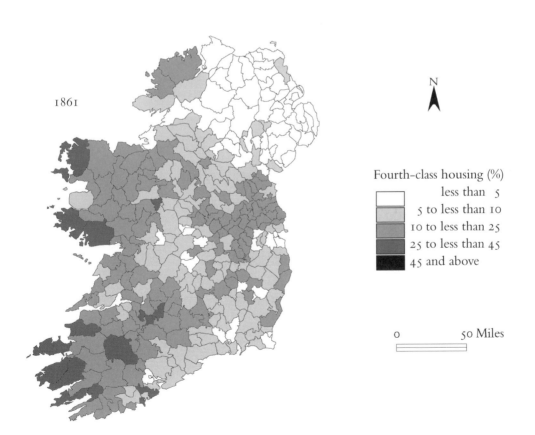

Fourth-class housing (%)

less than 5

5 to less than 10

10 to less than 25

25 to less than 45

45 and above

0   50 Miles

Map 36: Percentage fourth-class houses at barony level

CATHOLICS AND PROTESTANTS

Unlike the rest of the United Kingdom, where questions relating to religious worship were asked in only one census – that of 1851 – inquiries into religious adherence in Ireland formed a regular part of all Irish censuses from 1861. We do not have census statistics at county, poor law union or barony level to shed light on the geography of religion for the period before the Famine: we can only use the census to examine the post-Famine geography for 1861 and 1871. The Irish censuses vary in one other important respect. Whereas for England, Scotland and Wales, as part of the census in 1851, attendances at Sunday service on 30 March 1851 were recorded – and hence the census recorded the physical action of formal worship – Irish censuses concerned themselves simply with a profession of adherence. In other words, census enumerators were asked to inquire into the religious affiliation of every person in the country. So the figures here depict the extent of each religious community, not necessarily practising members of that community. Nor can the statistics reflect the complexities of the worshipping community, with some protestant adherents certainly attending the services of more than one denomination. For example, Church of Ireland adherents might well also attend Methodist services regularly. We are faced with one further problem. The census commissioners grouped denominations under eight headings (and just four from 1871). The Roman Catholic Church and the Church of Ireland were treated separately, but the various strands of Presbyterianism were amalgamated into one category, as were the Methodist denominations. Methodism in particular embraced a number of individual sects, including, for example, the Wesleyan Methodist Original Connexion and the Primitive Methodists. It would have been interesting, had the census recorded it, to examine the geography of these denominational subdivisions. Certainly in England and Wales the different strands of Methodism occur in distinct, and sometimes mutually exclusive, areas.[1] The remaining denominations recorded were the Baptists (again not broken down into distinct sects),

the Quakers, or Society of Friends, the Independents and the Jews. A further category was simply headed 'Others'. Data are available both at county and barony level allowing us to examine the geography of religion at a fairly local level.

Here we have included maps based on data from the 1861 census. Patterns of religious adherence in 1871 were almost unchanged (see Table 5), and their inclusion is not warranted therefore. So what do the maps show us? It is clear that the dominant denomination in 1861 was the Roman Catholic Church. It enjoyed its strongest support in the far-western counties of Connacht and Munster including Mayo, Roscommon, Galway, Clare and Kerry. Here Roman Catholic adherents exceeded 95% of the population. Throughout the rest of the country, excluding the six counties that today comprise Northern Ireland, the Ulster counties of Monaghan and Donegal, and County Dublin at the heart of the Anglo-Irish administration, Roman Catholics exceeded 60% of the population. Only in eastern Ulster was this dominant position challenged. In counties Antrim and Down, Catholics comprised less that 20% of the population; but with higher proportions in Londonderry, Tyrone, Armagh and Fermanagh. There was no overall change in this pattern in 1871. At barony level further resolution is added. Here we see that in only nine baronies outside the Province of Ulster did Catholic adherents fall below 80% of the population. In Ulster, catholicism was particularly strong in baronies within counties Cavan and Monaghan, together with two baronies in western Donegal and a further barony centred on the Antrim Glens. It was weak in baronies both to the north and south of Belfast.

The Church of Ireland was the second most widespread denomination in 1861. It was strongest in County Fermanagh and County Armagh. Throughout the remainder of the historic province of Ulster it was also relatively strong, with the proportion of adherents ranging from 20% of the population in Tyrone to 40% in Antrim. The Church of Ireland also enjoyed considerable support in much of southern Leinster, a product of the sixteenth-

[1] See K.D.M. Snell and Paul S. Ell, *Rival Jerusalems: the geography of Victorian religion* (Cambridge, forthcoming).

century plantations. The pattern becomes clearer at barony level. In only a handful of baronies did Church of Ireland adherents outnumber those of the Roman Catholic Church. They recorded between 40% and 60% of the population in three baronies to the south of Lough Neagh and a further three in central Fermanagh. They also achieved a relatively high percentage of adherents in central Ulster, along Antrim's north coast, in Dublin city and its southern hinterland as well as in a few other scattered baronies.

Presbyterianism in 1861 was confined largely to the northern and north-eastern counties. In county Antrim it accounted for almost 49% of the population. In the neighbouring counties of Down and Londonderry Presbyterianism enjoyed the support of 43% and 35% of the population respectively. In Donegal, Tyrone, Armagh and Monaghan it had above 10% of adherents. Elsewhere Presbyterianism was very weak, and weakest of all in Kerry where only 0.12% of the population were recorded as adherents in 1861. This figure had fallen still further to just 0.1% by 1871 – just 1 person in every 1,000. The barony map confirms these patterns. It is clear that Presbyterianism was confined to baronies at or close to the eastern seaboard of Ulster. Outside the Province Presbyterians nowhere exceeded 20% of the population.

Methodism was weaker still. It was strongest in county Fermanagh, but even here only 3.8% of the population were recorded as Methodists. It was especially weak in Clare where only one person in 2,000 belonged to the denomination. At barony level the same general pattern holds.

So far we have examined the geography of religion of the major denominations. There were a number of other groups that were extremely thin on the ground. These were the three Christian denominations – Quakers, Baptists, and Independents – and the Jews. The Quakers, Baptists, and Independents belonged to the Old Dissent dating from the sixteenth century. None of them commanded support from more than 0.5% of the population of any barony. For this reason their geographical distribution has been mapped using different class breaks from those employed for the major denominations. The Independents were widely dispersed, but there was some concentration in Ulster. The Baptists were also mainly a feature of Ulster. Quakers were scattered in baronies along the coastline of Leinster running into Munster and in a swathe of baronies running from Offaly, through Laois, Wicklow and Kildare to Dublin. There was also a concentration in

south Ulster, centring on Lurgan and Lisburn. These patterns reflected a process of settlement dating back to the late seventeenth century. As for Jews, the most striking feature of their distribution was the small number of baronies in which they were found.

Although the censuses of Ireland did not begin to gather statistics relating to religion until 1861, we can use an 1834 *Commissioners of Public Instruction* survey to shed some light on the patterns of religion in the pre-Famine period. Based on the enumerators' returns from the 1831 census, the original commissioners, of whom there were 22, were requested to return and ascertain the religious persuasion of every inhabitant of every parish in Ireland. They were further instructed to seek assistance from ministers of all religions. The results need to be handled with some caution. This survey was not a full census but an addition to the inquiries of 1831. As such, limited resources were available. In particular there was a problem in using in 1834 a list of individuals compiled in 1831: many people had simply moved elsewhere or died. This difficulty was severe in the urban centres of Belfast, Waterford, Limerick and Cork and especially so in Dublin. There was some confusion relating adherents within ecclesiastical parishes to the civil parish structure upon which the 1831 census population figures were based. Moreover, the classification of religions into just four groups – Established Church, Roman Catholics, Presbyterians and other protestant dissenters – adds to the uncertainties. The information was less detailed that that available in 1861 and there was particular confusion in distinguishing Wesleyan Methodists from adherents of the Established Church. Nonetheless the figures are all we have. The results are depicted in Table 5.

So, what can we say about changes in the geography of religion for the whole period 1834–71? Because of the nature of the data, the easiest period to deal with are changes between the census years of 1861 and 1871, as the statistics were collected largely in the same way. Table 5 shows the national percentage share of adherents for the four main denominations, with all others amalgamated, together with the 1834 data referred to above.

These figures bear out our earlier assertion that there was remarkably little change in the relative strengths of denominational adherence between 1861 and 1871. The percentage of Roman Catholic adherents declined slightly whilst those for other groups remained the same or increased a little. Changes between 1834 and 1861 were scarcely more marked, although we must bear in mind the limitations of the sources. The most notable changes were a decline in the percentage of Roman Catholic adherents from 80.9% in 1834 to 77.8% in 1861 and an increase in Church of Ireland adherents from 10.7% to 12%.

We can conclude, therefore, by making a number of observations. First, all of the major denominations had distinct and coherent geographies. Second, the Roman Catholic Church was dominant followed by the Church of Ireland and, in specific locations, Presbyterianism. Third, from the evidence available, there was remarkably little change in the national share of each denomination's adherents between the pre and post-Famine periods. Starvation, disease and emigration afflicted Catholics more severely than Protestants, a fact partly reflected in the 4.2% drop in the share of Roman Catholics in the overall population.

Table 5: National share of adherents of various denominations in 1834, 1861 and 1871

	1834	1861	1871
Roman Catholic	80.9	77.8	76.7
Church of Ireland	10.7	12.0	12.3
Presbyterian	8.9	9.0	9.2
Methodist	} 0.3	0.8	0.8
Others		0.5	1.0

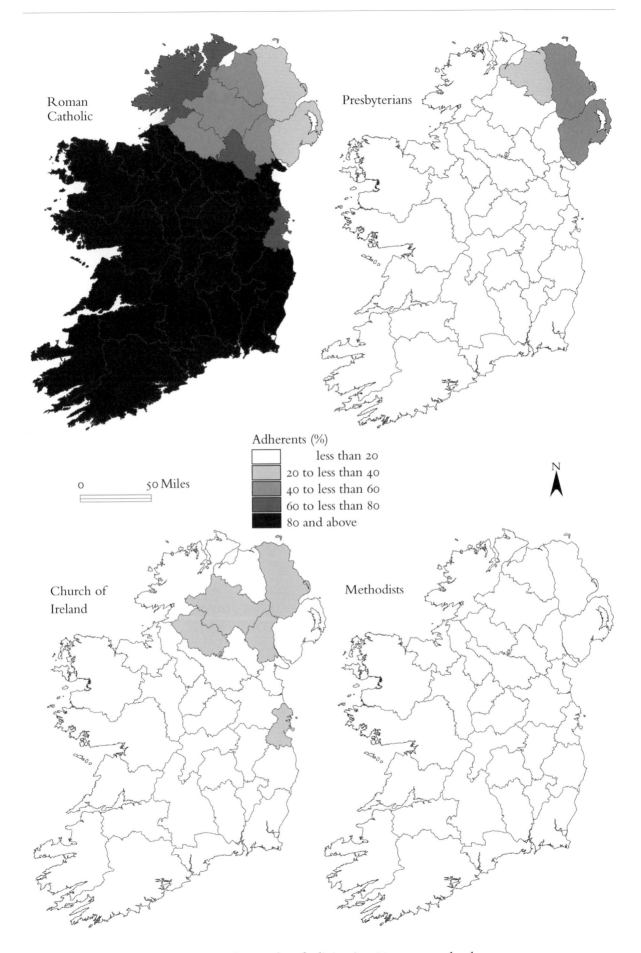

Map 37: Geography of religion in 1861 at county level

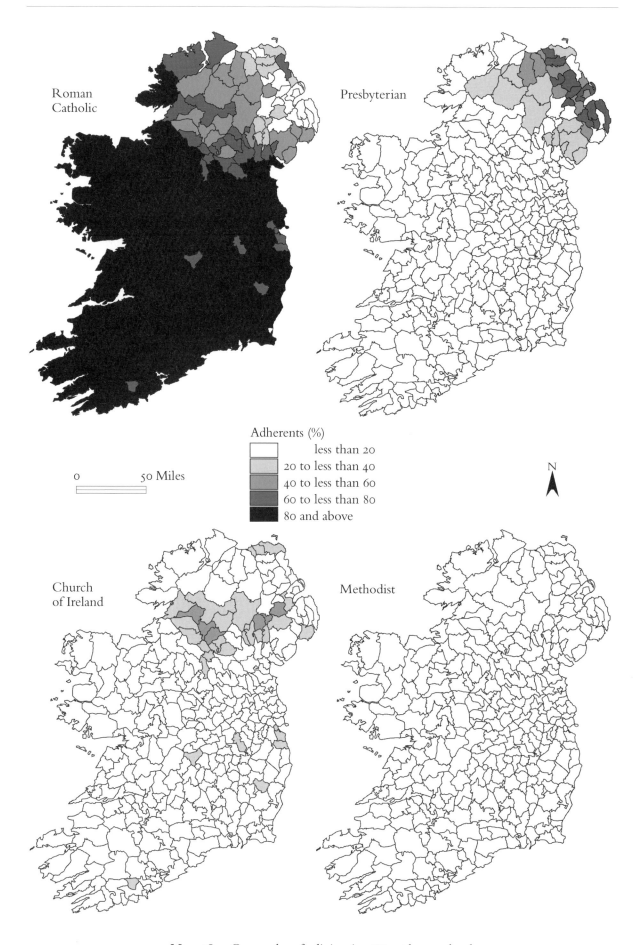

Map 38a: Geography of religion in 1861 at barony level

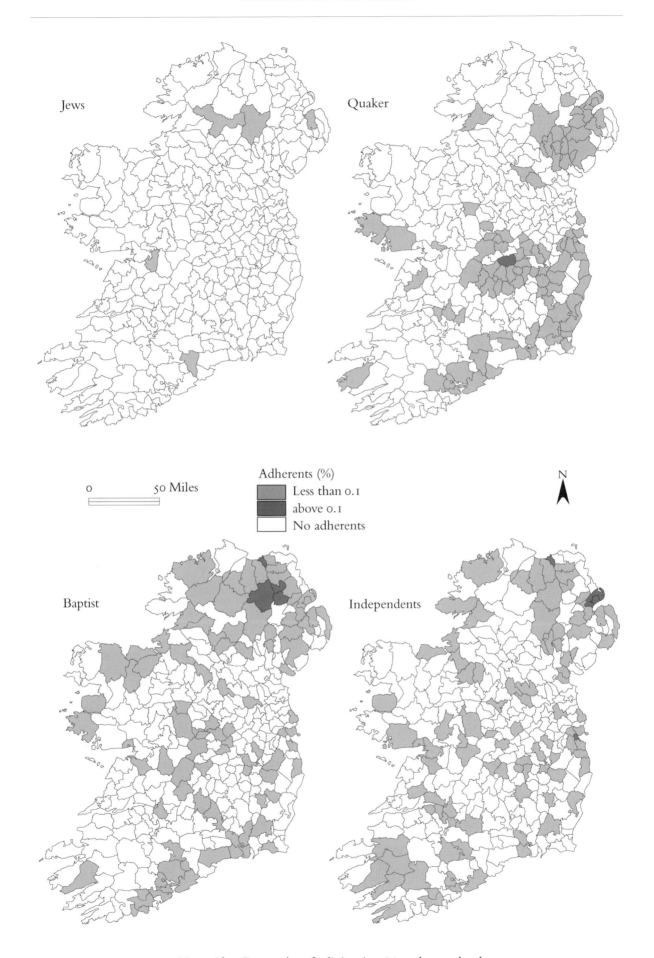

Map 38b: Geography of religion in 1861 at barony level

THE LITERATE AND THE 'IGNORANT'

Literacy, or some ability to read and write in the English language, was far from being the norm in many parts of Ireland in the mid-nineteenth century. Still, a solid base existed, with one in three Irish people, aged five years or older, claiming the ability to read and write in 1851. The origins of popular interest in formal education, including the acquisition of skills in reading and writing, may be traced back to the closing decades of the previous century. Indeed in Presbyterian communities a widespread demand for literacy, animated in part by theological considerations, reached deeper in time. Private initiatives to promote schooling for the poorer sections of Irish society were greatly enhanced by the formation of a state system for national education in 1831. The popularity of the system, for parents if not children, pointed to a public consciousness which valued schooling and literacy at all levels of society. These manifestations of cultural 'modernisation', it is clear, predated the Great Famine.[1]

Consistent with its interest in a national educational system which would promote the 'general intelligence and good conduct of the poorer classes', the British state collected information on the progress of schooling and literacy in Ireland.[2] The most comprehensive information on literacy and illiteracy before the Famine comes from the census commissioners, who collected data from 1841 onwards. The census divided the population into three categories: those able to read and write, those able to read only, and the illiterates (those who were unable to read or write). As there was no check by the census enumerators on claims to literacy – the classification was on the basis of self-assessment or the whim of the household head – there are some grounds for suspecting an upward bias. That is, the official figures reported in the 1841 and later censuses may well overstate the extent of literacy in Irish society. Moreover, the term literacy can span a wide range of knowledge and skills: one suspects modest abilities in reading or writing sufficed to justify a claim to literacy. By contrast, one seems safe in assuming that few who admitted to being illiterate

were exaggerating their ignorance. The proportion illiterate may, therefore, be a particularly useful variable to use in exploring both literacy and illiteracy, and it is the one mapped here.

The most extreme examples of illiteracy (or 'ignorance' as the commissioners unceremoniously labelled it) on the eve of the Famine were to be found along the western seaboard. The counties of Sligo, Mayo and Galway in Connacht, and of Kerry in Munster, all showed levels of male illiteracy in excess of 60%. A band of counties, consisting of the north midlands and most of Munster, constituted an intermediate zone in terms of male literacy. The most literate males were to be found in the north-east, the south-east, and in Dublin. The extent of illiteracy among women was even more pronounced. In the western counties of Mayo, Galway and Kerry more than four out of every five females were classified as illiterate in 1841. Sligo, Roscommon and Clare trailed only a little behind these in the illiteracy stakes. The midlands and the east generally claimed higher levels of literacy, though a sharp distinction between them is hardly tenable. In county Louth, for example, it was reported that seven out of every ten females were unable to read and write, a much higher proportion than farther inland in Longford, Westmeath or Offaly. By contrast, two out of every three females in Down and Dublin were classified as literate, in the loose sense of being able to read (though many of these could write as well). The top position went to Antrim which contained the town of Belfast, once dubbed the 'Athens of the North'. Here most females, three out of four, enjoyed literate status.

The trend over time was towards greater literacy. Focusing on women, where the greatest changes were taking place: on the eve of the Famine a majority of Irish females (six out of ten) lacked basic skills in reading and writing English. Two decades later, this position had been exactly reversed, with six out of every ten women being classified as literate in the census of 1861. Thus, as the national school system diffused literacy to the younger

1 L.M. Cullen, *The emergence of modern Ireland, 1600–1900* (London, 1981), pp. 235–8.   2 John Logan, 'Sufficient to their needs: Literacy and elementary schooling in the nineteenth century', in Mary Daly and David Dickson (eds), *The origins of popular literacy in Ireland: language change and educational development 1700–1920* (Dublin, 1990), p. 132.

generations, illiteracy became a minority phenomenon and there was a general levelling-up of literacy levels throughout the island. Despite these changes, the ranking of the counties in terms of literacy did not change very much. The western counties still had noticeably higher proportions illiterate in 1871. In fact geographic inequalities in access to literacy proved difficult to erode. Between 1841 and 1861 the proportional decline in illiteracy in Connacht actually lagged behind the decline nationally. It was not until the end of the century that the literacy experience of the western counties came to approximate that of the east. Catching-up was a slower process than might have been expected.

The geographical patterns and the process of change over time can be followed in greater detail using the spatial unit of the barony. For males it is abundantly clear, as indicated earlier, that the most pronounced instances of illiteracy lay along the western seaboard. The outstanding example is west Galway. The barony of Ross reported a remarkable 87% illiteracy rate in 1841, the highest in Ireland. It was closely followed by the neighbouring baronies of Moycullen (84%) and Ballynahinch (81%). At the other extreme, on the other side of the island, lay the barony of Dufferin, bordering Strangford Lough in county Down. Inverting the position found in Ross, almost 90% of males in Dufferin were classified as to some degree literate (able to read). Other districts with similarly high literacy rates were to be found nearby, with Castlereagh Upper and Castlereagh Lower reporting literacy rates in excess of 85%. One suspects that the association with presbyterianism and presbyterian settlement was not accidental. A different type of association, one between urbanisation and literacy is suggested by the relatively higher literacy rates to be found in the

hinterlands of Belfast, Dublin, Waterford and Cork. Galway city, to some extent, went against the grain. A majority of females in the town, for example, were returned as illiterate in 1841, though rates of recorded illiteracy were higher still in the surrounding districts. The case of Galway, and the west of Ireland more generally, raises the distinct possibility that Gaelic culture and Gaelic speaking acted as a barrier to the penetration of literacy.

A test of this hypothesis, using simple regression analysis, shows that this appears to have been the case. In Figure 19 the proportion of illiterate males is regressed on the proportion of Gaelic speakers in the year 1851. The observations used relate to the counties of Ireland, with the exception of Antrim and Dublin where the counties have been further subdivided into urban and rural components and entered separately. The total number of cases, therefore, is 34. If there was no relationship between illiteracy and Gaelic speaking, then one would expect a random scattering of values. In fact, illiteracy generally increases with the rising proportion of Gaelic speakers except where the share of Gaelic speakers is minuscule as in some eastern coastal counties. The Pearson product-moment correlation coefficient turns out to be 0.84, which is high. The result for females is strong also, yielding a correlation coefficient of 0.85. The relationship for females is presented in Figure 20. On the basis of the findings, which suggest a negative relationship between Gaelic speaking and literacy, one might conclude that the adoption of literacy was inhibited by the presence of large concentrations of Gaelic speakers. One should add, though, that the test, while highly suggestive, is not conclusive since no attempt has been made to control for other variables.

Figure 19: Percentage of illiterate males related to the proportion of male Gaelic speakers, 1851

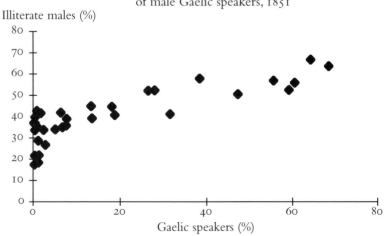

Figure 20: Percentage of illiterate females related to the proportion of female Gaelic speakers, 1851

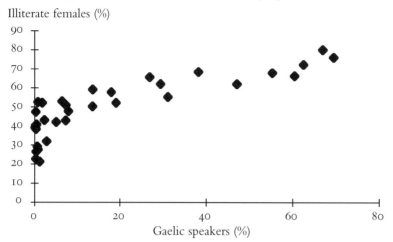

If one regards the acquisition of literacy as valuable, and many contemporaries did, then the position of men and women on the eve of the Famine (and for some decades thereafter) was markedly unequal. The baronial maps illustrate clearly a strong gender dimension to the question. The extent of illiteracy among females was deeper than in the case of males, and the geographical incidence of illiteracy more pronounced. In Ross in county Galway in 1841, some 95% of females were enumerated as illiterate, placing the barony at the top of the female illiteracy tree. Ross also topped the male tree, as we noted, but the altitude was a bit lower. The lowest rate of female illiteracy was to be found in Dufferin in county Down, again echoing the finding for males. More generally, one can say that female and male illiteracy rates were highly correlated at the local level: the 'ignorant' cohabited with the 'ignorant'.

The story over time, for females as well as males, was of the gradual advance of literacy westwards towards the Shannon and the erosion of clumps of high-illiteracy areas in the north midlands. But the rates of change varied. We notice, for instance, that the Cooley peninsula adopted female literacy only slowly while several baronies in west Waterford made a similarly slow transition to a literate culture. Regional differences, and earlier geographical patterns, still persisted in 1861. The baronies along the south-western and the western seaboard still obtruded as enclaves of female illiteracy. The contrast remained with the baronies of south Leinster and of course east Ulster, where literate females were proportionately much more numerous. But, taking a longer view, the tendency was from an oral culture towards a more literate one. The extent to which this involved changed mentalities is of course another matter. There is no necessarily fixed relationship between the one and the other. Still, over time, one

would be surprised if the acquisition of skills in reading and writing English did not reshape world views to some degree. This could of course take an ironic twist. It is known, for instance, that the major mobilisations of popular opinion in protonationalist and nationalist movements during the nineteenth century relied heavily on the use of written English for propaganda purposes.

The gender gap, while narrowing in the years after the Famine, by no means disappeared. It is worth reminding ourselves that in Ireland generally in 1861 some 42% of females could not read or write, as measured by the census takers. This compared with a substantially lower level for males of 35%. In some regions the gap was wider still. In county Mayo in 1861, for example, the rate of female illiteracy, at 72%, compared unfavourably with the male rate of 59% (in itself high by national standards). The likelihood is that these gender differences reflected different attitudes towards male and female children, not just in terms of educational investment decisions, but more widely in relation to their respective roles in Irish society.

The direction of change in literacy in the period 1841–71 is not in doubt. Explaining the course of change is more difficult. A short-term factor was the Famine, one of whose effects was to reduce the numbers and proportions of illiterate people in the population. Of longer-term significance, there was the wider exposure of Irish economy and society to market forces. Increasing monetisation and a deeper involvement in production for the market made rudimentary numeracy and writing skills more important in the post-Famine decades. Literacy was also perceived to be a useful preparation for the labour market. For many this meant work outside Ireland, where the ability to speak, read and write English could be a distinct advantage. This may have been especially true in the case of women, as so many female emigrants sought work abroad as servants and housekeepers. Presumably there were also pressures and incentives, of a social nature, towards the adoption of literacy. The higher-status elements in Irish society, such as strong farmers, ministers, priests, doctors, solicitors, bank clerks, teachers and state officials, carried with them the trappings of literate culture. In the more socially-stratified communities of eastern Ireland it is likely that some of these acted as role models, or partial role models, for the young and the aspiring.

Literacy could of course be an end in itself. If the writer William Carleton (whose career spanned the divide of the Great Famine) is to be believed, country people placed a high value on education. One may reasonably wonder, though, if the undoubted demand for skills in reading and writing was ever entirely divorced from a perception of opportunities and advantages of a material or symbolic kind. Then, of course, the motivation to acquire literacy could be fired by religious motives: the desire to read the sacred scriptures is sometimes cited as a reason for the high levels of literacy to be found in presbyterian communities. These are all factors on the demand side. On the supply side, one must attach primary significance to the role of the state and the major churches, who, for a variety of (sometimes competing) motives, created an infra-structure of educational provision in Irish society which diffused literacy to the young generations. These two sets of forces helped shape the new society which emerged in the later nineteenth century, one already in the process of formation before the mid-century debacle.

Figure 21: Percentage of females and males who were illiterate in 1841 and 1871

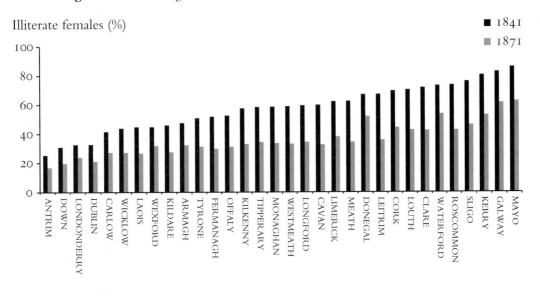

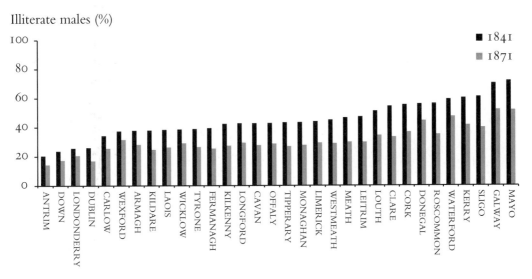

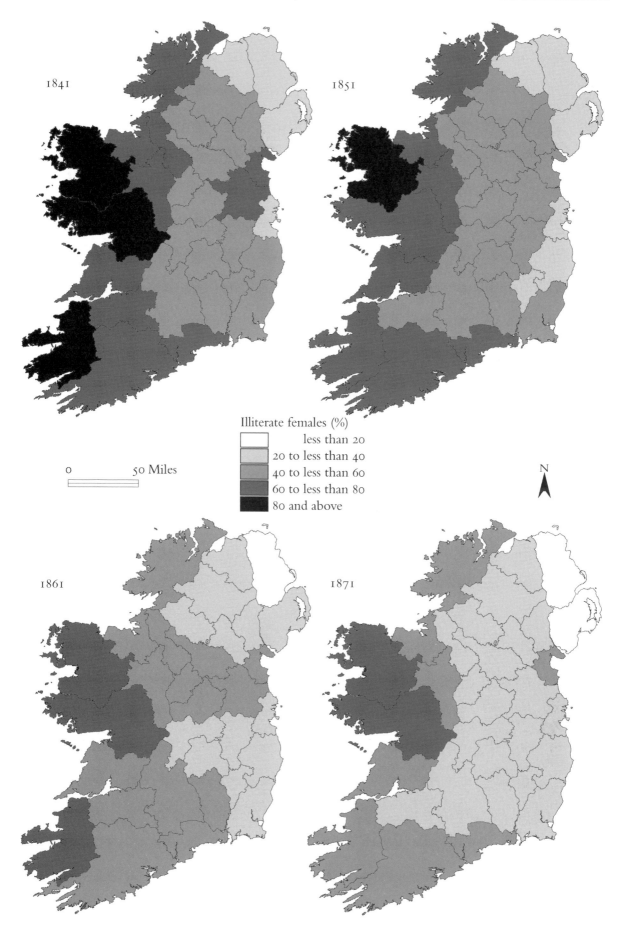

Map 39: Percentage of illiterate females at county level

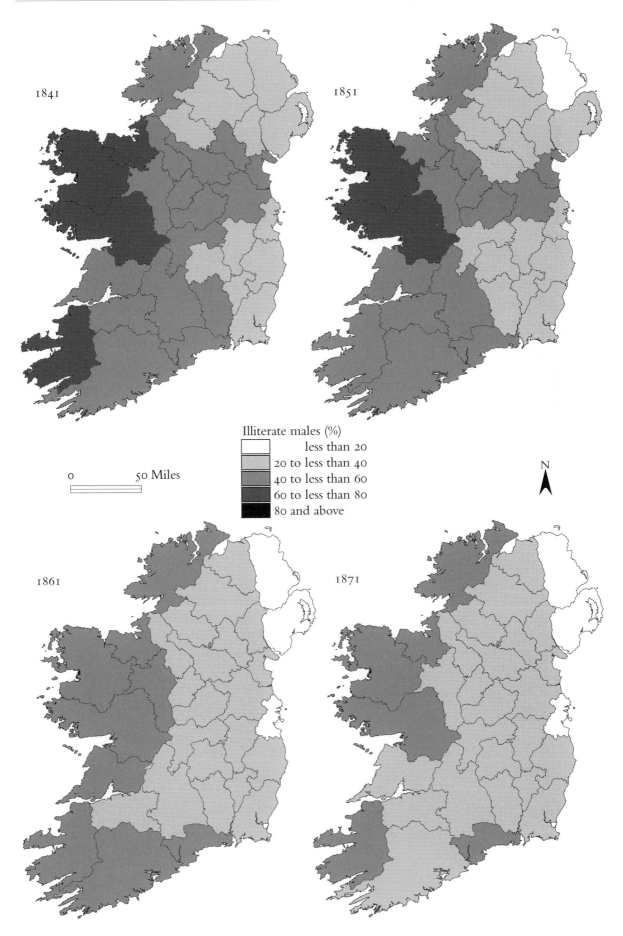

Map 40: Percentage of illiterate males at county level

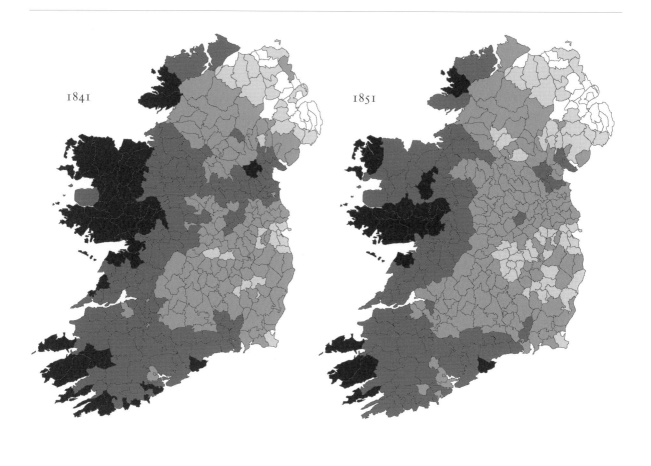

Illiterate females (%)

☐	less than 20
☐	20 to less than 40
☐	40 to less than 60
☐	60 to less than 80
■	80 and above

0   50 Miles

Map 41: Percentage of illiterate females at barony level

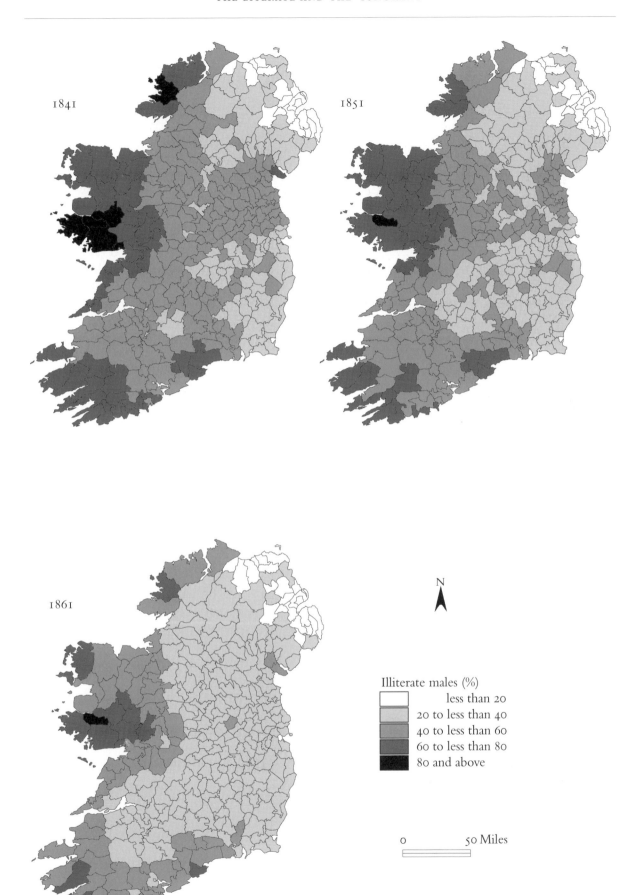

Map 42: Percentage of illiterate males at barony level

'AN BÉAL BOCHT': THE DECLINE
OF THE GAELIC LANGUAGE

There is little doubt about the course of language change in Ireland during the nineteenth century. The shift was inexorably from speaking Gaelic (or Irish) to English speaking. Yet the course of that change is not so easily traced in detail.

A language question was not included in the census of Ireland until 1851, hence there are no good data for the first half of the century. Even with the rich resources of the census, one may wonder about the accuracy of the returns. The prevailing social climate favoured responses which indicated proficiency in English and downgraded the ability to speak Gaelic. English was the language of polite society, of the drawing room, the school, the court-house, the market place and, above all, of the labour markets to which Irish people migrated.

The proportions of males and females able to speak Gaelic in each county were very similar. This was true at each of the three census points in time. It is not obvious, in advance, that this should be so. Differential access to education or the market place, for instance, might have produced distinctive patterns along gender lines. But this is not evident from the data, at least at the aggregate level of the county. In view of the essential similarity of the male and female spatial patterns, the maps present the patterns for females only.

On the eve of the Famine the likelihood is that a third or more of the population could speak Gaelic. These were heavily concentrated in the lower strata of the social structure, among the cottiers, labourers and servants. In view of the close association between Gaelic speaking and social class, Gaelic speakers were especially vulnerable to the ravages of the Great Famine. Moreover, Gaelic speaking was much more common in the western half of the island which suffered disproportionately during those terrible years, further compounding the destructive impact on Gaelic-speaking communities.

At the first census after the Famine, just under a quarter of the population admitted to having a knowledge of Gaelic. Most of these could also speak English, some of the older ones perhaps only after a fashion. But it is revealing in relation to the fortunes of the language, then and later, that only 5% were monoglot Gaelic speakers in 1851. The strongholds of the language were in the west, but even there marked regional contrasts could be found. West Donegal and west Cork, for example, had large proportions of Gaelic speakers, while the eastern parts of those counties were largely English speaking. In Donegal the matter of language was not simply one of geography and social class. While some members of the protestant communities of Donegal spoke Gaelic (even as late as 1900), this was untypical: protestantism and anglicisation were closely related, as was true more generally of Ulster.

After the Famine the proportions of Gaelic speakers continued to shrink. By 1871 Galway and Mayo were the only counties where more than 50% of the population were enumerated as being able to speak Gaelic. At the other end of the spectrum lay counties like Dublin, Antrim and Down, where those who claimed a speaking knowledge of the language numbered less than one person in a hundred.

The tide of anglicisation did not sweep uniformly from east to west. It is noteworthy that county Waterford in the south-east had a majority of Gaelic speakers before the Famine and this distinctiveness persisted. In 1851 some 55% of males and females in Waterford could speak Gaelic. Two decades later, although the share of Gaelic speakers had fallen, it was still almost 40%. On the east coast of Ireland, in county Louth, almost 20% of males and females could speak Gaelic in 1851 (though these declined rapidly to a rump of 5% by 1871). Within county Louth, as we know from other evidence, the rugged Cooley peninsula was an outpost for Gaelic speaking. This illustrates a wider point: the Gaelic language, under continuous threat from the forces of anglicisation and modernisation, tended to survive only in the more inaccessible and remote parts of the island. Hence the association in popular mentality between Gaelic speaking and back-wardness, a belief which itself served to accelerate the erosion of Gaelic language and culture. Finally, one might note that the decline of Gaelic was part of a wider process of decline among minority languages throughout the British and Irish Isles. The nineteenth century witnessed the decline, not only of Irish Gaelic, but of Scottish Gaelic, Lallans and Welsh as well.

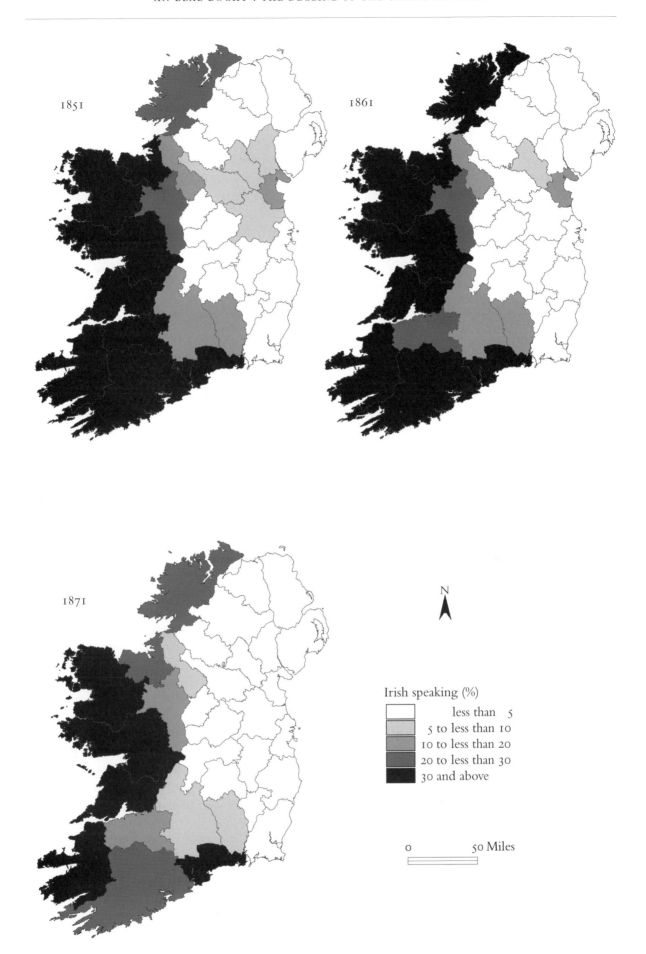

Map 43: Percentage of females who could speak Irish at county level

During the Famine more people died from disease than from starvation. We know this from the monumental work of Sir William Wilde, who compiled three volumes of data on disease and death as part of the census of Ireland for the year 1851.[1] Because the information was gathered from the recollections of surviving householders and others looking back over the previous ten years, it underestimates the true extent of disease and mortality. Death and emigration had swept away entire families, leaving few survivors to answer the questions of the census enumerators. Another area of uncertainty lies in the disease descriptions given by householders as to the cause of their relatives' deaths. Nevertheless, Wilde's work provides us with a framework for inquiring into the medical history of the Great Famine.[2]

The diseases that afflicted the population fell into two broad categories: diseases of nutritional deficiency, and famine-induced diseases. The nutritional deficiency diseases most commonly experienced were starvation and marasmus, as well as another condition called at the time dropsy.[3] Other nutritional disorders were also present, though only one, the vitamin C deficiency disease, scurvy, was explicitly discussed by the medical profession. The presence of other nutritional diseases has to be inferred from the symptoms described by travellers' accounts, government reports and from articles and commentaries in the medical journals of the day. Xerophthalmia, an eye disease caused by a deficiency of the vitamin A, is one example. It was described by contemporaries, who diagnosed a common eye ailment called ophthalmia. The true identification and cause of this disease was not uncovered until the twentieth century.

The greatest mortality, however, was not from nutritional deficiency diseases, but from famine-induced ailments All were infections, some viral, others bacterial. Many infections, nevertheless, were strongly influenced by the nutritional state of the famine victims. The undernourished were very susceptible to infections, and, furthermore, they were more severe when they occurred. Measles, diarrhoeal diseases, tuberculosis, most respiratory infections, whooping cough, many intestinal parasites, and cholera were all strongly conditioned by nutritional status.[4] Potentially lethal diseases, such as smallpox and influenza, however, were so virulent that their activity was independent of nutrition.

An important cause spreading disease during the Great Famine was social dislocation. The best example of this phenomenon was fever, which exacted the greatest toll of death. In the popular mind, as well as among much medical opinion, fever and famine were closely related.[5] This opinion was not totally wrong, but the most crucial connection was the congregating of the hungry at food depots, soup kitchens, overcrowded houses of industry and workhouses where conditions were ideal for spreading infectious diseases such as typhus, relapsing fever and typhoid. As for the diarrhoeal diseases, their presence was the consequence of poor hygiene, bad sanitation and dietary changes. The final assault on a population debilitated by famine was delivered by Asiatic cholera. Cholera had visited Ireland, briefly, in the 1830s. But in the following decade it spread uncontrollably across Asia, through Europe, into Britain and finally reached Ireland in 1849.

The scale of sickness during the Famine was unprecedented. Hospitals, charitable institutions and workhouses were overwhelmed by an influx of sick and hungry people. Even the gaols were inundated by hoards of starving men and women. The attraction of regular meals induced many people to commit

1 *Census of Ireland for the year 1851* part III, *Report on the status of disease*, BPP, 1854, lviii; part V, *Tables of Deaths*, vol. 1, BPP, 1856 [2087–I], xxix; vol. II, 1856 [2087–II], xxx. 2 A major source is the 'Report upon the recent epidemic fever in Ireland', *Dublin Quarterly Journal of Medical Science* [*DQJMS*], vol. 7 (1849), 64–126, 340–404; vol. 8, 1–86, 270–339. This report contains responses to a questionnaire circulated by Wilde. His aim was have a record of the fever epidemic and accompanying illnesses. Because of sickness Wilde was aided in the preparation of this report by Drs J. Moore Neligan and John Aldridge. 3 Dropsy was a popular name given for a symptom we today would call oedema. Oedema can be a symptom of several diseases, one of which, kwashorikor, is associated with starvation. 4 M. Levi-Bacci, *Population and nutrition: an essay on European demographic history* (Cambridge, 1991), p. 38. 5 D.J. Corrigan, *Famine and fever as cause and effect in Ireland* (Dublin, 1846); Henry Kennedy, *Observations on the connexion between famine and fever in Ireland and elsewhere* (Dublin, 1847).

petty crimes in the belief they would be saved from a starvation death. This was a misplaced faith. Death from another cause awaited them. Prisons, like workhouses, and even hospitals harboured a host of infections deadly to an impoverished population. The horrors of sickness and death in the Tralee gaol were movingly described by Dr Crumpe:

> In this horrid den those labouring under local disease, those ill from fever, those dying, and the dead from fever and dysentery, were promiscuously stretched together. So insufferable was the atmosphere of the place, so morbidly fetid and laden with noxious miasma, notwithstanding constant fumigation … that on the door being opened I was uniformly seized, on entering, with most violent retching; and it is singular that I should be so affected, who dissected so much, have opened so many bodies, performed so many operations, and see often such forms of loathsome disease: yet the fact is so … The mortality was enormous, deaths often taking place a few hours after admission; but this occurred in the most exhausted and worn-down subjects.[6]

Fleeing to foreign fields carried its own risks. Hungry emigrants carried with them unseen baggage in the form of typhus, relapsing fever, diarrhoea and dysentery. Many of those who were not sick on leaving Ireland became so on the journey. Others, again, fell ill after they had arrived in Liverpool, Boston, New York or Quebec. It is worth remembering, though that the majority of emigrants did survive the perils of the journey and made new lives for themselves in the New World.

In sections that follow, the most important diseases have been selected for detailed examination, making use of the statistics gathered by William Wilde. These data are imperfect for the reasons stated earlier; nevertheless, they provide an insight into the scale and severity of the Famine. The maps present death rates of diseases which were pertinent to the Famine, on a county basis. Some diseases are mapped for 1847, a few for 1849 and one for 1850, depending on which year had the greatest mortality. For example, cholera is mapped for 1849, the year in which the disease reached its zenith. The aim is to provide an idea of the regional distribution of specific diseases, while the accompanying diagram shows how their virulence varied from year to year.

Figure 22: Deaths from selected diseases in Ireland, 1844–51

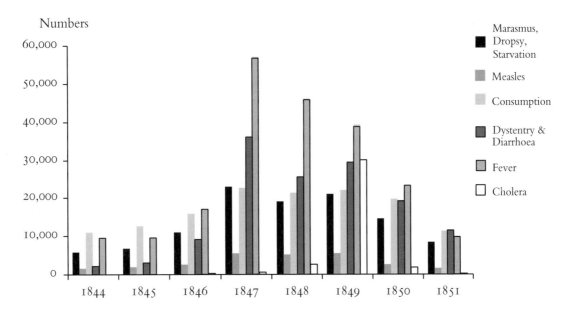

6 'Report upon the recent epidemic fever in Ireland', *DQJMS*, vol. 7 (1849), 86–7.

THE NUTRITIONAL DISEASES:
STARVATION, DROPSY AND MARASMUS

Emaciation from starvation is the most overt sign of famine. In 1847 starvation accounted for 1 in 41 of all recorded deaths. Over the decade 1841–51, 21,770 deaths were attributed to starvation and of these 91% occurred between 1846 and 1850. Only 117 starvation deaths had been recorded for the previous decade of 1831–41. The much higher figures for the mid-1840s indicated a crisis of cataclysmic proportions. Nevertheless, these figures are a poor indicator of starvation mortality. During the 1840s either entire families were wiped out by starvation or remaining survivors emigrated, and so there was no-one left in 1851 to record their demise. There was also a reluctance on the part of the authorities to accept and return verdicts of 'death by starvation' at inquests. We might inflate the starvation deaths by adding mortality from marasmus and dropsy. Even so, the total of around 100,000 deaths for the famine years is only about half that caused by fevers. Unfortunately, deaths categorised as marasmus (wasting) cannot always be assumed as arising from hunger. As Wilde explained, 'marasmus was adopted as a generic term [for] all those various afflictions of infancy and early youth returned … as "consumption (infantile), wasting, decay, decline, emaciation, general debility and loss of strength." '[7] The same is also true of dropsy. This was a common term for ascites and anasarca, that is a swelling of the body as the result of fluid retention. Thus dropsy was a symptom of several diseases, although it could indicate famine oedema caused by the nutritional deficiency disease that today we call kwashiorkor.

The annual distribution of marasmus and dropsy mortality statistics suggest that very many of these cases during the Great Famine were indeed the result of a shortage of food. Deaths from marasmus greatly outnumbered those from starvation and dropsy. Over the period 1846–50 49,166 deaths were registered as caused by marasmus, while starvation and dropsy deaths numbered 19,886 and 20,306 respectively. The considerably larger figure for marasmus can partly be attributed to the ambiguity of the term 'marasmus'. However, the fact that marasmus mortality almost doubled between 1846

and 1847 and remained high for the next two years, suggests that a substantial proportion of these deaths was hunger related. Dropsy deaths almost doubled between 1846 and 1847 and remained high during 1848 and 1849, though not quite at the 1847 level. The twelve fold increase in starvation mortality between 1845 and 1847 was even more dramatic. In the years 1848 and 1849 starvation deaths also remained elevated, though not at the 1847 level (see Figure 23). As deaths from starvation diseases occur only after prolonged periods without food, the severity of the Irish famine is reinforced by these mortality data.

Collectively marasmus and kwashiorkor are now referred to as protein-energy malnutrition (PEM), and children are the most vulnerable in society to these conditions because their nutritional needs are very exacting. Identifying these diseases 150 years later can be difficult. However, the descriptions of philanthropists, travellers, doctors and clergy help nutritionists and medical historians, not only to identify these ailments, but also to evaluate and explain in greater detail features of the Irish Famine formerly not fully understood. For example, children described by the Quaker, William Bennett and the Revd Dr Traill Hall, a Church of Ireland rector in Schull, as having endured prolonged periods of inadequate nourishment, were certainly exhibiting symptoms of nutritional marasmus and kwashiorkor. Bennett wrote movingly of 'three children huddled together, lying there because they were too weak to rise, pale and ghastly, their little limbs … perfectly emaciated, eyes sunk, voice gone, and evidently in the last stages of actual starvation.'[8] Traill Hall, described 'the aged, who, with the young – are almost without exception swollen and ripening for the grave.'[9] Marasmic children also made an indelible image on Joseph Crosfield, another Quaker. In 1846 he witnessed, a 'heart-rending scene [of] poor wretches in the last stages of famine imploring to be received into the [work]house … Some of [the] children were worn to skeletons, their features sharpened with hunger, and their limbs wasted almost to the bone.'[10] And William Forster noted in Carrick-on-Shannon that 'the children exhibit the effects of famine in a remarkable degree, their faces looking wan and haggard with hunger, and seeming

7 *Census of Ireland for the year 1851*, part V, *Tables of deaths*, vol. 1, BPP, 1856, xxix, p. 455.   8 *Transactions of the Central Relief Committee of the Society of Friends during the Famine in Ireland in 1846 and 1847* (Dublin, 1852), Account of William Bennett in county Mayo, p. 163.   9 'Report upon the recent epidemic fever in Ireland', *DQJMS*, vol. 7 (1849), 101 f/n.   10 *Transactions of the Central Relief Committee of the Society of Friends*, pp. 145–6.

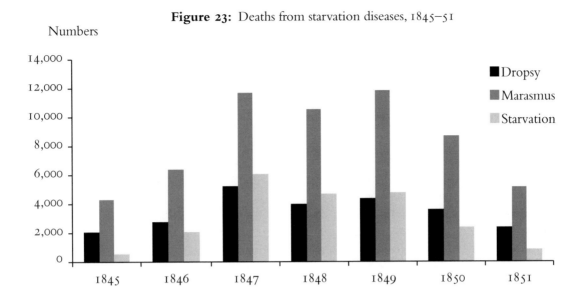

Figure 23: Deaths from starvation diseases, 1845–51

like old men and women.'[11] Such observations agree with the data collected by the census enumerators, who found higher starvation mortality among men than women and among the age group five to ten year olds and the over fifty-fives.

Many famine survivors bore the long-term scars of prolonged food deprivation. The need for particular nutrients, especially during the growing phase of life, was not understood in the nineteenth century. Consequently, in all probability children remained stunted throughout their growing years, eventually becoming small adults. Historical evidence is limited, but Ó Gráda's work on Irish recruits to the East India Company born before the Famine shows a small but measurable height advantage over English and Scottish recruits, but this diminished as the population became increasingly impoverished.[12]

One of the most detailed expositions on the medical aspects of starvation was written by Dr Daniel Donovan, working in the Skibbereen district at the time of the Famine. His observations were very acute. Not only did he describe in detail the physiological changes which took place in the victims of hunger but he also noted the psychological degeneration. Of the early stages of hunger he stated:

I have made particular inquiry from those who have suffered from starvation relative to the sensations experienced from long fasting; they described pain of hunger as at first very acute, … [which] subsided, and was succeeded by a feeling of weakness and sinking … with

insatiable thrist, for cold water particularly, and a distressing feeling of coldness …

In a short time the face and limbs become frightfully emaciated; the eyes acquire a most peculiar stare; the skin exhaled a peculiar and offensive foetor, and was covered with a brownish, filthy-looking coating, almost as indelible as varnish. This I was at first inclined to regard as incrusted filth, but further experience has convinced me that it is a secretion poured out from the exhalants on the surface of the body.[13]

Of the psychological changes resulting from starvation Dr Donovan, vividly expressed harrowing events in Skibbereen.

Want of food produced a very different effect on the young and infant population: the same cause that paralysed the faculties of the adult served to sharpen the instinct of the child: babies scarcely able to speak became expert beggars … Another symptom of starvation and one that accounts for the horrible scenes that famine usually exhibits, is the total insensibility of the suffered to every other feeling except that of supplying their own wants. I have seen mothers snatch food from the hands of their starving children; known a son to engage in a fatal struggle with a father for a potato: and have seen parents look on the putrid bodies of their offspring without evincing a symptom of sorrow.

11 *Transactions of the Central Relief Committee of the Society of Friends*, p. 146. **12** C. Ó Gráda, *Ireland: a new economic history 1780–1939* (Oxford, 1994), pp. 18–23, 106–10. **13** Daniel Donovan, 'Observations on the peculiar diseases to which the famine of last year gave origin …', *Dublin Medical Press*, 19 (1848), 67.

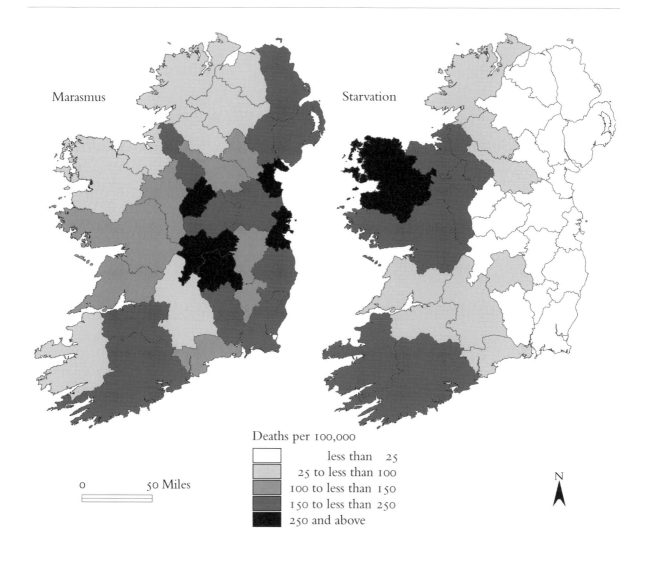

Map 44: Death rates in 1847 at county level

The map of starvation death rates for 1847 demonstrates a clear west-east gradient confirming the severity of food shortages in the extreme west and south-west. In Galway, Leitrim, Mayo, Roscommon, Cork and Kerry deaths rates exceeded 200/100,000 of the population, the peak rate occurring in Mayo at 289/100,000. Sligo had a rate of just over 150/100,000, while in the rest of the country values ranged from 78/100,000 in Fermanagh to 1.95/100,000 for Kildare. Leinster and Ulster counties were not in the same league.

Dropsy and marasmus show a less clear cut pattern. True, Galway headed the dropsy death rates when averaged over 1847–9, as was the case with starvation deaths, but it was closely pressed by Dublin City (see Figure 24). Then came Cork, immediately followed by the two eastern counties of Antrim and Louth. Mapping the distribution of dropsy death rates for the

year 1847 only clouds rather than clarifies the picture. Highest death rates were found in Dublin, followed by Antrim, Fermanagh, Longford and Galway. None of the values were outstandingly high and no particular regions stood out as particular black spots.

Similarly marasmus death rates exhibit highly unstable patterns (see Figure 25). Offaly had the dubious distinction of the highest average marasmus death rates in 1847–9, followed by Dublin City, Longford, Louth, and Laois. At the tail end were the Ulster counties of Donegal and Londonderry, followed by Kerry, Mayo and Sligo in the west. Mapping death rates for the single year of 1847 illustrates just how volatile the statistics are. The map shows the highest rate of marasmus deaths in the east along with Limerick and Cork in the south west, rather than the west where destitution was

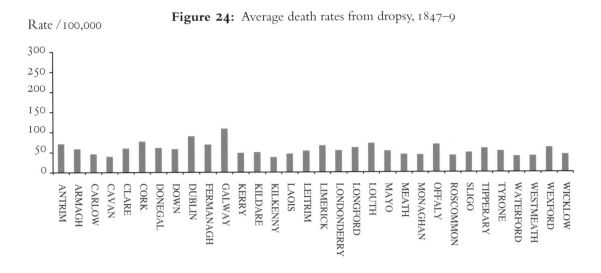

Figure 24: Average death rates from dropsy, 1847–9

Rate / 100,000

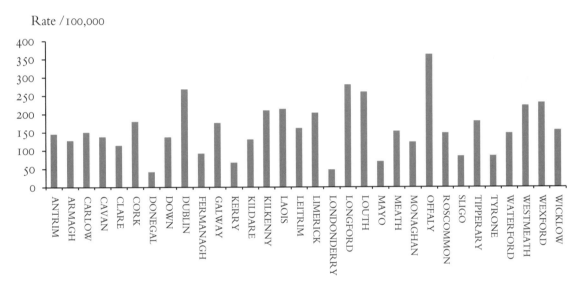

Figure 25: Average death rates from marasmus, 1847–9

Rate / 100,000

greatest. The most likely explanation is the all-inclusive nature of the description, 'marasmus'.

What can be concluded from this detailed analysis? The clearest spatial pattern is found in deaths from starvation. The west and south-west suffered most. The labouring classes in that part of Ireland had greatest dependence on the potato in their diet. Moreover, many of the poor law unions in both these regions were so overwhelmed by the scale of the catastrophe that the workhouses quickly filled to a point of overflowing, leaving many of the destitute with no means of sustenance until out-door relief was commenced in February 1847. There is a strong relationship between the distribution of poor law unions officially declared as 'distressed' and the areas where starvation deaths were high.

Turning to marasmus and dropsy, these were, as we have seen terms that were used in a loose fashion, although the high rates prevalent in the mid-1840s clearly suggest that many cases of marasmus and dropsy were famine deaths. Counties in which there was a major port, such as Dublin, Louth, Cork, Limerick, Galway and Antrim had higher death rates from dropsy than inland counties. These pockets of high death rates in the east coast counties of Dublin, Louth and Wexford are explained to some extent by the influx of rural labourers to the ports of Dublin, Drogheda, Dundalk and Wexford in search of food, employment or a ship in which to emigrate. The lower rates in Ulster reflect the relative prosperity of the northern people.

THE NUTRITIONAL DISEASES: VITAMIN DEFICIENCIES

The most insidious illnesses to afflict Ireland during the Great Famine were vitamin deficiency diseases. Common among these were scurvy and xeropthalmia, though only scurvy was recognised for what it was. Because scurvy had not been prevalent in Ireland before 1845 some doctors were not immediately aware of what they were up against. Others, however, did recognise the disease and consequently the presence of scurvy during the Great Famine was well documented.[14] Its incidence, however, cannot be measured, its geographical distribution cannot be mapped, and despite its lethal potential, scurvy mortality cannot be measured. The census figure of 167 deaths between 1841 and 1851 simply cannot be believed, if only because so many scurvy victims died from other ailments before scurvy claimed them.

Scurvy is caused by a lack of vitamin C in the diet. Rich sources are fruit and vegetables. The pre-Famine diet of the labouring classes contained high levels of vitamin C by virtue of the large quantities of potatoes consumed daily. Nutritional analysis of their diet reveals that between 300 and 400 mg of vitamin C was consumed each day, though modern nutritional research has demonstrated that 30 to 40 mg daily is sufficient to forestall scorbutic symptoms. The demise of the potato cut the population off from their only source of the vitamin, since neither milk, milk products nor herrings, all adjuvants to the diet, contain vitamin C. Nor did the use of grains, such as Indian meal and oatmeal help since these also are devoid of vitamin C.

Scorbutic patients complain of tiredness, breathlessness, and mental depression. Later cutaneous haemorrhages, from bleeding under the skin surface, produce purple blotches (purpuric spots) which usually appear first on the limbs and then on other parts of the body. Joints become swollen and painful as a result of bleeding. Gums turn red, soft, spongy, swollen, easily bleed, and eventually the teeth loosen and fall out. Scurvy unrestrained is a killer disease, death being the result of haemorrhages into the heart muscle or brain.

The Irish cases displayed all these classical symptoms. Initially scorbutic symptoms were mistaken for an ailment of a 'gastro-enterite' nature. Some doctors blamed the eating of diseased potatoes, others, the lack of food. A few physicians, however, made the right connection, identifying the lack of potatoes, not the eating of diseased potatoes, as the problem. The enormous amounts of potatoes eaten daily had in fact placed the Irish labourers' diet in the mega-dose league. One doctor even spotted the strong similarities between the scorbutic symptoms seen in Ireland at this time and those observed among sailors by Lind in the 1770s.

If the vitamin C content of the Irish diet was so good when food supplies were adequate why did scurvy appear so quickly when the Famine struck? There are several answers to this question. First, unlike some vitamins, dietary supplies are the sole source of vitamin C; it cannot be manufactured endogenously. Secondly, it is not storable, and so must be replenished regularly. Thirdly, a wealth of research confirms that often diseases, particularly infections and gastrointestinal disorders, rapidly deplete vitamin C. Typhus, relapsing fever, diarrhoea, and dysentery were all rife in Ireland during the Famine and, coupled with the sharp drop in dietary intake of vitamin C, the speed of the onset of scurvy is not surprising.

Even more crucial, the exceptionally high levels of vitamin C in the potato diet operated to the disadvantage of the Irish in times of potato shortages. People accustomed to saturated levels of vitamin C deplete more quickly than those used to a low intake, because the body becomes conditioned to high levels and sudden withdrawal does not allow for adaptation to a lower intake. The Irish peasants fell into this trap. Had their usual intake of vitamin C been at a lower level before the Famine – say between 20 and 30 mg daily – deficiency symptoms would have appeared more slowly.[15]

Particularly strong evidence supporting the 'withdrawal syndrome' theory can be found from medical records of the Irish in Scotland. Dr Christison of the Edinburgh Royal Infirmary had 149 scurvy cases over a period of three months in 1847.[16] All but three were Irish, fleeing the Famine, who had arrived in the early summer of that year to work on the railways. All railway labourers had to purchase their food rations in the company's store,

14 J.O. Curran, 'Observations on scurvy as it has lately appeared throughout Ireland and in several parts of Great Britain', *DQJMS*, 4 (1847), 84–134. **15** See E. Margaret Crawford, 'Scurvy in Ireland during the Great Famine', *Journal of the Society for the Social History of Medicine*, 1, 3 (1988), 281–300. **16** R. Christison, 'On Scurvy', *Monthly Journal of Medical Science*, New Series, 13 (1847), 1–22.

and on inquiry it was discovered that potatoes were not eaten by any of the navvies; yet it was only the Irish who experienced the effects of a potato-less diet and hence vitamin C withdrawal.

There is a further reason that may explain the speed with which scurvy symptoms appeared. A link is suspected between heavy exertion and early onset of scurvy symptoms. Many of the hungry Irish men and women got employment on the public works schemes. The projects involved heavy labouring such as road works, harbour construction and the like. Thus we may have an explanation for the many reports of labourers dropping dead on the job. A plausible comparison can be made with the scorbutic seamen who dropped dead on the deck having fallen from the mainsail.

Scurvy vanished as quickly as it appeared once the potato supply was restored. Despite the lethal potential of scurvy, its mortality during the Famine can never be measured, if only because so many scurvy victims died from some other ailment before scurvy claimed them. For this reason, therefore, we have not been able to chart the course of scurvy during the Great Famine.

Another vitamin deficiency disease that emerged towards the end of the Famine, though not recognised at the time, was xerophthalmia. This is an eye affliction caused by a prolonged lack of vitamin A in the diet. Reference to William Wilde's historical survey of diseases in Ireland reveals that a disease, which contemporaries called ophthalmia, had been endemic in Ireland. Several severe outbreaks either coincided with, or immediately followed periods of food shortage, for example, in 1701, 1740, 1758, 1801, 1825, 1840 and 1849–50. The problem in 1849–50, however, was not ophthalmia, an infectious eye disease, but xerophthalmia.

Xerophthalmia damages the iris, conjunctivae and cornea of the eye, and ultimately causes blindness. The earliest symptom of xerophthalmia is night blindness, frequently followed by Bidôt's spots and dryness (xerosis) of the conjunctiva. The next stage is irreversible damage to the eye caused by ulceration leading in advanced cases to complete perforation of the cornea.

Fish-liver oils, such as cod-liver oil, are rich sources of vitamin A. Liver, butter, cream, cheese, whole milk, and egg yolk are also good sources. As long as the Irish diet included whole milk, xerophthalmia was not present. Furthermore, vitamin A is a storable vitamin, reserves being located in the liver. However, when famine is both severe and prolonged, as in 1845–9, the chances of xerophthalmia occurring increases, especially among children whose reserves of vitamin A are small and their demands great to facilitate growth.

One chink in the nutritional armour of the Irish labourer's diet before the Great Famine was the poor levels of the fat soluble vitamin A. The Irish were totally dependent on diet for vitamin A. Potatoes contain only tiny quantities of the vitamin, and although whole milk is a good source, skimmed milk and buttermilk are not. Herrings also provide plenty of vitamin A, but they were eaten only seasonally. For many labourers and their families, therefore, diets were poor in vitamin A for much of the year. Thus when the harvest failed, this weakness left the young extremely vulnerable to nutritional deficiencies, in this case xerophthalmia.

Conclusive evidence for the presence of xerophthalmia in Ireland during the late 1840s comes from the Poor Law records. In 1849 the Irish poor law commissioners were greatly alarmed by an epidemic of, what they termed 'ophthalmia' among the paupers in the overcrowded and insanitary workhouses (see Table 6). It was particularly rife in the south and west of the country and was especially common among the workhouse children. Two eminent physicians, Professor Arthur Jacob and Sir William Wilde, were invited by the Poor Law authorities to investigate the disease.

Table 6: Number of so-called ophthalmia cases treated in Irish workhouses

	1849	1850	1851	1852
Cases arising in workhouse	11,368	24,882	42,067	28,765
Cases admitted to workhouse with ophthalmia	532	758	963	1,360

SOURCE: *Annual Reports of the Poor Law Commissioners, 1850–3*

Table 7: Statistics of blindness in Irish workhouses, 1849–51

	1849	1850	1851
One eye lost	114	202	656
Both eyes lost	37	80	263

SOURCE: *Annual Reports of the P.L.C. 1851 and 1852*

Similarities between the classical symptoms of xerophthalmia and the eye disease examined by Wilde and Jacobs were strong. For example, Wilde found the highest incidence of the disease among children.[17] In the Tipperary workhouse 96% of cases were children; their ages ranged from 4 to 14 years.[18] Secondly, often blindness occurs in one eye only. The pattern once again reflects that found by Wilde.[19] This feature was also present in the statistics on blindness for all the workhouses in Ireland at this time.

Recent research has revealed that the workhouse diets were grossly deficient in vitamin A over a prolonged period.[20] Sir William Wilde's treatment provides final proof that he was dealing with xerophthalmia. He recommended:

> where the patient is much broken down in health, and … the disease is in a chronic stage, I beg to suggest the plentiful use of *cod-liver oil*, of which medicine a large supply should at once be procured, and a tablespoonful given to each child, two or three times a day. I saw I am sure fifty cases among those under your care which would be greatly benefited by the use of this remedy.[21]

Wilde's recommendation predated by sixty years the recognition that cod-liver oil was an effective treatment for vitamin A deficiency.

THE INFECTIONS: MEASLES, SCARLATINA AND CONSUMPTION

From the experience of modern famines we have learnt that a strong interaction exists between mal-nutrition and infection. Malnutrition affects the character and development of infections. It lowers resistance, exacerbates the severity of acute infections and raises mortality from infectious diseases. In addition, infections adversely affect nutritional status by depleting the body of essential nutrients thus precipitating deficiency diseases, such as kwashiorkor, scurvy and xerophthalmia.[22]

Turning to Ireland in the mid-1840s, we find mortality from infections greatly increased. Dr John Colvin of Armagh, for instance, observed measles, quinsy and whooping cough to be very rife among the children of his locality as early as 1846.[23] Selecting three infections, measles, scarlatina and consumption (tuberculosis), a rise in mortality is shown in Figure 26.

Between 1845 and 1849 deaths from measles rose almost three fold, and over the period recorded deaths were 67% higher than the average of the previous decade. Scarlatina was a late comer. Mortality more than doubled between 1844 and 1850, the highest year being 1850. Between 1841 and 1851 scarlatina affected 1 in 67 of the population compared with measles at 1 in 46. Of greater magnitude was consumption. Over the famine decade at least 153,098 people died from consumption, placing it as the second highest killer disease recorded after fever. Tuberculosis of the lung was the most common form of the disease, called phthisis in medical circles. Another name for lung tuberculosis, often used in common parlance was 'consumption', the name used in the census.

Measles and scarlatina are highly contagious child-hood diseases, though one episode usually provides life-time immunity. Over the decade 1841–51

17 *Fourth Annual Report of the Commissioners for Administering of the Law for Relief of the Poor in Ireland* (1851), p. 145 **18** Ibid. **19** Ibid. p. 140. **20** E. Margaret Crawford, 'Dearth, diet and disease in Ireland 1850: A case study of nutritional deficiency', *Medical History*, 28 (1984), 159. **21** *Fourth Annual Report*

P.L.C., p. 137. **22** See Nevin S. Scrimshaw, 'Malnutrition and infection' in Jean Mayer (ed.), *World nutrition: a US view* (Washington, 1978), pp. 118–19. **23** J. Colvan , 'Report of the Armagh Dispensary for 1846', *Dublin Medical Press*, 17 (1847), 223.

Figure 26: Deaths from infections in Ireland, 1844–51

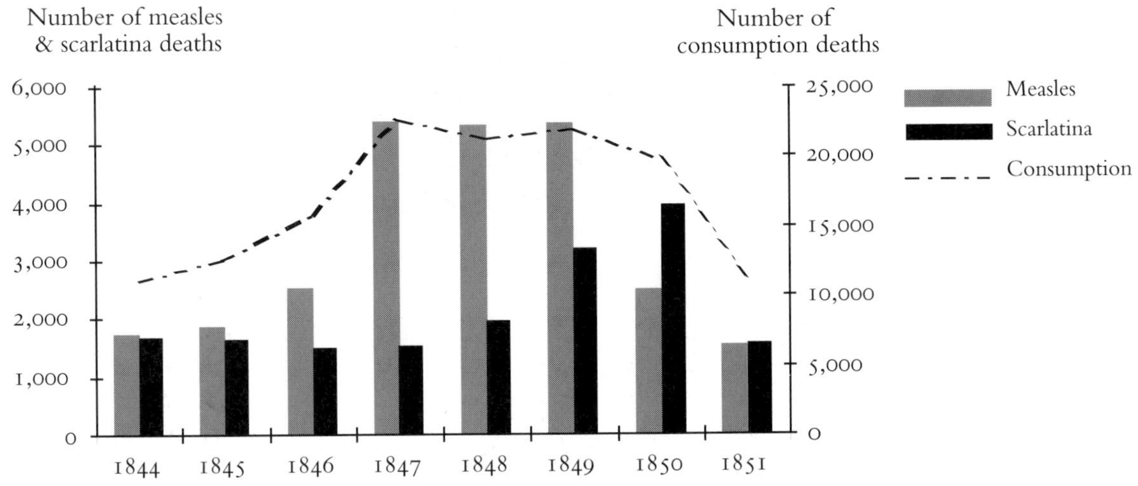

SOURCE: *Census of Ireland 1851 and 1861*[24]

children under 5 years old accounted for 67% of all measles deaths and children under 10 years old for 91%.[25] A similar mortality pattern was displayed by scarlatina with 88% of all deaths from this disease occurring among children under 10. While measles and scarlatina swept away the children, consumption eliminated young adults. Of all consumption deaths, 35% occurred among the 10 to 25 year olds, the peak cohort being the 15 to 25 year olds.

The spatial distribution of measles mortality was erratic for no obvious reason. In 1847 the highest death rates occurred in Dublin City, and in Kerry, Armagh, Fermanagh, Londonderry, Monaghan, Louth and Laois. The cramped living conditions of city tenements explain the high rate in Dublin, but for the remaining seven counties explanations are harder to find. Louth, Monaghan, Armagh and Fermanagh have common boundaries, and form an east-west corridor in the north of the country. With a disease as infectious as measles it is not surprising, therefore, to find adjacent counties with high death rates. By the following year the disease had travelled south and west where in the counties of Galway, Mayo, Sligo, Clare and Kerry death rates were considerably higher than in 1847, and the highest in the country for that year. During 1849 measles waned in all Ulster counties except Monaghan. However, for a number of locations 1849 remained or became a

bad year. Counties Dublin, Westmeath and Longford had the highest death rates of the epidemic, and in Longford, a county hitherto little affected, the measles death toll was the highest of any county throughout the crisis. In the south-west, in Clare, Cork, Kerry, Limerick and Tipperary, as well as Galway in the west death rates exceeded 100/100,000. In addition to northern counties, Carlow and Laois also had low death rates. We do not have morbidity figures, but it is possible that those who caught measles in these eastern counties survived the episode better than the impoverished inhabitants of the west and south-west. In the case of Wicklow and Wexford, for example, local doctors commented that the local populations were not in 'actual starvation', thus strengthening the suggestion that the better diet there enhanced chances of surviving a measles' attack.[26]

Over the decade 1841–51 mortality from scarlatina was greatest in the east and lowest in the west. In Leinster the ratio was 1 in 37, of all deaths, while in Connacht it was 1 in 271. In Ulster and Munster the proportions were 1 in 72 and 1 in 62 respectively. The highest rates in these provinces occurred in counties with large urban centres – Limerick, Waterford, Antrim and Down. Smaller towns too experienced the ferocity of scarlatina. Lisburn, in county Antrim and Tullamore in county Offaly, for example, suffered severe epidemics in 1846. All

24 *Census of Ireland for the year 1851*, part V, *Tables of deaths*, vol. 2, BPP, 1856, xxx; *Census of Ireland for the year 1861*, part III, *Tables of deaths*, vol. 2, BPP, 1863, viii.   25 *Census of Ireland 1851*, p. 664.

26 'Report upon the recent epidemic fever in Ireland', *DQJMS*, 8 (1849), 82.

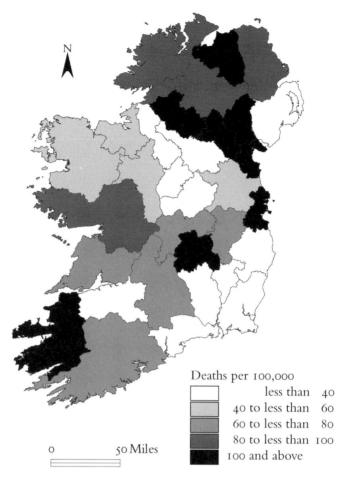

Deaths per 100,000

☐	less than 40
▨	40 to less than 60
▨	60 to less than 80
▨	80 to less than 100
■	100 and above

0   50 Miles

Map 45a: Death rates from measles at county level, 1847

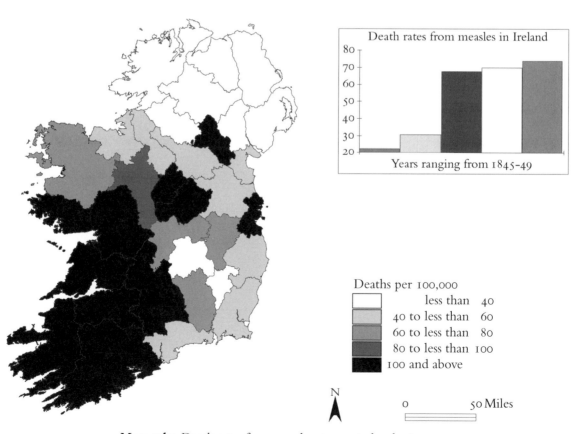

Death rates from measles in Ireland

Years ranging from 1845-49

Deaths per 100,000

☐	less than 40
▨	40 to less than 60
▨	60 to less than 80
▨	80 to less than 100
■	100 and above

0   50 Miles

Map 45b: Death rates from measles at county level, 1849

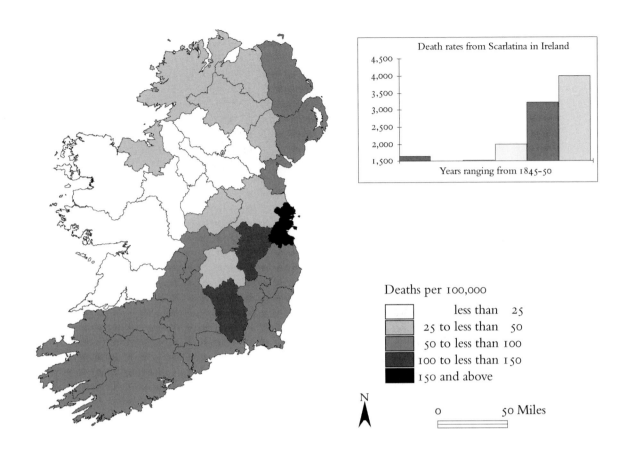

Map 46: Death rates from scarlatina at county level, 1850

communities greatly feared scarlatina. It was highly infectious and consequently spread quickly in crowded towns and cities and was said to wipe out the children of entire villages within days.[27] Robert Law, a Dublin Professor of Medicine observed that the current epidemic had indeed 'assumed a character of violence to which we had ... been utter strangers, sweeping away entire families of children, and not sparing adults.'[28]

The map shows the distribution of scarlatina deaths in the year 1850, the year of highest scarlatina mortality. Dublin City and county had the highest

death rate by a large margin, followed by Kilkenny and Kildare. Lowest rates occurred in the western counties of Clare, Galway, Leitrim, Mayo, Roscommon, Longford, and northwards into Cavan, Monaghan and Fermanagh. The census commissioners expressed doubts about the large disparity between mortality in the east and west. Their explanation for this regional pattern was ignorance of the symptoms of scarlatina by the lower classes in the west, with the result that scarlatina deaths were under-recorded.

27 *Census of Ireland for the year 1851*, part V, *Tables of deaths*, vol. 1, BPP, 1856, xxix, p. 424.

28 'Report upon the recent epidemic fever in Ireland', *DQJMS*, 8 (1849), 311.

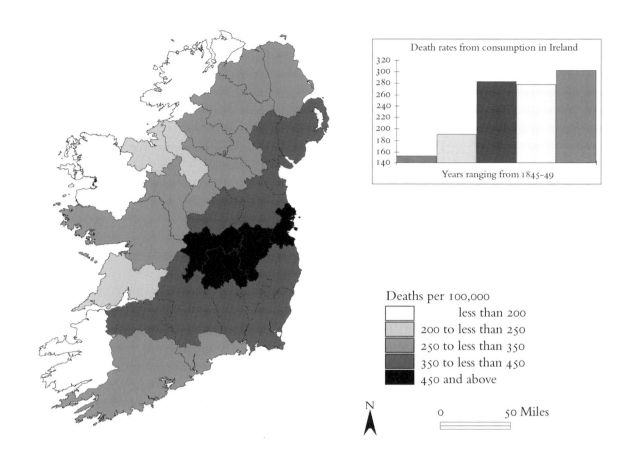

Map 47: Death rates from consumption at county level, 1849

Turning to consumption, the pattern of mortality was an inverted image of that displayed for starvation: high death rates in the east, low rates in the west and south-west. Tuberculosis is an airborne infection, and the overcrowded, filthy tenements of the city fostered the dissemination of the disease. High death rates occurred in Dublin and the nearby counties of Kildare, Offaly and Laois, with lower levels radiating out northwards to Meath, Louth, Down and Armagh, southwards to Wicklow, Carlow, Kilkenny, Wexford, and westwards to Tipperary and Limerick. Lowest mortality levels occurred in the rural counties of Mayo, Kerry and Donegal. Consumption was particularly lethal in poorly-fed and crowded communities.[29]

In summary, mortality statistics of infectious diseases and contemporary medical reports demonstrate the strong influence of prolonged starvation on the incidence and character of infectious ailments. Mortality from all the infections we have examined rose during the hungry years. There was a two-way relationship. Lack of food triggered a process of nutritional depletion, which, in turn, made the starving more prone to infections. But as the infections ran their course, they accelerated the excretion of vital nutrients from the body. This exposed further the victims to nutritional deficiency diseases. At the same time, the virulence of their infection was heightened, increasing chances of death. It was the unusual severity and duration of the Irish Famine which produced such a plethora of disease that decimated a vulnerable population.

29 Alex Mercer, *Disease mortality and population in transition* (Leicester, 1990), p. 98.

INFECTIONS: FEVERS

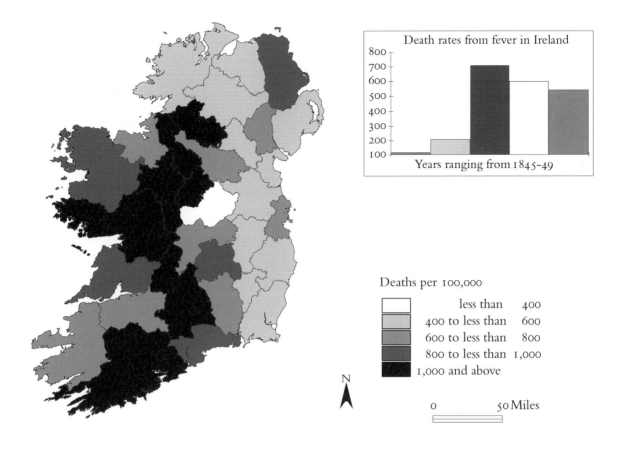

Map 48: Death rates from fever at county level, 1847

During the Famine years the population was subjected to a battery of infections. Fevers were the greatest killers of all. In the nineteenth century 'fever' was a general name given to several febrile conditions, and a wide variety of names was associated with the condition. Some referred to the environments in which the fevers flourished, such as road, gaol, camp or ships' fever. Other names were suggested by the symptoms. Typhus, for example, was sometimes called 'brain fever', 'fever of the spirits' 'spotted fever', 'petechial fever', 'maculated fever', and 'miliary fever'. Typhus was also called the 'Irish ague', because it was endemic. For relapsing fever the names of gastric fever and yellow fever were common, and the term 'famine fever' was used both for typhus or relapsing fever. In short, 'fever' was an omnibus term that embraced many conditions.

The most common fevers to afflict the population were typhus and relapsing fever. Both exhibited the febrile symptoms of high temperature, headaches, loss of appetite and general malaise. At this point the similarities ended. Typhus attacked the blood vessels of the skin and brain, causing skin rashes and delirium. With relapsing fever the episodes were sharper and shorter, and, as the name indicates, there were several relapses. Relapsing fever was also characterised by vomiting and sometimes jaundice. Faced with a multiplicity of symptoms during the epidemic of 1846–9, doctors struggled to give accurate names to the fevers they treated. Typhus fever was common in some regions and relapsing fever in others. To complicate matters further, it was not unknown for the predominant fever to start as typhus, be displaced by relapsing fever, and revert back to typhus. Sometimes the two coexisted.[30]

---

30 W.P. MacArthur, 'Medical history of the Famine' in R. Dudley Edwards and T.D. Williams (eds), *The Great Famine: studies in Irish history 1848–52* (Dublin, 1956), pp. 277–8.

As we noted earlier, doctors and laymen saw a direct association between famine and fever. The relationship, however, was complex. Poverty, squalor and overcrowding were somehow implicated but the connection between famine and typhus and relapsing fever was complex: the culprits were not cesspools, stagnant air, nor even hunger, but infected body lice. Lice eggs lodged in the folds, creases and seams of the poor's ragged and dirty clothing where they found an ideal habitat. When the eggs hatched the lice fed on their host's blood several times daily. If a louse bit a person unfortunate enough to be infected with either typhus or relapsing fever the micro-organisms multiplied rapidly within the body of the louse. Diffusion to humans was usually through skin broken by scratching, or the conjunctiva of the eyes or by inhaling infected dust.

Everybody was vulnerable to fevers; they did not respect age, sex or social class. Variations in the pattern of fevers, however, occurred within social classes. The poor caught both typhus and relapsing fever, the better-off, primarily typhus, and rarely relapsing fever. The explanation rested with the mode of transmission. Because the active typhus micro-organisms lodged in dust, direct contact with lice was not necessary to contract the disease. Thus armies of workers such as doctors, clergy, lawyers, magistrates, jurors, workhouse officials, hospital staff and relief workers and others involved tending the sick and in philanthropic endeavours, often succumbed to typhus by inhaling infected dust Of all the professions the medical fraternity was the most exposed to typhus and they paid a high price for their vocations.[31] The agent causing relapsing fever, on the other hand, entered the body through broken skin or the conjunctiva of the eye; thus direct contact was necessary to contract the disease.

Among the poor typhus spreads throughout the entire household; in better class families it was confined to the victim. The relative cleanliness, and more spacious living conditions of better-off homes, as well as the inability of lice to survive at room temperature, halted the propagation of typhus. Despite cleaner environments, the resistance of the wealthy was low, and the rich suffered higher mortality.

Death rates among the poor were estimated at 1 in 30, but 1 in 3 among the wealthy.[32] There are several possible explanations for class differences in mortality. The endemic nature of typhus among the poor gave them a two-fold advantage. Earlier, less virulent episodes provided immunity for survivors that lasted several years, and milder subsequent attacks enhanced chances of survival.[33] Higher ranking victims tended to be older, and MacArthur suggests that 'the strain thrown on the heart' was too great for them to bear.[34]

The map shows high death rates in the west, south-west, and in counties with high population concentrations. Cork and Tipperary in the south and Galway, along with Leitrim, Roscommon, Longford and Fermanagh in the west, displayed very high rates indeed. Observations from doctors practising in these counties, who responded to Wilde's fever questionnaire, emphasized the prevalence of fever in these areas. One physician, Dr Pemberton of Ballinrobe, commented that 'there was not a village and scarcely a cabin in this district that escaped its desolating influence.' Pemberton continued, 'I have seen whole families consisting of seven or eight individuals, lying in the fever at the same time, with perhaps a child of eight or nine years of age the anxious nurse tender of its father, mother, and ... brother and sisters ... the child itself scarce able to walk from starvation.'[35] At the other end of the scale were Westmeath, Kildare, Londonderry, Donegal, and Tyrone, all with death rates below 500/100,000. Once again the medical reports concur with the mortality statistics. A Londonderry physician, Dr Rogan, observed that 'no starvation existed in the city ... and in the county only few instances of fever from its effects are recorded.'[36] Dr Hamilton of Omagh, County Tyrone, calculated that the proportion of cases in his area was 1 in 85,[37] a figure considerably lower than that for the whole nation of 1:6. Although the highest fever mortality occurred in 1847, in Carlow, Offaly, Meath, Wexford, Clare, Limerick, Cavan and Galway the greatest number of fever deaths took place in 1848. Fever was waning by 1849, yet epidemic levels were still experienced in pockets of the country up to 1850.

31 Peter Froggatt, 'The response of the medical profession to the Great Famine', in E. Margaret Crawford (ed.), *Famine: the Irish experience 900–1900* (Edinburgh, 1989), p. 148.   32 D.J. Corrigan, *Famine and fever as cause and effect in Ireland* (Dublin, 1846), p. 5.   33 Anne Hardy, 'Urban famine or urban crisis? Typhus in the Victorian city', *Medical History*, 32, 4, (1988), 406.   34 W.P. MacArthur, 'Medical history of the Famine', p. 280.   35 'Report upon the recent epidemic fever in Ireland', *DQJMS*, 7 (1849), 368.   36 Ibid. p. 105.   37 Ibid. p. 107.

DIARRHOEAL DISEASES

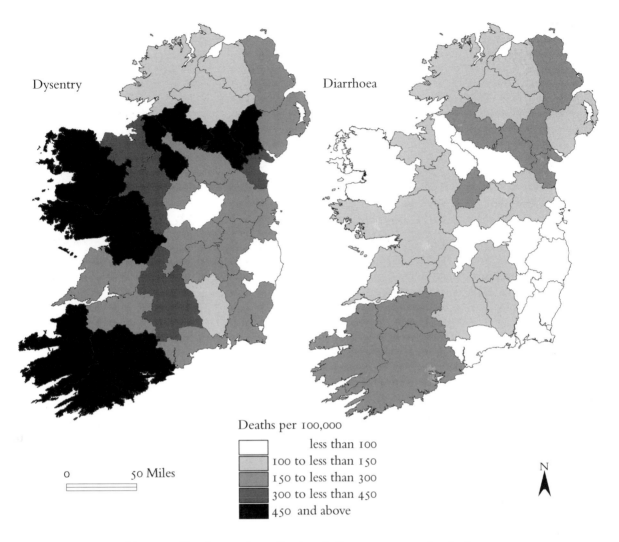

Dysentry

Diarrhoea

Deaths per 100,000

less than 100
100 to less than 150
150 to less than 300
300 to less than 450
450 and above

0   50 Miles

N

Map 49: Death rates from diarrhoeal diseases at county level, 1847

Dysentery and diarrhoea exacted a high toll among famine victims. At times of food crises they were particularly virulent and during the Famine mortality from these diseases was as high as 1 in 7 of recorded deaths in 1847. Several causes were responsible. Severe malnutrition of itself triggered non-infective famine diarrhoea. Eating contaminated food, insanitary conditions and overcrowding resulted in dysentery. Furthermore, the introduction of inadequately ground Indian meal as relief food gave many people diarrhoea. Statistical data are flimsy, not least because there can be little confidence in the accuracy of recording the distinction between diarrhoea and dysentery. Nevertheless the census recorded a marked rise in diarrhoeal deaths during the Famine.

Famine diarrhoea was the terminal stage of malnutrition. It was non-infective, the result of a paper-thin digestive system being unable to absorb food of any kind, let alone the scraps of dubious food scavenged by the starving. Doctors who carried out post mortems during the Great Famine found victims with empty and translucent intestines and colons, suggesting that some of the diarrhoea cases had in fact been suffering from famine diarrhoea.[38]

38 D. Donovan, 'Observations on the peculiar diseases to which the Famine of last year gave origin, and on the morbid effects of insufficient nourishment', *Dublin Medical Press*, 19 (1848), 67–8.

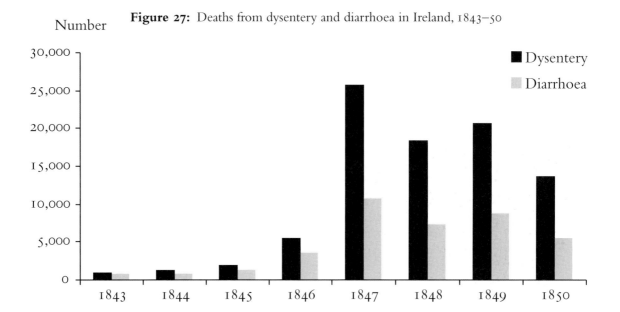

Figure 27: Deaths from dysentery and diarrhoea in Ireland, 1843–50

Dysentery was highly infectious and was transmitted easily by food, fingers, and flies.[39] So intense was hunger in the mid-1840s that rotted vegetation and carrion were devoured with gruesome consequences. Putrid potatoes, in particularly, were singled out for blame.[40] Insanitary conditions also aided in the spread of disease. Bowel discharges from infected paupers likewise transmitted disease to others and so the infection spread with great rapidity. Moreover the virulence of dysentery was intensified by the famine conditions and so weakened by hunger the population fell prey to severe attacks.

Indian meal at first added to people's misery. Its great attraction as a substitute for the potato was its cheapness compared with oatmeal. Early shipments were stale, dry and inferior and people did not know how to grind and store it. The grain was hard, requiring steel grinders to render it fit for consumption. Furthermore, although Indian meal was imported as relief food in the early 1800s and again in the 1820s, most people did not know how to cook it. Some even attempted to eat Indian meal raw. The consequences were serious. The flint-hard grain caused severe intestinal disorders. The medical profession recognised that the people were experiencing difficulty in digesting Indian meal. Dr Dillon of Castlebar in Mayo, noted important differences between the symptoms he witnessed and what he termed 'true dysentery'. He blamed Indian meal, asserting that 'the quality of the Indian meal, all of

which, *ground in this country*, contains a large proportion of the husk or skin; [compared to] that prepared in America being closely sifted, and quite as pure as our best flour.'[41]

Diarrhoea is a symptom of the vitamin B (niacin) deficiency disease, pellagra. It was common among people heavily dependent on Indian meal. We have no direct evidence of pellagra during the Famine, but as many Irish were getting less niacin in their relief rations than is required to prevent the disease, the chances of the Irish being afflicted with diarrhoea associated with pellagra were high.[42]

Medical evidence confirms that dysentery was rife in every county and the spatial distribution, shown on the map, indicates that the counties hardest hit by famine experienced the highest mortality from dysentery. Thus counties Cork and Leitrim had the highest rates of mortality from dysentery with values exceeding 750/100,000 of the population, though Kerry, Galway and Armagh had high rates too, all in excess of 500/100,000. Even counties with lower death rates, such as Tyrone, Westmeath and Wicklow, were not immune to the disease. For instance, a Tyrone doctor commented that 'dysentery was frequent in all stages';[43] but the better nutritional condition of the labouring classes in the east and north aided in survival from dysentery whereas their western counterparts succumbed. Recorded diarrhoea mortality was lower. The highest levels were returned for the south-west, as well as a

39 W.P. MacArthur, 'Medical history of the Famine', in R. Dudley Edwards and T.D. Williams (eds), *The Great Famine: studies in Irish history 1848–52* (Dublin, 1956), p. 268.   **40** Ibid, pp. 284–5.   **41** 'Report upon the recent epidemic fever in Ireland', *DQJMS*, 7 (1849), 367–8.   **42** E. Margaret Crawford,

'Indian meal and pellagra in nineteenth-century Ireland' in J.M. Goldstrom and L.A. Clarkson (eds), *Irish population, economy and society: essays in honour of K.H. Connell* (Oxford, 1981), pp. 113–33.   **43** 'Report upon the recent epidemic fever in Ireland', p. 116.

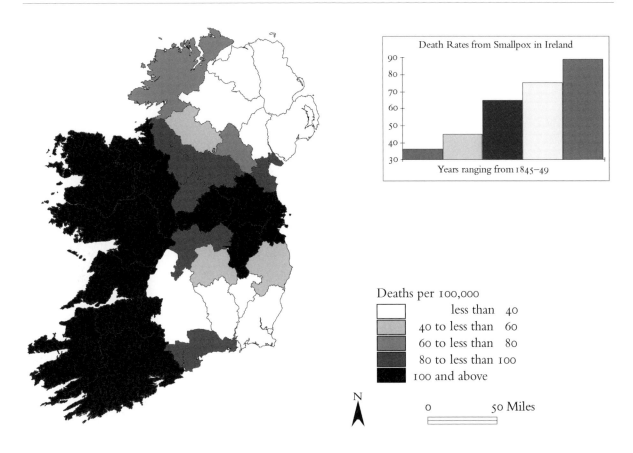

Map 50: Death rates from smallpox at county level, 1849

small pocket along the north-east border counties of Armagh, Louth and Monaghan, and also Longford and Antrim.

INFECTIONS: SMALLPOX

Smallpox was a greatly feared disease. It was generally a killer, and those who survived carried the stigma of disfigurement for the rest of their lives. The symptoms of the disease were headache, vomiting, high fever and a skin rash. It was this rash which produced unsightly pock marks. In some cases an additional legacy was blindness. Smallpox is a viral disease and has no direct association with famine. Indeed the disease was no respecter of class or wealth; thus rich and poor alike contracted smallpox. There was possibly more than one strain of the smallpox virus which varied in virulence; and survival, even of a mild attack, usually gave lifetime immunity. By the eighteenth century populations

had reached a size enabling them to sustain the disease. Furthermore, the immunity provided by the practice of inoculation protected many adults, leaving mainly children vulnerable.[44]

Smallpox epidemics, nevertheless, coincided with periods of food shortages. Increased incidence was recorded in 1740, 1757, 1817 and 1847–9, all years of scarcity. If smallpox had no direct link with famine why was there an increase in morbidity and mortality when food was in short supply? Several factors contributed. First, famine is a time of social dislocation. Swarms of starving people leave their homes in search of food and congregate at food relief centres. Because smallpox is an air-borne, density-dependent infection the opportunity for the disease to spread was greatly enhanced at these centres.[45] Secondly, in urban centres where smallpox was periodically rife some would have acquired immunity; in addition opportunities for vaccination were greater in towns. Country folk, on the other

44 Alex Mercier, *Disease, mortality and population in transition* (Leicester, 1990), p. 47   **45** William H. Foege, 'Famine, infection and epidemics' in G. Blix (ed.), *Famine: a symposium dealing with nutrition and relief operations in times of disaster* (Uppsala, 1971), p. 64.

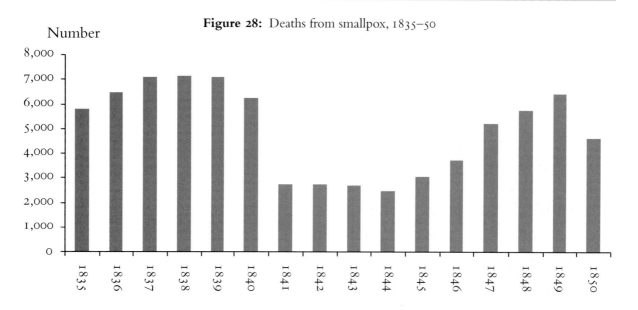

Figure 28: Deaths from smallpox, 1835–50

SOURCE: *Censuses of Ireland for 1841 and 1851.*

hand, and particularly the young, crowding into towns and cities for the first time, were vulnerable to the disease. Besides, although the first centre of vaccination opened in Dublin in 1800, legislation on vaccination for Ireland was not passed until 1840 and 1841. The responsibility for vaccination was placed with the poor law authorities, but the legislation was permissive rather than mandatory, and so in many unions the scheme was not in place at the outbreak of the Famine. Consequently thousands slipped through the net.[46] Nevertheless the impact of the legislation is reflected in the mortality statistics, shown in Figure 28.

Although the years 1841–44 show a marked decline in smallpox deaths, throughout the famine years an increase in mortality is evident. For the year 1849 alone a total of 7,319 cases was returned to the Commissioners of Health, a figure much below the true number, since the recorded cases were only those who sought medical attention. The Commissioners commenting on this increased incidence, attributed it 'in some degree to the continuance ... of inoculation, but [also] more to the want of an efficient system of vaccination'.[47] Yet it was realised that alone these factors could not explain both the substantial rise in incidence and its 'peculiarly malignant character'.[48] From 1845 the

number of deaths rose, reaching a peak in 1849 with 6,436 recorded deaths. In the years leading up to the Famine the average deaths amounted to just over 30 per 100,000, though by 1849 mortality had risen three fold to 89 per 100,000. Wilde, in preparing the 1851 census, was surprised to find deaths from smallpox so high when vaccination was available. It 'can only be accounted for', wrote Wilde, 'by the disease being maintained and propagated in the country districts, by [the more dangerous] inoculation with small-pox virus, as well as the general neglect of vaccination.'[49] Ignorance and fear among the poorer classes were more likely explanations rather than an increasing carelessness or aversion to vaccination.[50]

The geographical distribution of smallpox mortality shows high death rates in the west and south-west during the period 1847 to 1849. Belfast and Londonderry were blackspots in 1847, though it was in 1849 that highest mortality occurred. Not only had the west and south-western counties of Clare, Cork, Kerry, Limerick, Galway, Mayo, Roscommon, and Sligo high death rates, but also Dublin and a corridor of counties – Kildare, Meath, and Westmeath – due west from Dublin where mortality rates exceeded 100/100,000 of the population. The north-east and south-east corners of the country escaped the worst of the epidemic.

46 Boards of Guardians viewed vaccination programmes as an additional expense on already overstretched financial resources. **47** *Report of the Commissioners of Health (Ireland)*, BPP, 1852–3, xli, p. 17.   **48** *Report of the Commissioners of Health*, p. 17.

49 *Census of Ireland for 1851*, part III, *Report on the Status of Disease*, BPP, 1854, lviii, p. 116.   **50** *Census of Ireland for 1851*, p. 264.

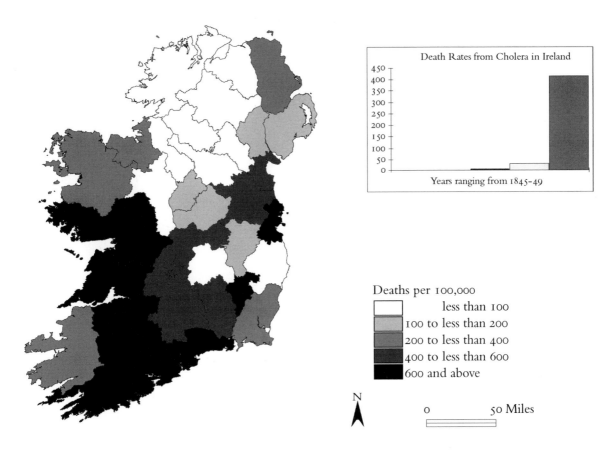

Map 51: Death rates from cholera at county level, 1849

CHOLERA: THE FINAL ASSAULT

During the final year of the Famine many survivors fell victim to Asiatic cholera. The epidemic originated in Afghanistan in 1845, migrated across the Middle East, appeared in Europe in 1847, moved westwards during 1848, and arrived in Ireland in November 1848. During 1849 it spread across the whole country. Its progress was monitored by the medical profession, their journals reporting regularly on the latest locations to be stricken. Mindful of the devastating earlier epidemic of 1832–4, there was great fear of a repeat performance. In response, the Government passed legislation in 1848 aimed at preventing the spread of cholera. Also the Central Board of Health circulated to all authorities involved in the care of cholera patients procedures intended to ameliorate the impact of the epidemic.

Cholera aroused panic reminiscent of the plague scares of earlier eras. This fear was not misplaced.

Cholera was a killer, with a short and sharp life span. Sufferers usually died within three or four days of the symptoms appearing; sometimes death took place within hours. Approximately fifty per cent of people in Europe who contracted the disease died.[51] In Ireland the mortality during the 1849 epidemic was calculated at 42%,[52] though this figure is probably an underestimation. The fact that cholera affected the healthy as well as the weak, the young and the aged, also heightened anxiety.

The main symptoms of cholera are vomiting and diarrhoea. Death resulted from dehydration. The appearance of cholera victims was particularly shocking; they were comatosed, their eyes were sunken, and their skin had a blue-grey hue.

Cholera is transmitted by water and by food. The most common mode of dissemination was by drinking contaminated water. Public sanitation was crude or non-existent. In such conditions the public water supply readily became contaminated by

51 Richard J. Evans, 'Epidemics and revolutions: cholera in nineteenth-century Europe', in T. Ranger and Paul Slack (eds), *Epidemic and ideas* (Cambridge, 1992), p. 154. **52** *Report of the* *Commissioners of Health, Ireland on the Epidemics of 1846 to 1850*, BPP, 1852–3, xli, p. 30.

Table 8: Cases and deaths from cholera in major towns, 1849

	CASES REPORTED BY BOARD OF HEALTH	DEATHS REPORTED BY BOARD OF HEALTH	DEATHS AS A % OF BOARD OF HEALTH CASES	DEATHS REPORTED IN THE CENSUS 1851	DEATHS AS A % OF BOARD OF HEALTH CASES
Dublin	3,813	1,664	43.6	3,482	91.3
Cork	3,176	1,329	41.8	1,571	49.5
Limerick	1,500	746	49.7	1,638	109.2
Belfast	2,705	969	35.8	857	31.7
Waterford	522	294	56.3	629	120.5
Galway	897	426	47.4	570	63.5
Kilkenny	1,046	529	50.5	410	39.2

SOURCE: *The Census of Ireland for the year 1851*, Table of Deaths, vol 1, p. 323 & vol. 2, pp. 202, 354, 398, 434, 386, 588, 232, *Report of the Commissioners of Health, Ireland, On the Epidemics of 1846–50*, BPP 1852–3, xli, p. 35.

excreta from infected patients. Where raw sewage seeped into the water supply cholera swept through communities with great speed.

Some victims contracted cholera from food contaminated by flies or infected hands as well as from infected clothing. Cholera consequently spread most rapidly in dirty and overcrowded locations and in institutions such as workhouses and prisons where sanitation was particularly bad. In addition there was the Famine. Although not caused by hunger, the depleted nutritional state of many people intensified the impact of cholera. Table 8 provides some indication of the incidence and mortality of cases in the principal towns and cities where many of the starving poor congregated.

Doctors of the day did not understand how cholera was transmitted, and certainly the importance of hygiene was not appreciated. Debate raged within the medical profession on whether it was contagious. The fact that carers of cholera victims were not particularly prone to catching the disease, confirmed in the mind of some that it was not contagious. A leading proponent of the non-contagionist theory was Dr Dominic Corrigan. He was a member of the Central Board of Health, and was therefore influential in shaping the public health policy. The non-contagionist policy pursued by the Board had far reaching effects on Irish cholera mortality.[53] For example, the Board advocated the treatment of cholera patients in their own homes. If hospitalised, they were to be treated alongside other patients. Policies such as these, in fact, aided rather than abated the spread of cholera.

The first reported cases came into Ireland via Belfast in November 1848, yet northern counties suffered less compared to other regions of the country. High mortality occurred in Clare and the counties with major ports. Hence Dublin city and its hinterland, and Galway recorded the highest death rates. Limerick, Cork and Waterford, all counties with ports engaged in trade with Britain, Europe and beyond, also had high cholera death rates. The coastal counties of Louth, Meath and Antrim felt the sting of the epidemic too as did land-locked Tipperary, Kilkenny, and Offaly. Kerry, Mayo, Sligo and Wexford recorded death rates of a lower order, and the Ulster counties of Londonderry, Tyrone, Fermanagh, Donegal, Cavan, Monaghan as well as Leitrim, Roscommon, Wicklow and Laois escaped the ferocity of the disease, with mortality rates not exceeding 65/100,000.

In 1849 cholera ranked second as a major killer disease after fevers. More than 44,000 cases were reported to the Board of Health; mortality was returned at 19,325.[54] The census figure for 1849, however, showed a higher mortality figure of 30,156, suggesting that morbidity was also higher than the Board of Health recorded.[55] The cholera epidemic lost its vigour in the summer of 1850 as the surviving population looked forward to a blight-free harvest of potatoes.

53 *Report of the Commissioners of Health*, p. 30; J. Robins, *The miasma: epidemic and panic in nineteenth-century Ireland* (Dublin, 1995), p. 137.   54 *Report of the Commissioners of Health*, p. 29.

55 *The Census of Ireland for the year 1851, Table of deaths*, vol. 2, BPP, 1856, xxx, p. 660.

THE PLIGHT OF THE POOR

THE POOR LAW

The Poor Law was inextricably involved in the famine crisis by virtue of its function. Set up in 1838 to alleviate the distress of the 'deserving' poor, it consisted initially of the network of 130 unions, subdivided into 2,049 electoral divisions, with a workhouse in each union to accommodate the paupers. Relief was to be received only inside the workhouse and accommodation was planned for 100,000 paupers within the entire system. On the eve of the Famine the network of unions was almost complete with 123 workhouses open, the final seven following before the end of 1846.[1] No sooner was the network finished than it was put under extraordinary pressure because of the failure of the potato in 1845. With the reappearance of a blighted potato crop in 1846 and 1848 the poor law commissioners realised that workhouse relief would be inadequate to cope with the developing calamity, and some contingency plans should be implemented. Initially, emphasis was placed on the importance of extracting the poor rate from rate payers, who were finding it more and more difficult to meet their tax obligations.

By the spring of 1847 workhouses in the west and south were filling quickly and soon the occupancy exceeded the number the system was designed to cater for. As the stream of paupers into the workhouses increased to a torrential flood from 1846 to 1850 boards of guardians sought additional accommodation. More sleeping galleries were erected, wooden sheds put up, extensions added to existing workhouse buildings, unused buildings commandeered for the duration of the crisis, and houses hired on a temporary basis. These plans were inadequate, made evident by the ever increasing numbers of able-bodied paupers who became eligible to receive outdoor relief because workhouses were filled to overflowing.[2] This state of affairs prompted the appointment of a Boundary Commission in 1848 to examine expansion of the union network. Consequently one union was added in 1848, a further 32 unions were added by 1850 making a total of 163 union and 3,439 electoral divisions. During 1847–8 accommodation was extended to cater for 150,000 paupers, further expanded to over 250,000 during 1848–9, and to over 300,000 by 1851. The numbers of destitute availing of workhouse shelter rose dramatically between 1847 and 1849, reaching a peak of almost one million (932,284), the result of yet another bad harvest in 1848 and the increasing pace of evictions. Numbers remained high during 1850 and 1851, but there was a marked decline thereafter (see Table 9).

Table 9: Total numbers relieved in the workhouses, 1844–53

YEAR	NUMBER OF WORKHOUSES IN OPERATION	TOTAL NO. OF PERSONS RELIEVED DURING THE YEAR	YEAR	NUMBER OF WORKHOUSES IN OPERATION	TOTAL NO. OF PERSONS RELIEVED DURING THE YEAR
1844	113	105,358	1849	131	932,284
1845	123	114,205	1850	163	805,702
1846	130	243,933	1851	163	707,443
1847	130	417,139	1852	163	504,864
1848	131	610,463	1853	163	396,438

SOURCE: George Nicholls, *A History of the Irish Poor Law* (London, 1856), pp. 323 & 395

1 G. Nicholls, *A history of the Irish Poor Law* (London, 1856; reprint New York, 1967), p. 304.   2 Provision was made in the new Poor Law Act of 1847 to allow outdoor relief under particular circumstances; see the entry on Outdoor Relief.

1847 marked a turning point in poor relief policy. Formerly the Government had put money into a number of schemes, such as public works and soup kitchens to aid the crisis. From 1847 all relief was to be directed through the Poor Law. The new Poor Law Act of 1847 contained some provisions aimed at ameliorating the pressure within the system, such as outdoor relief and hospital accommodation, as well as establishing strong budgetary control. The financial burden of famine relief was to be met by the local rates. Irish property must pay for Irish poverty. Where there was dissatisfaction with union administration, such as failure to provide necessary relief or a misapplication of the union funds, the Act gave power for the dissolution of boards of guardians, and their replacement by paid officers. Meanwhile, the numbers seeking relief were increasing, and the revenue from the poor rates falling. The heaviest burden of poor relief was in the poorest unions whose populations were the least able bear the financial burden of high poor rates. Consequently, many poor unions, particularly those in the south and west, fell into deficit, some were declared bankrupt, and between August 1847 and March 1848 39 unions were dissolved. The majority of these unions were in the west, some in the south and midlands and one in Ulster.[3]

Reluctantly the Government accepted that it was far beyond the ability of certain unions to finance their own poor relief. A scheme was designed to bridge this gap between the financial shortfall from inadequate revenue from ratepayers and spiralling expense of poor relief. Under this scheme twenty-two unions were declared as 'distressed' and financial assistance was given to them.[4] Initially this money came from funds raised by the British Relief Association, part as grants and part as loans. Any additional Government finance was provided as loans, and then only when it became evident the local taxation could not meet the need. These twenty-two unions had a number of common characteristics. All were situated along the western seaboard, spatially quite large, contained a large population and had accumulated heavy debts. Their poor law valuations

were low. Prior to the arrival of blight the population depended heavily on the potato. Each contained a substantial number of small holdings. Distress in these unions was great in both 1845 and 1846, and by 1847 large numbers of the inhabitants no longer had the means to keep themselves and their families.[5]

Financial problems persisted. The blighted harvest of 1848, followed by the cholera epidemic in 1849, placed even further strain on an already overstretched relief system. To raise more money the Government expanded local responsibility for poor relief to a national liability by implementing a Rate-in-Aid Act (1849). This measure levied a rate to be paid by all ratepayers throughout the land based on the rateable value of property for 1849. The amount was assessed as 6d. in the pound. This money-raising exercise was repeated in 1850 when the rate was 2d. in the pound. There was a great outcry, particularly from the more prosperous regions of the country, who objected to subsidising relief in poor unions.

An aspect of the 1847 Act which was particularly painful was the 'quarter acre clause', or 'Gregory clause', whereby all landholders with more than a quarter acre of land had to forfeit their holding in order to qualify for relief. The aim of this clause was to clear estates of impoverished small holders. This clause was to prove a double-edged sword. Landlords used it to evict insolvent tenants and in so doing increased the flow of destitutes into the workhouse and increased the cost of poor relief. Some small holders, however, held on with great tenacity to the point of death.

The maps show the workhouse population (per 1,000 of the union population) in 1847 and 1849.[6] It is immediately apparent that in 1849 the workhouses contained many more paupers than two years previously. In 1847, although there was a general clustering of higher densities in the south-west and north-west, there was no sharp contrast. In 1849, however, there was a clear concentration in the south-west of the country. The prolonged famine, accelerated evictions and increased burden of sickness induced by cholera all added to the strain imposed on the workhouses.

3 Dissolved unions were: Athlone, Ballina, Ballinrobe, Bantry, Cahirciveen, Carrick-on-Shannon, Castlebar, Castlereagh, Cavan, Clifden, Cootehill, Enniskillen, Ennistimon, Galway, Gort, Granard, Kanturk, Kenmare, Kilkenny, Kilrush, Longford, Loughrea, Lowtherstown, Mohill, Newcastle, New Ross, Roscommon, Scariff, Trim, Tuam, Tullamore, Waterford, Westport, followed by Boyle, Cashel, Listowel, Mullingar, Thurles and Tipperary. **4** Distressed unions were: Ballina, Ballinrobe, Bantry, Cahirciveen, Carrick-on-Shannon, Castlebar, Castlereagh, Clifden, Dingle, Ennistimon, Galway, Glenties, Gort, Kenmare, Kilrush, Mohill, Roscommon, Scariff, Sligo, Swineford, Tuam, Westport. **5** C. Kinealy, *The great calamity: the Irish Famine 1845–52* (Dublin, 1994), p. 206. **6** Data for maps from *First and Third Annual Reports of the Commissioners for administering the laws for relief of the poor in Ireland, 1848–1850*.

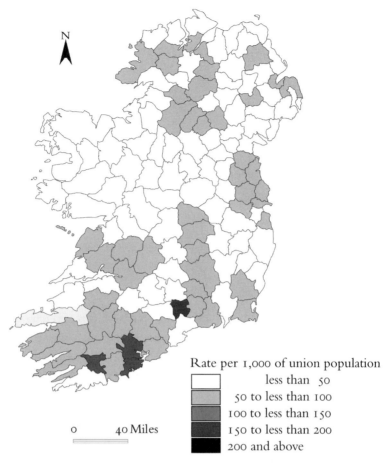

Rate per 1,000 of union population

less than 50
50 to less than 100
100 to less than 150
150 to less than 200
200 and above

0   40 Miles

Map 52: Workhouse relief during the year ending 29 September 1847 at poor law union level (130 unions)

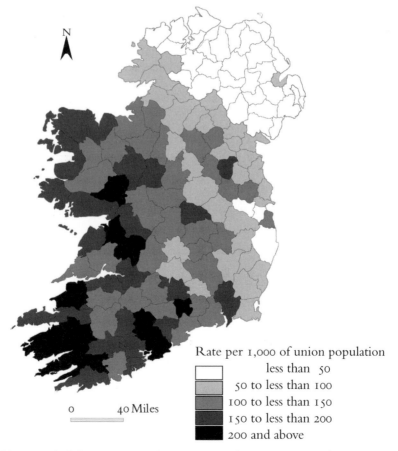

Rate per 1,000 of union population

less than 50
50 to less than 100
100 to less than 150
150 to less than 200
200 and above

0   40 Miles

Map 53: Workhouse relief during year ending 29 September 1849 at poor law union level (131 unions)

SICKNESS AND DEATH IN THE WORKHOUSES

Sickness and death stalked the workhouses. Mortality increased more than twelve-fold during the Great Famine. About 50% of deaths were from infections of various kinds and roughly 30% from diseases of 'uncertain seat' (including old age). Within these categories fevers, dysentery and diarrhoea were significant killers (see Table 10).

Although workhouses were equipped with infirmaries in which the sick were nursed, they were totally inadequate to cope with the influx of ailing paupers. The healthy and the sick were huddled together, and disease spread to the healthy with great rapidity. Many destitutes arrived in the workhouse sick and not far short of death in order to ensure a coffin burial. At its most extreme 'the whole workhouse was changed into one large hospital'.[7] The Ballina workhouse, for instance, had 84% of its inmates in its infirmary. Between October 1846 and April 1847 average weekly mortality rose six fold from 4/1,000 to 25/1,000 inmates.

Guardians could accept fever patients for treatment in the workhouse infirmaries irrespective of destitution by an amendment to the Poor Law Act in 1843. The guardians also had three other options for the treatment of fever patients. They could be removed to the nearest fever hospital; premises could be rented specifically for the treatment of fever patients; or a separate building could be constructed within the workhouse compound for use as a fever hospital. For containment of the disease, separate accommodation was preferable but by the outbreak of the Famine only a limited number of unions had separate fever hospitals. In all 222 temporary fever hospitals and numerous dispensaries were erected during the years 1847, 1848 and 1849, which aided in reducing workhouse mortality.[8] By September 1848 rates had dropped to 3/1,000. The cholera epidemic was responsible for mortality rates rising again to a peak of 12/1,000 in May 1849. Despite preparations for fever patients, it was dysentery which proved to be the greatest killer in the workhouses.

The map shows mortality in workhouses for the week ending 3 April 1847, a week in which an extremely high number of deaths occurred. Ballina union had the highest mortality by a considerable margin at 94/1,000, followed by Bantry in the south-west with 76/1,000. The coastal unions of Clifden, Galway, Gort, Ennistimon, Kilrush, Cahirciveen, Bantry, Skibbereen, and Bandon, and also the coterminous unions of Macroom, Dunmanway, Fermoy, Middleton, and Mallow, along with pockets of adjacent unions in the west and midlands, had high death rates compared with the more prosperous eastern and northern unions. Two exceptions were the unions of Downpatrick and Dundalk which had high death rates compared with surrounding areas. The poor law system was never intended to cope with mass starvation and its attendant diseases and the pressure was too great for the scheme to meet the need of the famine victims.

QUAKER RELIEF

The Society of Friends was at the forefront of private philanthropic activity. Concerned by the growing food crisis, they formed their Central Relief Committee in November of 1846 with the aim of raising funds to purchase food for distribution to the starving, and 'to obtain authentic

Table 10: Deaths recorded from main killer diseases in workhouses, 1845–50

YEAR	FEVER	DYSENTERY	DIARRHOEA	STARVATION	TOTAL DEATHS	RATIO OF DEATHS TO NUMBERS RELIEVED
1845	421	391	415	4	5,979	1 in 19.10
1846	1,334	1,354	1,358	8	14,662	1 in 17.11
1847	10,397	13,531	4,760	83	66,890	1 in 6.62
1848	6,645	9,500	3,081	56	45,482	1 in 13.42
1849	7,026	12,602	5,316	73	64,440	1 in 14.47
1850	6,478	9,238	3,555	63	46,721	1 in 17.24

SOURCE: *Census of Ireland for the year 1851*, part V, vol. II, p.116, 118; part V, vol. I, p. 401

---

7 G. Nicholls, *A history of the Irish Poor Law* (London, 1856; reprint New York, 1967), p. 326.

8 *Census of Ireland for the year 1851*, part V, Table of Deaths, vol. 1, BPP, 1856, xxix, p. 370.

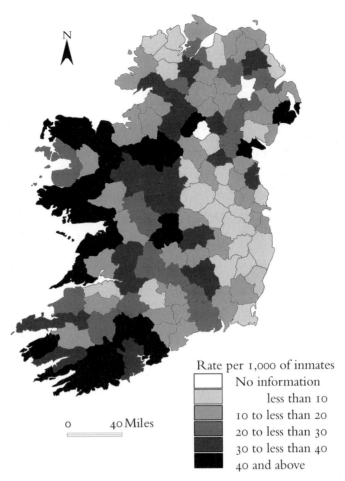

Rate per 1,000 of inmates

	No information
	less than 10
	10 to less than 20
	20 to less than 30
	30 to less than 40
	40 and above

o   40 Miles

Map 54: Workhouse inmate mortality rates for week ending 3 April 1847 at poor law union level (130 unions)

NOTES: There are no data for Ballinasloe, Cahirciveen, Enniskillen and Parsonstown for the week ending 3 April 1847. Data for the week ending 10 April 1847 has been used for the first three unions and a figure for the week ending 17 April for Parsonstown. Letterkenny and Clones submitted no returns for these weeks.   SOURCE OF DATA: *Correspondence relating to the State of Union Workhouses in Ireland*, Third Series BPP, 1847, LV.

information respecting the character of the distress in the different localities, in order that the best means might be devised for its alleviation.'[9] Details were gathered by a number of Quakers such as William Forster, William Bennett, James Tuke and Edmund Richards who toured the more inaccessible regions of the west, south-west and north-west. The purpose of these reconnaissance journeys was to identify the destitute who failed to qualify for government relief. These men witnessed unspeakable suffering, and the reports they sent back to the Relief Committee were moving and informative, and have left us an enduring record of the Great Famine.

The endeavours of the Society of Friends centred on several types of projects; soup kitchens, food supplies, provision of boilers, distribution of seeds, and clothing. Initially they were cautious, aware that

funds could be wasted and not achieve the maximum benefit to the starving. Their policy, therefore was to assist the funding of existing food distribution schemes and in rural districts where these were lacking, encourage and aid local residents to establish and run food centres. Grants of money, boilers and food were, therefore, provided by the Central Relief Committee. There were two benefits to this approach: it did not identify relief with any one religion, averting a charge of souperism; and it prevented wasteful duplication of effort and resources.

Relief efforts were also undertaken in towns, cities and densely populated locations. They opened soup shops, the first was in Charles Street, Dublin where on average 1,000 quarts of soup were sold daily at 1 old penny a quart or 1½d. with a piece of bread. Similar large-scale soup kitchens were

9 *Transactions of the Central Relief Committee of the Society of Friends during the Famine in Ireland in 1846 and 1847* (Dublin, 1852), p. 33.

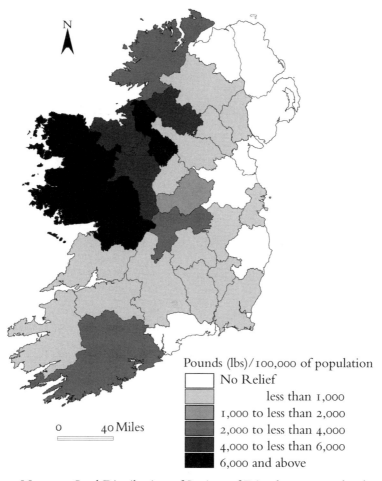

Pounds (lbs)/100,000 of population

- No Relief
- less than 1,000
- 1,000 to less than 2,000
- 2,000 to less than 4,000
- 4,000 to less than 6,000
- 6,000 and above

0   40 Miles

Map 55: Seed Distribution of Society of Friends at county level

DATA SOURCE: *Transactions of the Society of Friends during the Famine in Ireland 1846 and 1847* (Dublin, 1852), Appendix XVI, pp. 386, 388–9

opened in Cork, Waterford and other urban centres. The Quaker soup shop enterprise was a model for other such schemes and indeed demonstrated to the government their value in feeding large numbers efficiently. Once the Temporary Relief Act became operational the Quakers wound down their relief operations.

Food relief was not only in the form of soup. Rice was distributed in large quantities too. This grain was particularly suitable for the many people suffering diarrhoea and dysentery; furthermore, it was less damaging to local trade. Ship loads of peas, biscuit, American beef and Indian meal were also purchased abroad by Quakers and landed along the west coast. Food relief was an immediate solution to the crisis. Longer term help was given in the form of seeds and funds to start small-scale industrial enterprises. Turnip, carrot, mangel-wurzel and green crop seeds were distributed. Funds were given to foster a number of fisheries, agricultural projects and industrial endeavours.

During the period of their operation the Quakers purchased 294 boilers, 7,848 tons of food, 122,872 lbs of seeds and granted over £20,700 in cash.[10] The counties of Connacht and Munster were the greatest receivers of aid, whether money, food or seeds. For example, 50% of food aid went to Munster and 29% to Connacht, totalling 79%: the west and the south-west got 76% of boilers granted to relief kitchens: and three-quarters of the money aid went to that region also. Elsewhere, only Donegal received substantial sums of money, seeds and food, while Fermanagh was granted sizeable quantities of seeds, as also was Offaly. The need was greatest in the west and south-west and the Quaker aid programme reflected this. Although Cork received the largest sum of money, the greatest amount of food and more boilers than any other county in Ireland, yet when evaluated on the basis of population size, the greatest money relief and seed distribution was granted to Mayo. As regards food relief, Kerry got most with Mayo a close second.

10 *Transactions of the Central Relief Committee of the Society of Friends*, pp. 389, 473. Data for maps from: Appendix XVI, pp. 386, 388–9 and Appendix XXVIII, pp. 472–3.

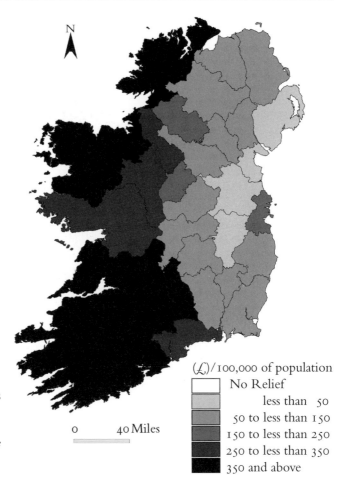

Map 56: Money granted by Society of Friends
at county level

DATA SOURCES: *Transactions of the Society of Friends during the
Famine in Ireland 1846 and 1847* (Dublin, 1852), Appendix
XXVII, pp. 472–3.

o   40 Miles

(£)/100,000 of population
No Relief
less than 50
50 to less than 150
150 to less than 250
250 to less than 350
350 and above

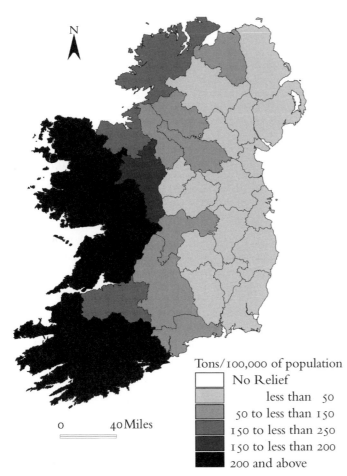

Tons/100,000 of population
No Relief
less than 50
50 to less than 150
150 to less than 250
150 to less than 200
200 and above

Map 57: Food relief granted by Society of
Friends at county level

DATA SOURCES: *Transactions of the Society of Friends during
the Famine in Ireland 1846 and 1847* (Dublin, 1852),
Appendix XXVII, pp. 472–3.

o   40 Miles

PUBLIC WORKS

Early famine relief centred on public works schemes. This type of aid was not new in Ireland; it had been used during earlier food shortages. The aim was to provide work for the starving population in return for a money wage. In Ireland labourers frequently existed in a partly monetised economy; they exchanged their labour in lieu of rent for a parcel of land on which they grew their staple food, the potato. By providing public works schemes when harvests failed the government was giving hungry labourers the means to purchase food to tide them over until the new crop matured. Between March 1846 and February 1847 there were two phases of public works schemes. The first phase was implemented under legislation of Peel's government in March of 1846.[11] The second was introduced by fresh legislation of Lord Russell's Whig government in August of 1846.[12]

The Act of March 1846 set in place the financing of the schemes, identified suitable types of projects and set out procedures for employing and paying labour. Projects to enhance the economy were envisaged, such as pier, harbour and railway construction, drainage and land improvement schemes. In reality, the vast majority of public works were road building and repair works.

Schemes were supervised either by the Board of Works or county grand juries. The financing of the schemes differed, depending on which of these two bodies were the sponsors. If a public works scheme was undertaken by a county grand jury the total cost was financed from the county cess, the Government initially putting up the money as a loan to be repaid over a number of years. The Board of Works schemes were funded from two sources. Half the cost was met by the government and charged to the consolidated fund; the other half was lent by the Treasury but had to be repaid from the county cess. The latter financing package became known as the 'half-grant scheme' and, being the more attractive, demand was high. Thus the Board of Works was the main agency for administering public works. On reflection, the government judged the 'half-grant scheme' a

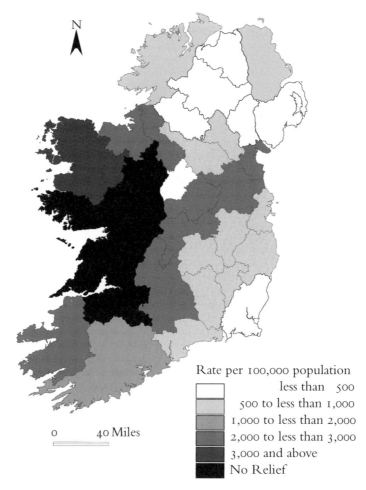

N

Rate per 100,000 population

	less than 500
	500 to less than 1,000
	1,000 to less than 2,000
	2,000 to less than 3,000
	3,000 and above
	No Relief

0   40 Miles

Map 58: Employment on public works for week ending 8 August 1846 at county level
DATA SOURCE: see footnote 13.

11 9 & 10 Victoria, cc 1–4 (5 March 1846).   12 9 & 10 Victoria, c. 107 (28 August 1846).

legislative mistake. Consequently applications were scrupulously vetted and projects were slow in starting, leading to great hardship.

The process of recruiting labour and the payment system were much criticised by administrators and labourers alike. Workers were selected by the local relief committee and issued with a ticket for presentation at the work site. Tickets were supposed to be dispensed to the destitute, but malpractice was rife and the most needy often failed to secure one. Wages were initially set at a daily rate. There were fears, however, that this system encouraged indolence; moreover, a daily wage rate of 9d., 10d., one shilling or more encouraged agricultural labourers to abandon their work on the land for employment on public works. Another concern was that wages on the public works schemes should not exceed the local rate.

By 8 August 1846 employment levels on relief works reached a peak when an average daily total of 97,617 was recorded. The accompanying map shows the distribution of employment on relief works during the first week of August, calculated as a rate per 100,000 of the population. The highest activity was in the west, where destitution was great. The county with the greatest number employed on public works was Clare. So great was the uptake there that the authorities put the county under particular scrutiny. Limerick had the second highest employment level, though only half that of Clare. High levels were also recorded for the western counties of Galway and Roscommon. Leitrim, Mayo and Sligo as well as Kerry, Tipperary, Westmeath, Offaly, Meath and Louth also had a significant participation in the schemes. The northeast and south-east corners of the country had a much lower level of activity in public works. Five Ulster counties, Armagh, Down, Fermanagh, Londonderry and Tyrone did not participate in the schemes at all.[13]

During the remaining weeks of August 1846 the numbers employed on public works schemes declined. Instructions were issued to terminate all

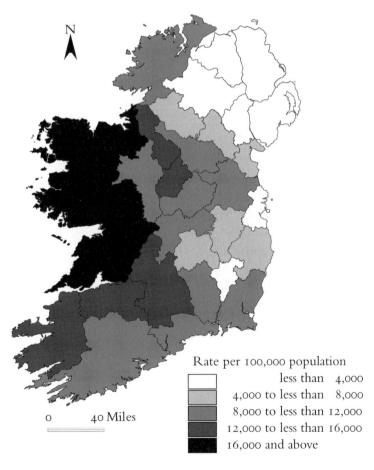

N

Rate per 100,000 population

less than 4,000
4,000 to less than 8,000
8,000 to less than 12,000
12,000 to less than 16,000
16,000 and above

0   40 Miles

Map 59: Employment on public works for week ending 13 March 1847 at county level
DATA SOURCE: see footnote 15.

13 See *Measures adopted for the relief of distress in Ireland* (Board of Works Series) BPP, 1847, 1, p. 80. In this table there are no employment figures for the counties of Longford and Wexford as well as the five Ulster counties referred to in the text, though there is evidence that labourers from the former two counties were employed on drainage projects.

relief works by 8 August, prompting an outcry. The new harvest was not the hoped for healthy crop. Meanwhile Trevelyan had been tinkering with the current public works legislation to eliminate waste, inefficiency and extravagance culminating in the new Act of August 1846. Several changes were made. Trevelyan's main purpose was to prevent the excesses of the 'half-grant scheme'. All the cost of relief works was to be met from local taxation, with repayment through the county cess. This local charge was to be assessed and levied by the same method used for the poor rate. Thus the cost was to borne by the owners of property in the distressed districts. The popular name for this revised legislation was the Labour Rate Act. Initially the Treasury put up the finance as a loan which was to be repaid by half yearly instalments of not less than four and not greater than 20 at a rate of 3½ % per annum.[14]

The Board of Works was to be the only agency for the administration of all relief schemes, the county grand juries being no more than identifiers of projects and compilers of lists of destitutes suitable for employment. All projects were scrupulously scrutinised by the Board of Works and it was an officer of the Board who determined to whom employment tickets were to be given. To meet its enhanced role in the administration of relief works the Board was reorganised and expanded.

In contrast to Peel's desire to promote 'productive' projects, Trevelyan favoured 'unproductive' schemes. Landlords greatly benefited under the old system, since projects they submitted, if accepted, enhanced the value of their property, and furthermore were half paid for by the Government. Trevelyan's intention was to eliminate this and so 'unproductive' schemes, such as road building and repairing digging and filling holes predominated.

Another feature of the new legislation was the method of paying wages. Wages were paid by task and not by a daily rate. This system had several drawbacks. Firstly, it was not fully understood by the labour force and so caused discontent. Secondly, those weakened by hunger were unable to do enough work to earn sufficient money to purchase adequate food. Thirdly, with rising food prices it became impossible to feed a family on the wages earned on the public works schemes, even by the ablest workers. Finally, administrative problems meant that wages were slow in filtering through to the labour force, leaving workers unpaid for a long period of time.

During this second wave of public works schemes even more people were employed and demand exceeded the number of places available. In March of 1847 a daily average of almost 730,000 workers depended on these schemes.[15] The highest uptake of public works employment was in the west. Clare, once again, stands out as the county where more workers were employed on public works schemes than elsewhere. The Connacht counties of Galway, Mayo and Sligo also had high rates. As before, the high dependency of the people on the potato and poor employment opportunities explain the high uptake. Ulster counties, by contrast, with the exception of Cavan and to a lesser extent Donegal and Monaghan, where the diet was more mixed and employment opportunities greater, had lower numbers resorting to public works employment. Dublin and Carlow also had low participation in schemes. The regional pattern of the first and second phases was very similar; the difference was one of degree. As the severity of the Famine intensified more labourers and indeed small farmers resorted to employment on public works schemes.

Ultimately public works schemes failed to feed the hungry and were costly to administer. The government finally recognised their failure and wound down this form of relief. Instead it introduced the Temporary Relief Act, the 'soup kitchen' Act in February of 1847.

14 *An Act to facilitate the employment of the labouring poor for a limited period in the distressed district in Ireland* 9 & 10 Victoria *c.* 107.

15 *Return showing daily average number of persons employed on public works in Ireland for week ending 13 March 1847*, BPP, 1847, liv, p. 1.

SOUP KITCHEN RELIEF

As the Famine intensified during 1846 and into 1847 neither the Poor Law facilities nor the Public Works schemes were adequate to cope with the rising tide of destitution and starvation. Workhouses were overcrowded and many unions were bankrupt. Public works schemes were failing. Ill-conceived projects, bureaucratic mismanagement and a starving population without the strength to earn enough money to purchase sufficient food, heightened the inability of this form of relief to meet the needs of famine victims. Aware of the success of the Quaker soup kitchens, the Government changed its relief policy and hastily set in place a new scheme, the Temporary Relief Act in February of 1847, pop-

ularly called the 'Soup Kitchen Act'. The scheme was organised within the existing poor law unions, with a relief committee in each electoral division. Four Ulster unions Antrim, Belfast, Newtownards and Larne did not participate in the scheme, confident of their ability to support their own poor.[16] The Soup Kitchen scheme was financed through the poor rate, though the Government gave loans to some unions and grants to the poorest unions to get the programme started.

The demand for government soup was great, and at its height these kitchens were providing over 2.6 million rations daily, which fed just over three million people. The map shows the distribution of daily rations issued gratuitously on Saturday 3 July 1847, at the peak of the scheme, presented as a % of

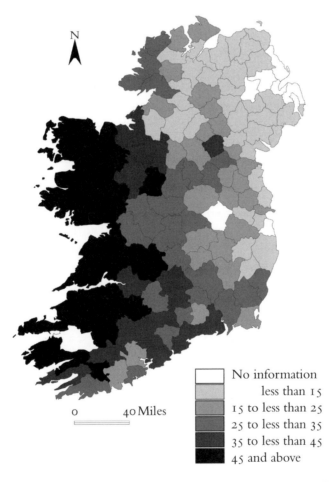

N

No information
less than 15
15 to less than 25
25 to less than 35
35 to less than 45
45 and above

0   40 Miles

Map 60: Number of daily rations dispensed in each poor law union by Relief Committees (under the Temporary Relief Act) as a % of the population on 3 July 1847

DATA SOURCES: see footnote 16

16 The *First Report of the Relief Commissioners* states there were 'only *three* [unions] into which the Act has not been introduced, namely: Antrim, Belfast and Newtownards', but in tables accompanying subsequent reports, showing number of persons fed under the 'Soup Kitchen Act' Larne is listed as supporting its own poor. The 4th Report states that Larne was 'not under the

Act'. See *First, Second, Third and Fourth Reports of the Relief Commissioners*, BPP, 1847, xvii. Christine Kinealy, however, found that one of Larne's electoral divisions opened a government soup kitchen. See C. Kinealy, *This great calamity: the Irish Famine 1845–52* (Dublin, 1994), p. 152.

THE CONDITION OF THE PEOPLE

the 1841 population. The uptake was greatest in the west and south-west of the country, where hunger was greatest and poor law unions stretched beyond solvency. At the top of the league were the Connacht unions of Ballinrobe, Clifden, Gort, Westport, Castlebar, Tuam and Swineford; at the bottom were the Ulster unions of Coleraine, Ballymena, Kilkeel, and Newtownlimavady. Broadly speaking there was an east-west split, the pattern closely resembling that of deaths from starvation. Three unions failed to submit returns, those of which are Killarney, Edenderry and Rathdown represented by white on the map.

Unemployed labourers, impoverished landholders, and the infirm got free rations; for the employed, irrespective of the wage, food rations had to be purchased for at least cost price. This policy was a disincentive to work and some people left employment to qualify for free rations, and some employers colluded with their employees by temporarily dismissing them to give them entitlement to free rations.

The regulation rations were 1 lb of meal or flour (of any grain), or 1 lb of biscuit, or 1½ lb of bread or 1 quart of soup thickened with a portion of meal plus one quarter of ration of either bread, biscuit or meal. Children under nine years old received a half-ration.[17] Whether the food dispensed to the starving should be cooked or uncooked caused controversy. The starving preferred uncooked rations. Pride was at stake; they were sensitive to the indignity of the entire family queuing each day at the relief centre, with a receptacle, awaiting their portion. Authorities favoured cooked food; while it was more expensive per ration to provide, nevertheless, it was more cost effective, since fewer made application for cooked rations and so less food was prepared. There were other reasons too why the authorities preferred supplying cooked food; the opportunity for fraud was less, and where Indian meal was provided, there was ignorance of the method of preparation and cooking.

The Temporary Relief Act was intended as an emergency provision only, aimed at bridging the gap between the winding up of the Public Works and the passing of new Poor Law legislation in June of 1847, in which there was provision for out-door relief under specified conditions. By the middle of August 1847 the soup kitchens were closing. Activity ceased entirely on 12 September, just a couple of weeks before the deadline of 1 October 1847, stipulated in the legislation.

OUTDOOR RELIEF

Under the Irish Poor Law Act of 1838 outdoor relief was illegal. As the Famine worsened in 1846–7 the numbers seeking relief greatly increased and workhouses filled quickly, many beyond official limits. In response, some Boards of Guardians flouted regulations and dispensed food to non-resident paupers. This practice was greatest in the south and west, although it was also adopted in a few eastern and northern unions. Despite Poor Law Commissioners' admonitions, many unions continued outdoor relief until financial constraints forced them to curb these activities.

The new Poor Law Act of 1847, however, provided for outdoor relief under very circumscribed conditions. One category was the infirm, the sick and widows with two or more legitimate children, (the impotent poor), who could be relieved either in or out of the workhouse at the discretion of guardians.[18] The second category was able-bodied paupers who qualified only when the workhouse was full or unfit to accept paupers because of infectious diseases. In exchange for outdoor rations paupers had to labour on arduous tasks, and if land holders of more than ¼ acre of land, forfeit it to be eligible for poor relief (the Gregory Clause).

Relief was in the form of food, preferably cooked food, as it was feared paupers would sell raw rations. For logistical reasons, many unions were unable to fulfil this directive, but since more claimants turned up wanting raw rations rather than cooked, the additional expense of cooked food was more than offset by fewer applicants. The ration was 1 lb of Indian meal per adult per day and ½ lb per child under 12 years, which the Central Board of Health judged sufficient to maintain health. A review in May 1848 revised the rations to 1¾lb. raw Indian meal or 2½lb of baked bread.

To dispense outdoor relief, orders from the Poor Law Commissioners were required by each union to sanction it. These orders were for a maximum of two months. Yet despite appalling conditions in the workhouses, it was November 1847 before the first orders were issued. By February of 1848 almost ½ million were receiving outdoor relief, and numbers steadily increased to reach a peak in the summer of 1848 of over 830,000 (see Figure 29). With the expectation of a healthy potato harvest numbers steadily declined

---

17 *First Report of the Relief Commissioners*, Appendix D, Regulations for Relief Committees, BPP, 1847, xvii, p. 23.

18 G. Nicholls, *A history of the Irish poor law* (London, 1856; reprint New York, 1967), p. 330.

during the early autumn so that by the first week in October only 199,603 rations were dispensed. Hopes were quickly dashed by the appearance of yet another blighted crop, and numbers on outdoor relief soared again during 1849 to a peak of 784,367.

The map shows the number of people in each poor law union registered for outdoor relief in the week beginning 1 July 1848,[19] expressed as a rate per 1,000 of the population. Western unions topped the league. Ballinrobe, Clifden, Ennistimon, Castlebar, and Westport unions had rates in excess of 400/1,000; in Ballinrobe and Clifden the rates exceeding 50 % of the population. All these unions were designated as 'distressed unions' in recognition of their financial difficulty. The unions with largest numbers on outdoor relief were also in areas where there was a high dependency of the population on the potato.

Twenty-five unions did not enter into the outdoor relief scheme, their guardians still being able to cater for their poor within the workhouses.[20] Seventeen of these were in Ulster where unions were smaller, and more numerous than in other provinces. Also the famine crisis was less severe in the north-east because of more diversified industry and farming.

As famine receded, the numbers relieved by outdoor rations markedly decreased. In 1848 1,433,042 people received outdoor relief. Numbers were still high at 1,210,482 in 1849, but by 1850 the figure had dropped to 368,565, and fallen further to 47,914 in 1851. The majority of those remaining on outdoor relief was the 'impotent' poor, who remained a 'deadweight' on the system far beyond the crisis.

Figure 29: Numbers of people receiving outdoor relief, 1848

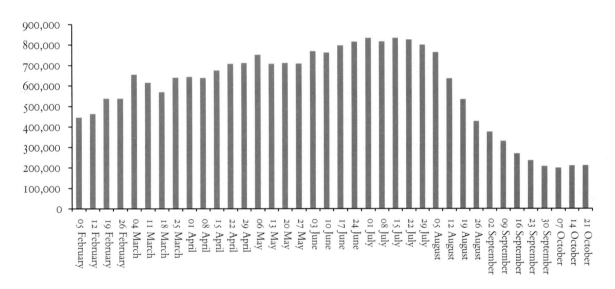

SOURCE: *First & Second Annual Reports of the Commissioners for Administering the Laws for Relief of the Poor in Ireland*

19 & *(Map 61) As no returns were received from Clifton and Glenties unions for 1 July, data for the week ending 15 July 1848 have been used. Map source: *Papers relating to the Relief of Distress* ... BPP, 1847–8, liv. **20** The following unions were not dispensing outdoor relief in the week ending 1 July 1848: Antrim, Ballycastle, Bandon, Belfast, Castlederg, Celebridge, Coleraine, Cork, Downpatrick, Dunfanaghy, Gortin, Kinsale, Larne, Letterkenny, Lisburn, Lisnaskea, Lurgan, Mallow, Middleton, Monaghan, Newtownards, Newtownlimavady, Parsonstown, Stranorlar, Wexford.

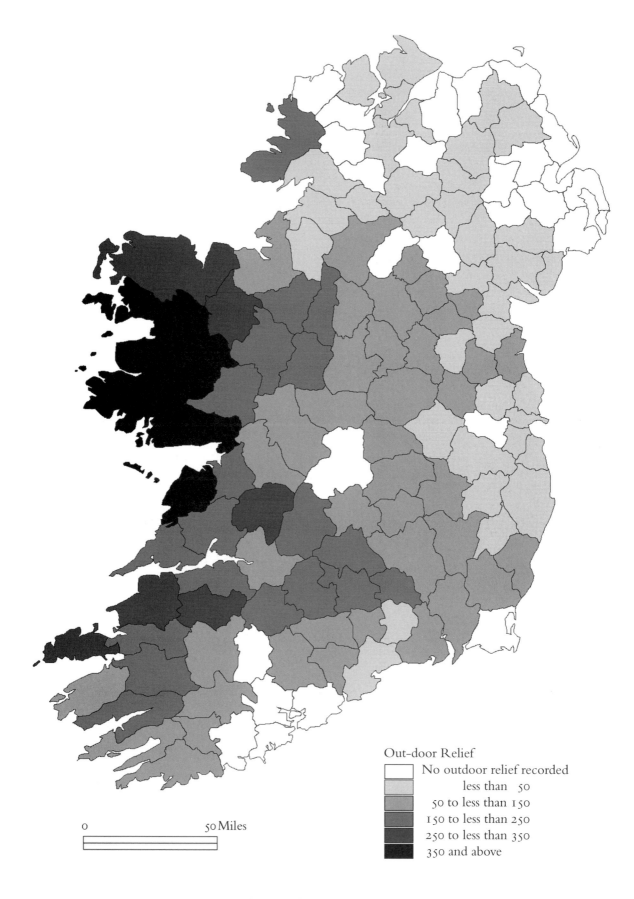

Out-door Relief

No outdoor relief recorded
less than 50
50 to less than 150
150 to less than 250
250 to less than 350
350 and above

0   50 Miles

Map 61: Persons receiving outdoor relief per 1,000 of the population in the week ending
1 July 1848★ at poor law union level

BOY AND GIRL AT CAHERA.

Illustrated London News, 20 February 1847

TOIL IN COUNTRY AND TOWN

The Great Famine had an obvious impact on the peoples of Ireland, on their numbers, mortality and migration, on their diet, the diseases they suffered from, and the houses that they lived in. It seems not to have disturbed their denominational allegiance and only gradually changed habits of marriage. The Famine probably accelerated the decline in the use of Irish and may have had a role in the growth of literacy. But what were its effects on the world of work?

On the eve of the Great Famine almost three-quarters of the male population were engaged in agriculture. The level of female employment in agriculture is more difficult to determine. The census of 1841 recorded 13%, but the true figure was much higher. By 1871 the proportion of males engaged in agriculture had declined by almost ten percentage points. The level of female employment remained more or less unchanged. Agriculture, nevertheless, remained the basis of employment, even though total employment declined by almost 700,000. However, the composition of agricultural activity altered a good deal. An army of cottiers had been wiped out by the Famine. There was, in addition, a switch from labour-intensive tillage to land-intensive pasture farming, a reflection not only of the decline in the size of the workforce, but also of changing markets for agricultural produce

The first essay in this section sheds important light on conditions in rural Ireland. Typically, rural labourers were remunerated by a mixture of payments-in-kind and money. Even with the former, the value of the payments – land, a cabin, food – were denominated in money, even when cash did not change hands. Substantial pools of rural labour were under-employed for portions of the year, with the result that annual incomes could be well below what the wage rate might suggest. The evidence is patchy; even so, it is clear that wages and incomes were lower in the west than in the east of the country. This helps to explain why the population of the west was most vulnerable to the Famine.

Between 1841 and 1871 male manufacturing employment remained more or less constant at around 15–16% of the workforce. This was not the case with females. In 1841 almost 60% of females recognised by the census commissioners as being in paid employment were in industry, the great majority of them working in the domestic textile crafts. By 1871 the proportion had almost halved as domestic industry declined.

The gross figures for manufacturing employment conceal important changes, particularly the concentration in the eastern towns and the growing importance of work in factories and engineering plants. The point should not be laboured; outside Belfast industrial employment remained largely a mosaic of small-scale enterprises. Still, as a whole the manufacturing sector became more capital-intensive and, one guesses, more productive.

Over the Famine decades there were substantial increases among males working in dealing, transport, and public and professional service. Collectively male employment rose from 5% to almost 15% of the total. Among females the tertiary sector – particularly domestic service – absorbed many females who previously might have worked in domestic industry. In all, employment in the tertiary sector increased by 180,000 men and women between 1841 and 1871, in spite of a 30% decline in the total workforce. This is one of the less noticed changes in the post-Famine economy, though some of the change is no doubt due to changes in classification.

It is probable that much of the change in the world of work would have taken place even had the Famine not occurred. Ireland was part of the United Kingdom and, as such, was locked into a web of international trade. So did the Famine have no effect? It swept away two million men, women and children in five short years. In terms of economics – the dismal science – this was the removal of a large quantity of surplus labour. In human terms it was a tragedy on a scale unprecedented.

WAGES BEFORE THE FAMINE

At one time it was thought that much of rural Ireland before the Famine hardly used money at all, and that markets, particularly labour markets, were weakly developed. This view has long since been displaced by a more complex picture of economic relationships during the first half of the nineteenth century. While it is true that cottiers and labourers within the rural economy frequently bartered their labour power to local farmers in exchange for potato land and other payments-in-kind, these transactions were calculated with reference to money values. The essence of these exchanges is captured in the following account from the parish of Templeboden, county Cork: 'wages for labour are usually paid by the labourer's holding a cottage from his employer, from whom he also takes some ground to grow potatoes, after which any wages remaining unpaid are paid in money.'[1] In Rathclaran, in the same county and before the same commission of inquiry, another witness declared that the usual wages of labourers hired for the whole year was 7 pence per day in the 1830s. He added immediately that employment for the whole year was rare: 'working farmers seldom pay any wages in money, as they charge high for cabins etc; they nominally give 6 pence with victuals, and 8 pence without'. In the towns, however, and in some of the more commercialised farming areas of the east, regular wage payments were the norm. The point to be borne in mind is that, irrespective of the existence of bargaining involving payments-in-kind, the idea and the practice of wage rates were widely diffused in pre-Famine society.

Wage rates varied depending on the time of the year. They were lower in winter than in the summer months, presumably reflecting shorter working days, in part dictated by fewer hours of light, and also the lower productivity of some forms of agricultural work in wintertime. Wages were highest at harvest time when the demand for labour peaked. Wages also varied depending on whether or not the diet of the labourer was included in the bargain. In the map shown here the wage rates used are those for the winter season, and exclude any entitlement to food. These daily wage rates have been weighted by the labouring population in each county, reflecting in a rough way the relative importance of wage

rates to the different local economies. The wage observations themselves have been calculated from data contained in the *Poor Inquiry (Ireland)*, whose report was published in 1836. This wage information needs to be treated with some caution, as it is based on the results of a survey conducted by the poor-inquiry commissioners. This in turn relies on the *impressions* of local correspondents rather than on actual wage accounts.

What emerges from the map of daily wages is that the counties of the eastern seaboard constituted a high-wage area, with Dublin wages above those of any other county (at about a shilling or 12 old pence per day). Antrim and Down were only a little behind. This, one may presume, reflects the effects of industrialisation and urbanisation, which were unevenly distributed on the island. A band of intermediate wage rates extended from Donegal down through the midlands to county Cork at the other end of the island. More refined data, at a parish or baronial level, would reveal differences within this great stretch of territory. The low-wage regions were to be found in the west of the island, a point of particular significance in terms of vulnerability to Famine. Thus, the regional pattern to wage rates is of interest, not just in its own right, but as a guide to the fault lines in the pre-Famine economy. These would soon be cruelly exposed by the mid-century crisis.

The accompanying map goes beyond daily wage rates to look at total income from wages over the course of the year. Thus it takes into account the frequency of work as well as the wage rate. Unemployment, or more typically underemployment, was a severe problem in the pre-Famine rural economy. Some labourers were hired by the year, as on the demesne farms of landlords or on the big commercial farms of the east. Many, however, got work whenever they could, which could be confined to the busy seasons of the farm year, at sowing and harvesting. For poor households in the west, or those living in the mountains, this could involve temporary migrations to the lowlands of the east. While it is difficult to generalise about the length of the working year, we can say with confidence that most labourers worked for wages for only a fraction of the year. The remainder of their time was spent tending a small potato patch, and living in enforced

---

1 *Poor Inquiry (Ireland)*, BPP, 1836, xxxi, Appendix D, p. 170.

Mean daily wage
(pence per day)

Annual
income (£)

o   50 Miles

Wage income
☐ No Information
less than   5
5 to less than 7
7 to less than 9
9 to less than 11
11 and above

N

Map 62: Income of a male labourer in 1835 at county level

idleness. The latter, incidentally, drew adverse comment from a number of ill-informed, comfortably-off contemporaries, who mistook underemployment for addiction to poverty and indolence. The culture of poverty in pre-Famine Ireland was a response to rather than a cause of low incomes, as the energy of Irish navvies on canal, road and railway construction in Victorian Britain amply testified.

As in the case of daily wage rates, the original source for annual wage income is the *Poor Inquiry* of 1836. The spatial patterns revealed are roughly similar in the two maps, though there are some anomalies such as the case of county Limerick. The latter may well be an artefact, the product of a small number of income observations and a biased sample. It may be noted also that there are no values for Galway and Leitrim owing to the limited information for these counties.

There is, however, a significant difference between the two sets of data which may not be immediately visible. There is much more variation in the data on wage income. The coefficient of variation for annual

(wage) *income* is much greater than it is for wage *rates*: 0.28 as compared to 0.17. This means that, while wage rates in the poorer west of the country were lower than in the east, income from wages was lower still, relatively speaking. The economic vulnerability of the western counties as compared to the eastern seaboard counties was even greater than the data on daily wages imply. In the west, labourers were employed for shorter periods of the year on wage labouring tasks. One should emphasise of course that income from wage labour was not the only source of income: cottiers and labourers produced much of their own food, their own fuel (from turf or peat), and often raised a pig or two for sale. Still, the large gap between east and west in terms of access to money income is a significant difference, replete with wider economic and social implications. When the primary means of subsistence failed, as in the later 1840s, the alternative of relying on purchased food simply did not exist. Men and women of the west stood penniless in the face of doom.

WORK IN FIELD, WORKSHOP AND FACTORY, 1841–71

The censuses of Ireland from 1841 onwards contain a rich quantity of information relating to occupations. The data exist at the level of the counties and five towns – Belfast, Cork, Dublin, Limerick and Waterford – and they provide the basis for a detailed picture of occupational distribution across the period of the Great Famine. The task of depicting changes over time, however, is complicated by two main problems. One is the immense amount of information gathered by the census commissioners. The other is changes in the classifications of occupations from one census to the next. Both issues need to be addressed before we consider the pattern of occupational evolution.

The 1841 census, which served as the template for subsequent censuses, listed at least 430 occupations throughout Ireland and this number increased in 1851, 1861 and 1871. Even 430 is a bewilderingly large number and the census commissioners attempted an eight-fold grouping of occupations:

> those 'ministering to food'
> (with three sub-divisions);
> those 'ministering to clothing'
> (with four sub-divisions);
> those 'ministering to lodging'
> (with five sub-divisions);
> those 'ministering to health';
> those 'ministering to charity';
> those 'ministering to justice';
> those 'ministering to education';
> those 'ministering to religion'.

There was an additional category – 'unclassified' – containing almost half a million workers. In 1886 Charles Booth re-ordered the occupations in the UK censuses between 1841 and 1881 into eleven divisions, in the process distributing the unclassified occupations into their appropriate categories; and in 1972 Professor Armstrong reduced these to nine.[1] In Table 11 these have been further combined into

six. On the whole, the names of the categories speak for themselves, except that 'industrial service' in the Booth/Armstrong system included writing clerks, caretakers and unclassified labourers. The appropriate place to put labourers is a critical point, as will become clear later. 'Public and professional' included government officials, teachers, lawyers, medical workers, ministers of religion and entertainers.

The categories inevitably overlap to some extent, but had they been used consistently by the commissioners this is not a major problem. Unfortunately they were not employed in a consistent manner, as an examination of Table 11 reveals. In 1861, for example, almost 50% of occupied males appear to be employed in agriculture, and 20% in industrial service, compared with 70% and 1% in 1851. There were even greater proportional shifts between the two categories among females, although involving smaller absolute numbers. More strikingly still, in 1841, 1851, and 1861, 27–28% of the female population were apparently gainfully employed, but in 1871 the proportion was 41%. The biggest increase had apparently occurred in agriculture which in 1861 seemingly absorbed fewer than 10% of occupied females but in 1871 employed more than one-third.

The explanation for these variations lies in the ways that the commissioners dealt with labourers and with the wives and other female dependants of employed males. In 1841 and 1851 most labourers were included in the category 'ministering to food' – that is they were treated as agricultural labourers. But in 1861 347,000 unspecified male labourers were included in the 'unclassified' category. In 1871 229,000 males were placed in the same category. A note in the 1871 census tells us that we can assume that the great majority of these were agricultural labourers. The problem also affected female labourers, but to a much smaller extent.

Turning to females who did not have specified occupations of their own, such persons (wives, daughters, sisters, etc. of working men) were assumed

1 Charles Booth, 'Occupations of the people of the United Kingdom, 1801–1841', *Journal of the Statistical Society*, 49 (1886), pp. 314–435; W.A. Armstrong, 'The use of information about occupation', in E.A. Wrigley (ed.), *Nineteenth-century society: essays in the use of quantitative methods for the study of social data* (Cambridge, 1972), pp. 226-310.

Table 11: Total occupied male population of Ireland from the censuses

OCCUPATION	1841		1851		1861		1871	
Agriculture, fishing, and mining	1,732,428	74.3%	1,315,474	69.5%	901,705	49.6%	890,911	53.5%
Dealing and transport	75,932	3.3%	93,850	5.0%	109,817	6.0%	127,879	7.7%
Domestic service	70,995	3.0%	90,902	4.8%	51,359	2.8%	26,034	1.6%
Manufacturing and building	360,576	15.5%	302,447	16.0%	288,131	15.8%	260,821	15.7%
Industrial service	42,993	1.8%	19,385	1.0%	369,736	20.3%	245,760	14.8%
Public and professional	49,850	2.1%	70,887	3.7%	98,509	5.4%	114,165	6.9%
OCCUPIED POPULATION	2,332,774	100.0%	1,892,945	100.0%	1,819,257	100.0%	1,665,570	100.0%
Whole population	4,019,576		3,190,630		2,837,370		2,639,753	
% OF POPULATION OCCUPIED	58.0%		59.3%		64.1%		63.1%	

Table 12: Total occupied female population of Ireland from the censuses

OCCUPATION	1841		1851		1861		1871	
Agriculture, fishing, and mining	144,839	12.7%	166,867	18.4%	81,703	9.8%	420,119	36.8%
Dealing and transport	32,344	2.8%	45,324	5.0%	45,811	5.5%	50,209	4.4%
Domestic service	270,705	23.7%	252,184	27.8%	322,410	38.6%	336,543	29.5%
Manufacturing and building	683,490	59.8%	429,960	47.4%	324,359	38.8%	264,567	23.2%
Industrial service	1,993	0.2%	818	0.1%	46,343	5.5%	20,723	1.8%
Public and professional	9,795	0.9%	12,770	1.4%	14,915	1.8%	50,171	4.4%
OCCUPIED POPULATION	1,143,166	100.0%	907,923	100.0%	835,541	100.0%	1,142,332	100.0%
Whole population	4,155,548		3,361,755		2,961,597		2,772,624	
% OF POPULATION OCCUPIED	27.5%		27.0%		28.2%		41.2%	

in 1841, 1851 and 1861, not to be in employment. In 1871, however, they were treated as though they were engaged in the same occupation as the male head of the household in which they lived. This was the case with all occupational categories, but the change affected agriculture most severely where there were very large numbers of such females.

Tables 11 and 12 show the occupations of males and females according to the censuses. Perhaps the most striking feature of these tables, as we have already noted, is that the proportion of females in employment apparently jumped from 28 to 41% in the ten years between 1861 and 1871.

It is important to be consistent if we wish to chart changes over time. Therefore, for the purpose of the county maps that follow, all but 28,000 of the unclassified male labourers in 1861, and all but 32,000 of the unclassified labourers in 1871 have been removed from 'industrial service' in Table 11 and added to agriculture. Similar, but much smaller adjustments have been made for females. For the towns, however, a different procedure has been adopted. There the bulk of general labourers (28,000 in 1861 and 32,000 in 1871) were probably working in building, on the roads or, in the case of port towns, as casual dock labourers. For the purpose of the town maps and charts they have been included in the manufacturing and building category, although a few should probably be placed among the dealers and transport workers.

To deal with the problem of dependent females, we need to remove them from the employed female workforce in 1871. They can be identified in the case of agriculture, shoemaking (within the manufacturing category) and some branches of dealing (shopkeepers, butchers, innkeepers, lodging house keepers), but not for public and professional services, nor from manufacturing apart from shoemaking. In all, more than 350,000 females have been taken from the workforce to bring the classification in 1871 in line with those of the earlier censuses. The adjusted occupational distributions for the country as a whole are shown in Tables 13 and 14.

Table 13: Total occupied male population of Ireland (adjusted figures)

OCCUPATION	1841		1851		1861		1871	
Agriculture, fishing, and mining	1,732,428	74.3%	1,315,474	69.5%	1,220,346	67.1%	1,068,157	66.2%
Dealing and transport	75,932	3.3%	93,850	5.0%	109,817	6.0%	127,879	7.9%
Domestic service	70,995	3.0%	90,902	4.8%	51,359	2.8%	26,034	1.6%
Manufacturing and building	360,576	15.5%	302,447	16.0%	316,306	17.4%	260,821	16.2%
Industrial service (exc. labourers)	42,993	1.8%	19,385	1.0%	22,920	1.3%	16,266	1.0%
Public and professional	49,850	2.1%	70,887	3.7%	98,509	5.4%	114,165	7.1%
OCCUPIED POPULATION	2,332,774	100.0%	1,892,945	100.0%	1,819,257	100.0%	1,613,322	100.0%
Whole population	4,019,576		3,190,630		2,837,370		2,639,753	
% OCCUPIED	58.0%		59.3%		64.1%		61.1%	

Table 14: Total occupied female population of Ireland (adjusted figures)

OCCUPATION	1841		1851		1861		1871	
Agriculture, fishing, and mining	144,839	12.7%	166,867	18.4%	116,387	13.9%	114,524	14.5%
Dealing and transport	32,344	2.8%	45,324	5.0%	45,811	5.5%	36,725	4.6%
Domestic service	270,705	23.7%	252,184	27.8%	322,410	38.6%	336,543	42.5%
Manufacturing and building	683,490	59.8%	429,960	47.4%	325,425	38.9%	253,544	32.0%
Industrial service (exc. labourers)	1,993	0.2%	818	0.1%	10,593	1.3%	387	0.0%
Public and professional	9,795	0.9%	12,770	1.4%	14,915	1.8%	50,171	6.3%
OCCUPIED POPULATION	1,143,166	100.0%	907,923	100.0%	835,541	100.0%	791,894	100.0%
Whole population	4,155,548		3,361,755		2,961,597		2,772,624	
% OCCUPIED	27.5%		27.0%		28.2%		28.6%	

In the case of males, the proportion employed in agriculture declined gradually from 74% to 66% and that in dealing and transport rose from 3% to 8%. There was little change in the other sectors, except for a fall in domestic service, which was never a big employer of male labour. Overall, the proportion of the male population in employment fluctuated at around 60%.

Figure 30: Total occupied male population (adjusted figures)

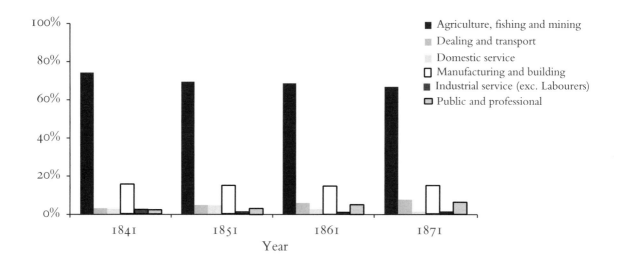

Figure 31: Total occupied female population (adjusted figures)

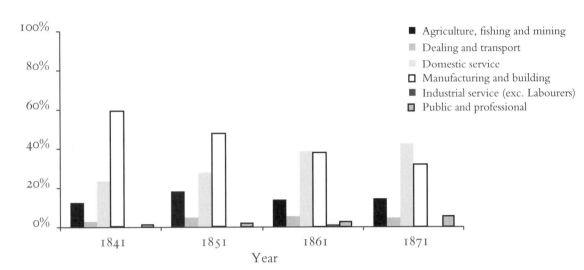

The female story is more complicated. In total 27% to 29% of the female population were in paid employment throughout the period according to the adjusted classifications. The proportion of the female workforce in manufacturing almost halved, from 60% to 32%, and the proportion in domestic service rose from 24% to 43%. The share of the female workforce in agriculture varied between 13% and 18%. There was apparently a sharp rise in the proportion of females employed in the public and professional sector between 1861 and 1871, but this reflects the inclusion of wives of professionals as part of the occupied population. The 'blackening' of the 1871 map (map 72) showing female employment in professional services is therefore misleading.

Because the occupational patterns in town and country were different, in the maps that follow the five towns of Belfast, Cork, Dublin, Limerick and Waterford have been presented separately from their host counties. At the county level agriculture was the dominant source of employment for males throughout the period 1841–71. The proportions were always higher in the west than the east of the country, and only in the three eastern counties of Ulster and counties Dublin and Kildare did they dip below 40%. The female distribution was rather different. Because the wives and daughters of male farmers and farm workers were not regarded by the census commissioners as employed (except in 1871), the proportion of women in agriculture – those with specified occupations – was low, usually 20% or less. By 1861 there was a slight concentration in a band running from Waterford to Mayo but the proportion rarely rose beyond a third of employed

females. The inter-county variations may have had as much to do with classification practices as with different modes of agriculture.

Manufacturing generally accounted for 15 to 16% of occupied males, with clusters only in east Ulster and county Dublin where industry gave employment to a third and more of males. Overall, the maps emphasise the extent to which nineteenth-century Ireland, outside a few favoured locations, remained a non-industrialised economy.

The female distribution in manufacturing emphasises a further dimension: that of de-industrialisation. In 1841 there was a broad band of female manufacturing occupations (50% and more), running north-east to south-west, but this belt retreated northwards into Ulster as time went on. This reflected the decline of the rural textile industry that had given so much employment to women, with only a limited compensation of a growth in factory employment in east Ulster.

The remaining county-level patterns require little comment. Domestic service always accounted for a high percentage of female employment and this increased as rural manufacturing employment declined. Domestic service was never an important source of employment for males. They filled superior positions in large households as stewards, butlers, coachmen and so on, but the maps reveal no regional patterns of interest.

Dealing was a category that overlapped with manufacturing; in the nineteenth century a shoemaker, for example, might well be a person who both made and sold shoes. As defined here, dealing and transport, including people such as shopkeepers, merchants, peddlers and railway workers, never accounted for more than 8% of male and 6% of female employment. There was some clustering around the towns but country dwellers as much as town dwellers depended on dealers and they were quite widespread.

Employment in the public and professional category increased over time. Included in this category were people working in education, the law and medicine, as well as officials in local and central government. They were scattered widely throughout the country, reflecting – among other things – the nation-wide distribution of post office officials, policemen and Poor Law officers.

The distribution of urban workers differed from that of the countryside in a number of ways. Figures 32 and 33 show the patterns for the five towns considered separately in the censuses (based on the adjustments discussed earlier). Among males, manufacturing and building accounted for around 50% of employment. Dealing and transport hovered around 20%, with some tendency to increase over time as railways became more important. Employment in the public and professional sector also rose. Agriculture and domestic service were not important sources of employment. The apparent increase in agriculture in 1851 may have been the result of agricultural labourers coming into the cities during the later Famine years.

Among females, manufacturing and domestic service dominated, each accounting for around 40% of the occupied female population. Dealing accounted for about 10%. The remaining categories were unimportant. The apparent increase in female professional employment in 1871 is misleading. It reflects the difficulty in that year referred to above of distinguishing wives of male professionals from women truly employed.

The pie charts illustrate the position in the five towns. The total employed populations of Belfast and Dublin both increased; the others contracted. The manufacturing and building sector among males was large in all places, but especially so in Belfast, which offered more factory-type employment. Dublin had somewhat greater shares of professionals than the other towns. Turning to females, Belfast had a decided advantage in manufacturing, reflecting the importance of the linen industry.

By no means all the changes in occupations described above can be attributed to the Famine. Indeed most of them probably occurred quite independently and were part of the wider processes of industrialisation at work within the British and Irish Isles and the Atlantic economy. The industrial revolution profoundly altered the economic geography of the British Isles. From the 1760s industry was becoming concentrated in south Lancashire, the West Riding of Yorkshire, the west Midlands, south Wales, the Clyde valley, and Ulster. Old industrial centres, such as the Weald of Kent and Sussex and East Anglia were in decline and their economies became increasingly agricultural. Ireland was no different from other parts of the British Isles in undergoing regional specialisation based on comparative advantage. This process ensured that mid-nineteenth century Ireland remained an agrarian society. The Great Famine changed the land/labour ratio and so emphasised the climatic advantages that Ireland possessed in pastoral farming. At the same time the persistent loss of population eroded the market for local industries. To that extent the Great Famine accelerated a trend already underway.

Figure 32: Male urban occupations, Belfast, Cork, Dublin, Limerick, Waterford

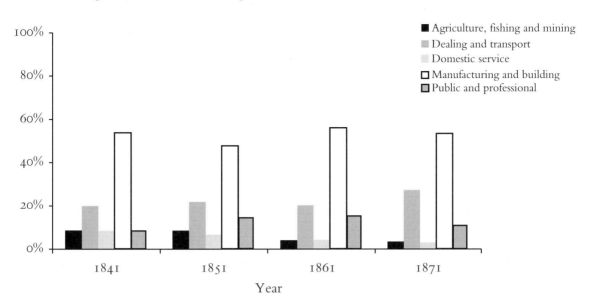

Figure 33: Female urban occupations, Belfast, Cork, Dublin, Limerick, Waterford

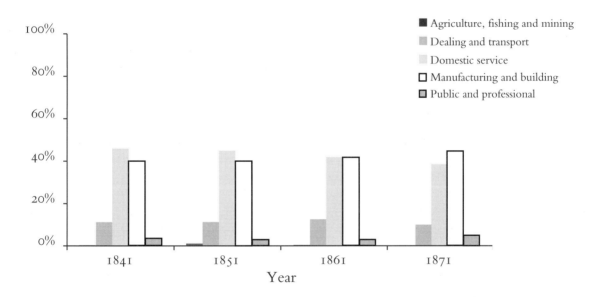

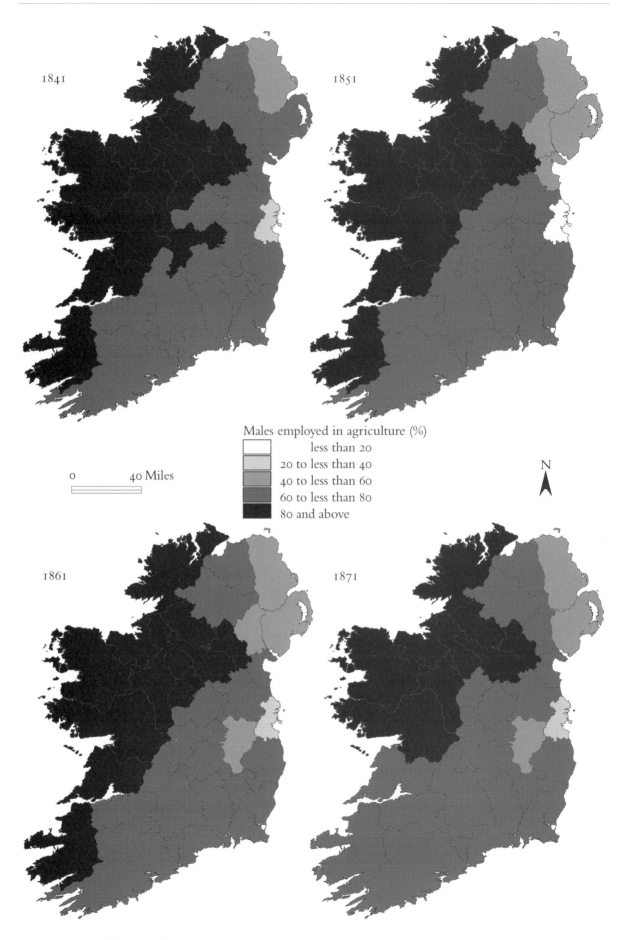

Males employed in agriculture (%)

less than 20
20 to less than 40
40 to less than 60
60 to less than 80
80 and above

0   40 Miles

N

Map 63: Percentage of occupied males engaged in agriculture at county level

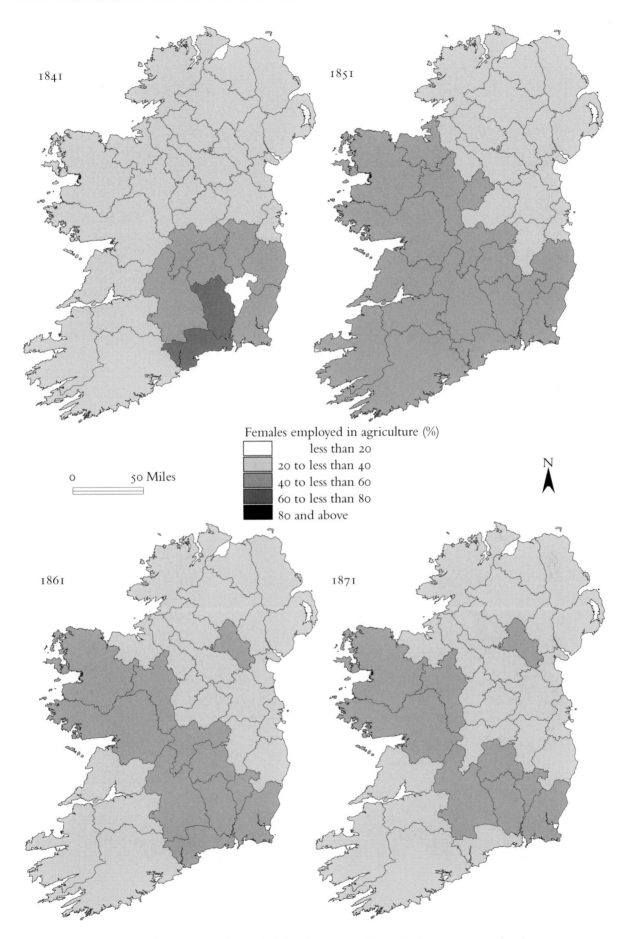

Map 64: Percentage of occupied females engaged in agriculture at county level

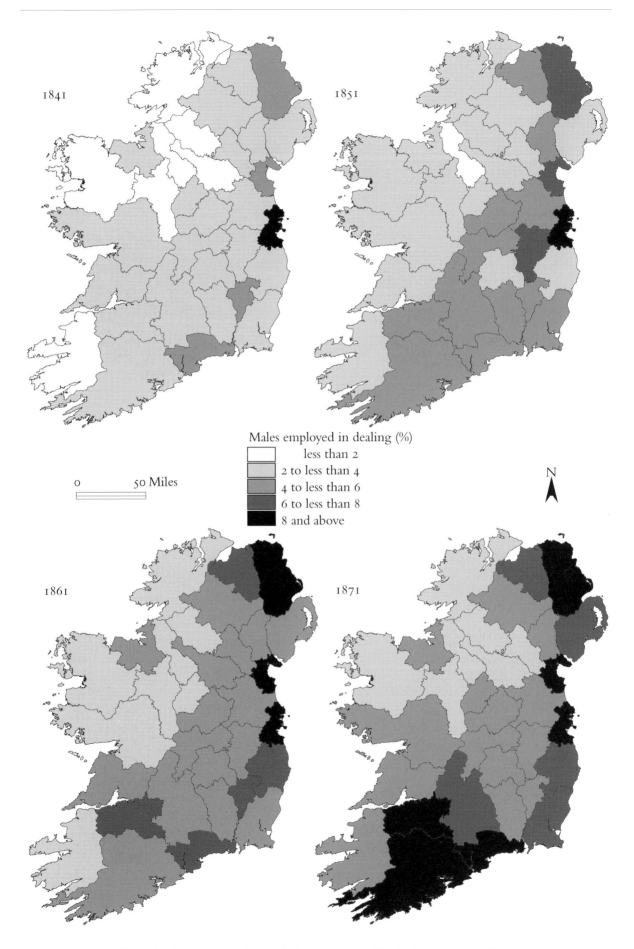

Males employed in dealing (%)

less than 2

2 to less than 4

4 to less than 6

6 to less than 8

8 and above

0   50 Miles

N

Map 65: Percentage of occupied males engaged in dealing at county level

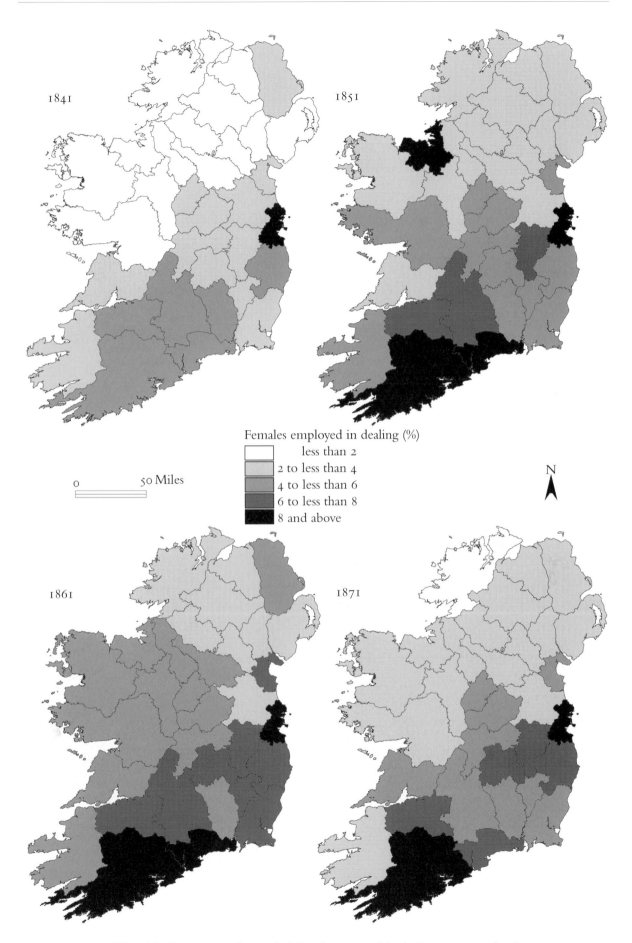

Map 66: Percentage of occupied females engaged in dealing at county level

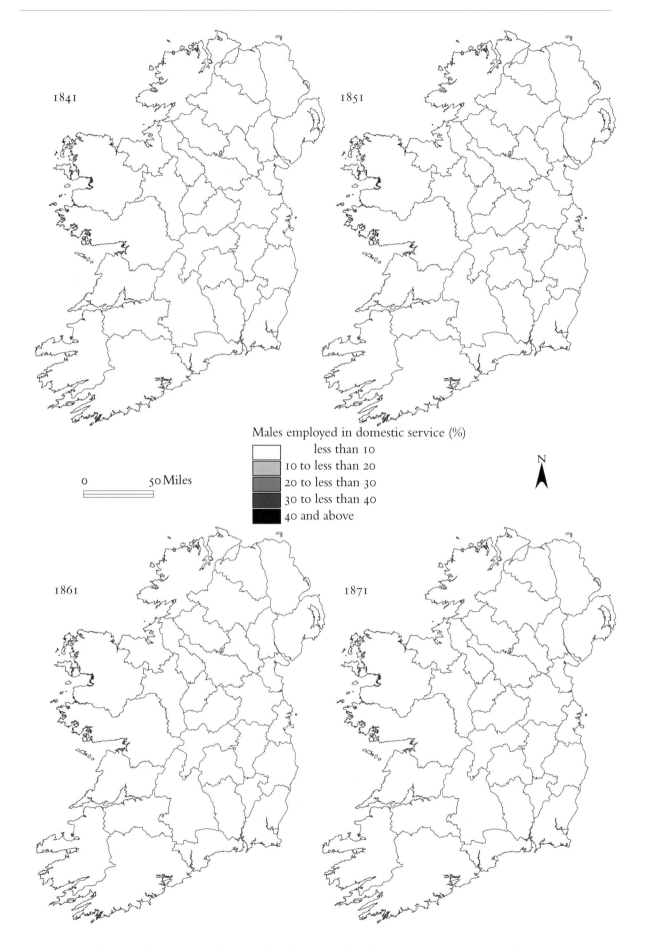

1841

1851

Males employed in domestic service (%)

less than 10

10 to less than 20

20 to less than 30

30 to less than 40

40 and above

0   50 Miles

N

1861

1871

Map 67: Percentage of occupied males engaged in domestic service at county level

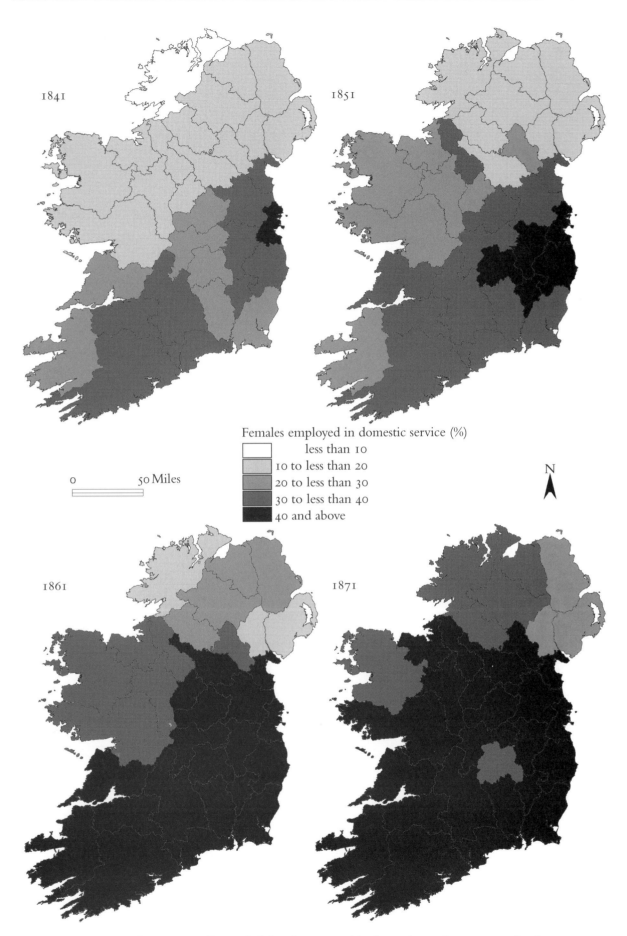

Females employed in domestic service (%)

less than 10
10 to less than 20
20 to less than 30
30 to less than 40
40 and above

0   50 Miles

N

Map 68: Percentage of occupied females engaged in domestic service at county level

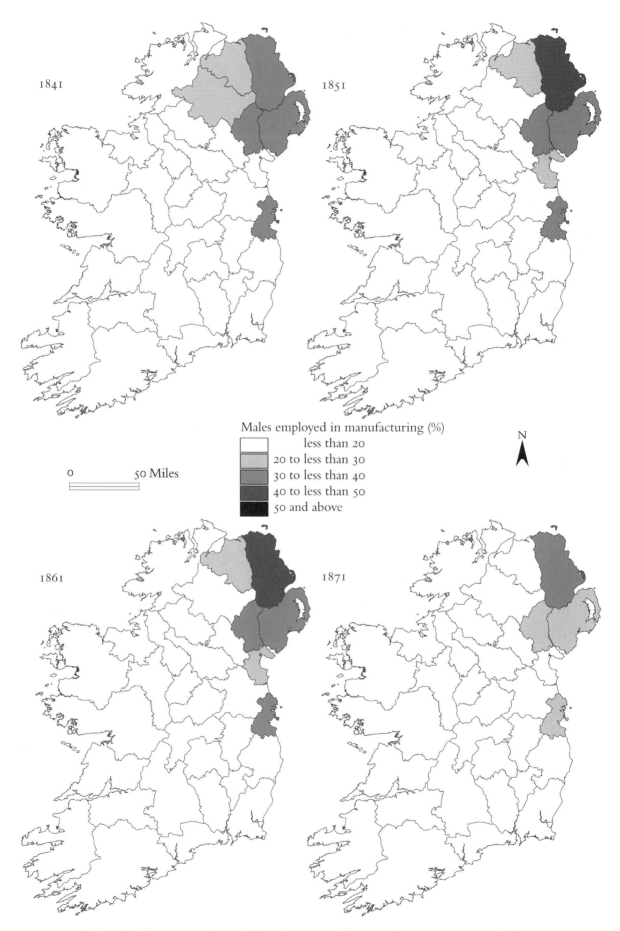

Map 69: Percentage of occupied males engaged in manufacturing at county level

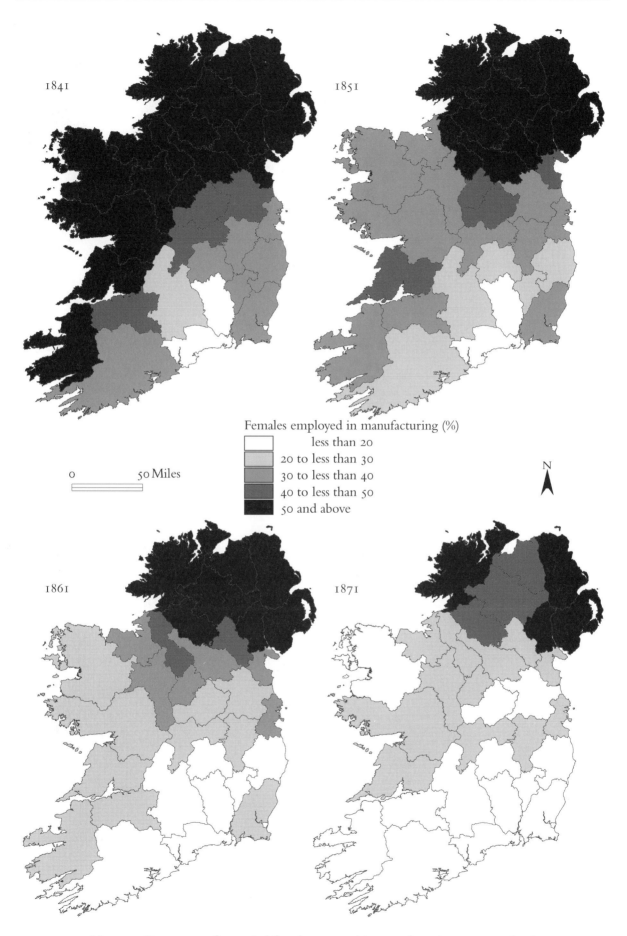

Map 70: Percentage of occupied females engaged in manufacturing at county level

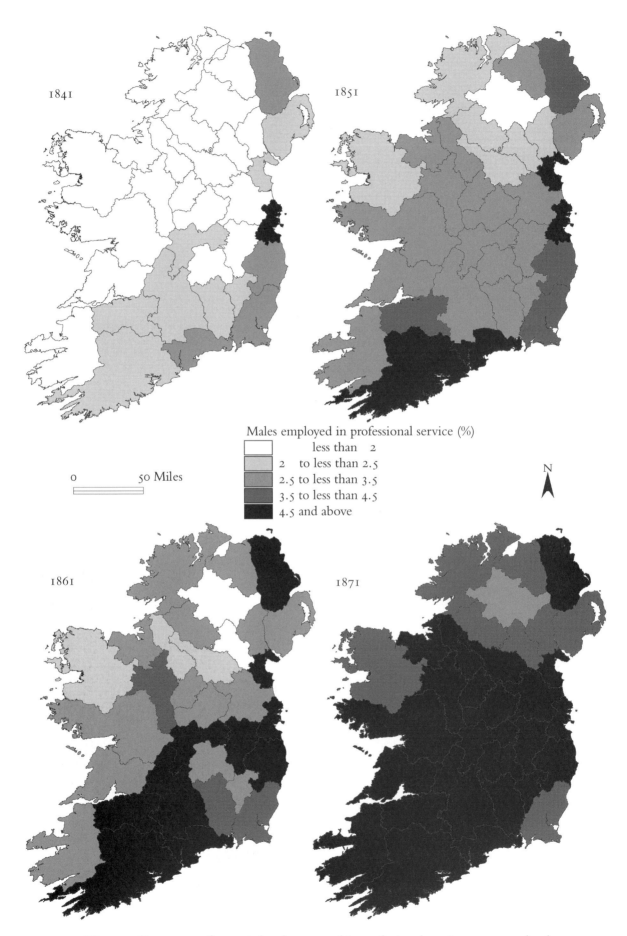

Map 71: Percentage of occupied males engaged in professional services at county level

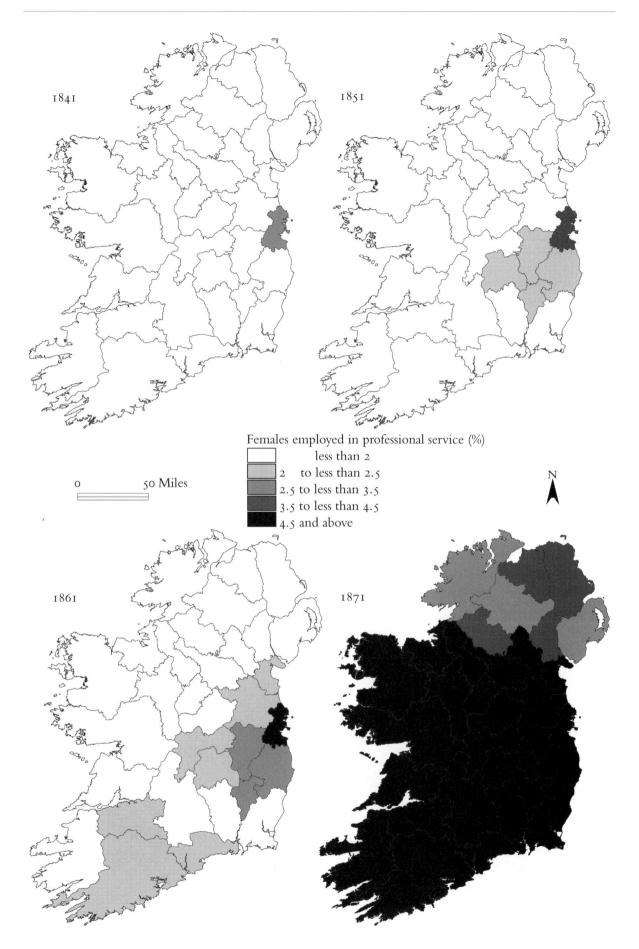

Map 72: Percentage of occupied females engaged in professional services at county level

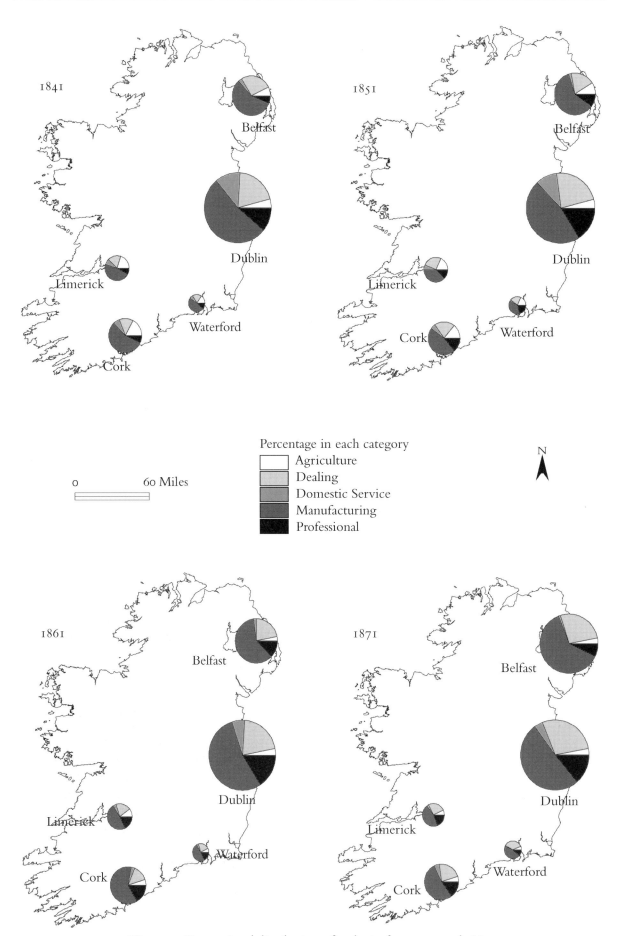

Map 73: Occupational distribution of males in five towns and cities

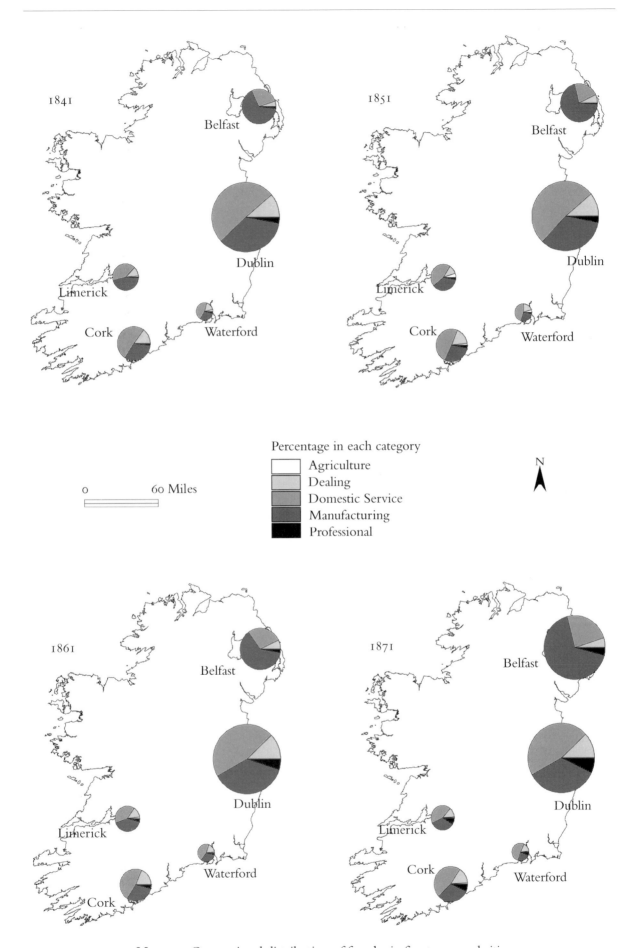

Map 74: Occupational distribution of females in five towns and cities

GARDENS AND FARMS: AGRICULTURAL HOLDINGS, 1841–71

Between 1841 and 1871 the population of Ireland fell by almost three million: 1.6 million during the 1840s; 800,000 during the 1850s; and 400,000 in the 1860s. The immediate effects of the Great Famine on the number and size of agricultural holdings were dramatic. During the Famine decade (and mostly between 1845 and 1847) tens of thousands of holdings – almost all of them under 5 acres in size – together with more than a million and a half people apparently vanished. Part of the seeming disappearance of so many smallholdings can be explained by the fact that in 1841 many plots had been measured in Irish acres – sixty per cent bigger than the statute acre – whereas from 1847 sizes were recorded in statute acres.[1] Had statute acres been employed consistently in 1841, fewer holdings not exceeding 1 acre would have existed than were in fact computed.

In the two decades after the Great Famine, the decline in the numbers of farms and gardens virtually ceased. There was, in fact, a small increase during the 1850s; almost all of this was accounted for by a recovery in the number of plots not exceeding 1 acre. This may have had as much to do with the problems associated with the measuring and counting of tiny bits of land as with underlying economic changes. During the 1860s there was a small decline in the total number of farms, although a continuing recovery in the numbers of holdings not exceeding 1 acre. By contrast, during the 1850s and 1860s there was a further shedding of 1.2 million people, most of it by emigration. In economic terms, Ireland on the eve of the Great Famine had been a labour-surplus economy. The labour was cruelly shaken out by hunger, disease and emigration and much land fell out of use. After 1851 labour was still surplus to agricultural requirements, but holdings abandoned by emigrants were incorporated into the gradually changing agrarian system, as their one-time occupants and descendants sought their salvation in the urban sprawls of Great Britain or North America.

What happened to farm size before 1847 is obscured by the problems of measurement and data gathering already referred to. Austin Bourke reworked the pre-Famine statistics and his results are reproduced in Table 15 (note, they relate to the numbers of persons holding land, not to the number of holdings).

Table 15: Number of persons holding land, 1845[2]

SIZE OF HOLDING	NUMBER
Less than or equal to 1 acre	135,314
Above 1 acre and not exceeding 5 acres	181,950
Above 5 acres and not exceeding 10 acres	187,909
Above 10 acres and not exceeding 20 acres	187,582
Above 20 acres and not exceeding 50 acres	141,819
Above 50 acres	70,441
Unclassified	30,433

1 P.M.A. Bourke, 'The Agricultural Statistics of the 1841 Census of Ireland. A critical review', *Economic History Review*, 2nd series, vol. XVIII (1965), pp. 377–81. The measures of farm size in 1841 also excluded waste, which was not the case in 1847 and subsequently. The 1841 census did not include a figure for holdings of up to 1 acre, but there was an estimate, relating to 1844 or earlier, made by the Devon Commission in 1845 and the Agricultural Returns, in 1847. 2 Bourke, 'The Agricultural Statistics of the 1841 Census of Ireland', 380.

Table 16: Number and sizes of holdings in 1847 and 1851

YEAR	1 ACRE OR LESS	ABOVE 1 ACRE AND NOT EXCEEDING 5 ACRES	ABOVE 5 ACRES AND NOT EXCEEDING 15 ACRES	ABOVE 15 ACRES AND NOT EXCEEDING 30 ACRES	ABOVE 30 ACRES	TOTAL HOLDINGS
1847	73,016	139,041	269,534	164,337	157,097	803,025
1851	37,728	88,083	191,854	141,311	149,090	608,066

Tables 16 and 17 summarise changes in holding size from 1847 to 1871. The figures are taken from the annual Agricultural Returns. Because different class breaks were used in the agricultural returns from 1852 onwards the data have been presented in separate tables. A comparison of tables 15 and 16 shows clearly the dramatic fall in the total number of holdings during the Famine. The biggest losses, as we have already noted, occurred among plots not exceeding one acre, the numbers of which declined by almost three-quarters. A reduction on a similar scale also took place among the holdings between 1 and not exceeding 5 acres. (Again, we must remember the caveats that the unit of land measurement.) There was a modest fall of 25% in farms in the category of 5 to not exceeding 15 acres. The total of farms above 15 and not exceeding 30 acres increased by almost 80%, whilst the farms bigger than 30 acres tripled in number.

From 1851 agricultural holdings were classified into nine categories: those not exceeding 1 acre; above 1 acre and not exceeding 5 acres; above 5 acres and not exceeding 15 acres; above 15 acres and not exceeding 30 acres; above 30 acres and not exceeding 50 acres; above 50 acres and not exceeding 100 acres; above 100 acres and not exceeding 200 acres; above 200 acres and not exceeding 500 acres; above 500 acres. For convenience these have been conflated into five categories as show in Table 17. Between 1852 and 1871 the number of tiny holdings (1 acre or smaller) rose by 13,000 (38%).

Insofar as this increase was not a mere statistical artefact is perhaps explained by a growing number of garden plots in or close to towns. In 1845 the Devon Commission had attempted a distinction within holdings of 1 acre or less between 'gardens where separately returned' and holdings 'for general tillage'. Among the 52,000 such holdings in 1845 where the distinction was made, 56% were garden plots. Between 1852 and 1871 there was a small decline of 7% in the total of holdings over 1 acre and up to 15 acres. There was an increase of 10% in the number of farms over 15 and up to 50 acres and a 7% increase in holdings above 50 and up to 200 acres. Very large farms, bigger than 200 acres, increased by 3% in number.

Notwithstanding problems with the evidence, it is clear that the greatest changes occurred during the Famine and among the smallest holdings. To gain some sense of the geography of the changes taking place in these terrible years the following two maps (Map 75 and Map 76) show the numbers of holdings in the two smallest categories in 1847. We focus on holdings not exceeding 5 acres because it was among these that the greatest changes occurred. Holdings not exceeding 1 acre were concentrated in the Midlands and the West, excluding the extreme south-west. Those above 1 acre and not exceeding 5 acres were found mainly in the West (again excluding the extreme south-west) and there was also a cluster in south Ulster, especially County Armagh, the seat of the linen industry.

Table 17: Number and sizes of holdings in 1852, 1861 and 1871

YEAR	NOT EXCEEDING 1 ACRE	ABOVE 1 ACRE AND NOT EXCEEDING 15 ACRES	ABOVE 15 ACRES AND NOT EXCEEDING 50 ACRES	ABOVE 50 ACRES AND NOT EXCEEDING 200 ACRES	ABOVE 200 ACRES	TOTAL HOLDINGS
1852	35,058	263,869	209,215	71,825	9,504	589,471
1861	41,561	269,400	213,700	75,464	9,919	610,045
1871	48,448	246,192	211,434	76,758	9,758	592,590

Moving on to the less calamitous decades of the 1850s and '60s, a series of maps illustrates the distribution of holdings in 1852, 1861 and 1871. As we noted at the beginning, there was a relatively little change in the number of holdings in the 1850s and 1860s, except for a notable recovery in the number of garden plots. The geographical distribution of holdings by size in 1852 echoed that of earlier years, with the highest percentage of very small farms and gardens in a stretch of countryside running south and towards the west. During the 1850s and 1860s holdings not exceeding 1 acre in size spread somewhat, and there was a growing concentration close to Dublin and Belfast. At the other extreme, counties in the south and the west contained the biggest number of holdings exceeding 200 acres. There had, in fact, been some further concentration of very large holdings in the west and south-west after the Great Famine, reflecting the process of clearance and consolidation and the shift to land-extensive pasture farming. The poor law union maps demonstrate the pattern in greater detail.

In conclusion, during the Great Famine and the decades immediately following, changes in the patterns of holding size occurred against a stable background of climate and topography. But demographic and economic conditions were altering dramatically. A declining population, a restructured agrarian system, profound changes in the international market for Irish farm products, all induced a fundamental restructuring of land-holding in Ireland. Initially this restructuring was swift and painful, the consequence of mass starvation and emigration. After 1850 the pace of readjustment was much slower, but it was inexorable.

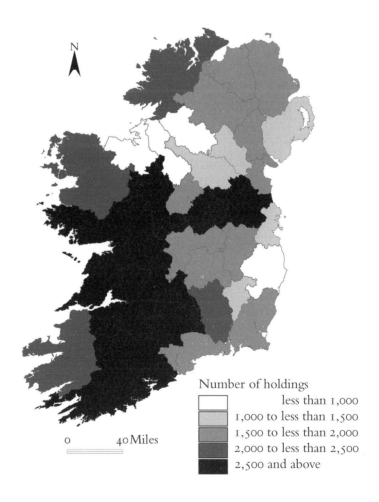

Number of holdings

☐	less than 1,000
☐	1,000 to less than 1,500
☐	1,500 to less than 2,000
☐	2,000 to less than 2,500
■	2,500 and above

Map 75: Number of holdings not exceeding 1 acre at county level, 1847

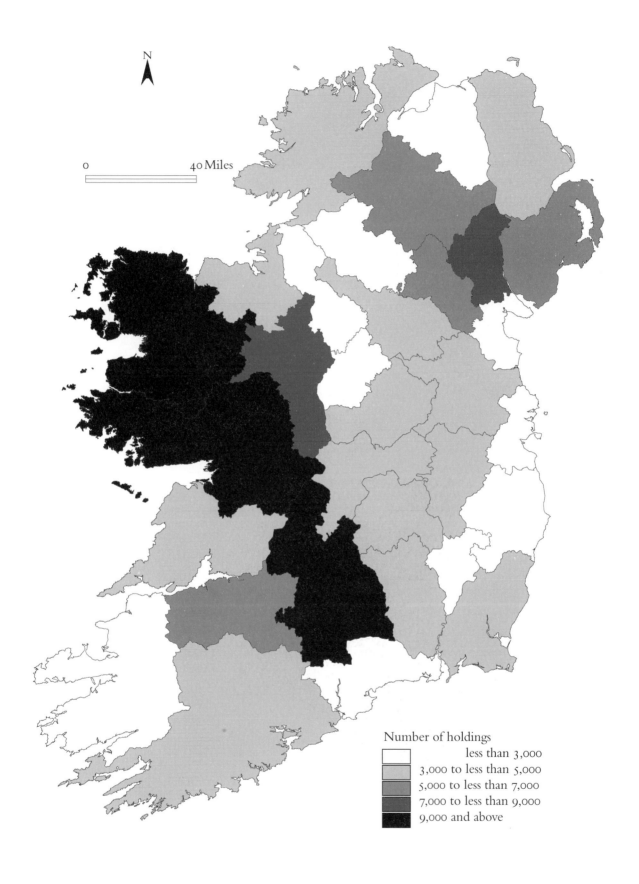

N

0   40 Miles

Number of holdings
less than 3,000
3,000 to less than 5,000
5,000 to less than 7,000
7,000 to less than 9,000
9,000 and above

Map 76: Number of holdings above 1 acre and not exceeding 5 acres at county level, 1847

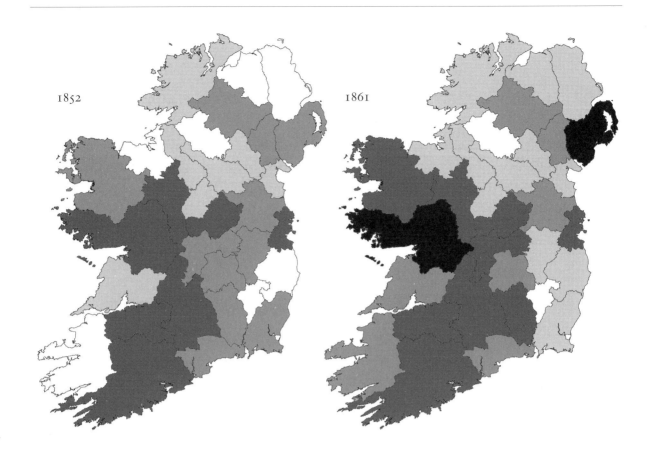

Map 77: Number of holdings not exceeding 1 acre at county level

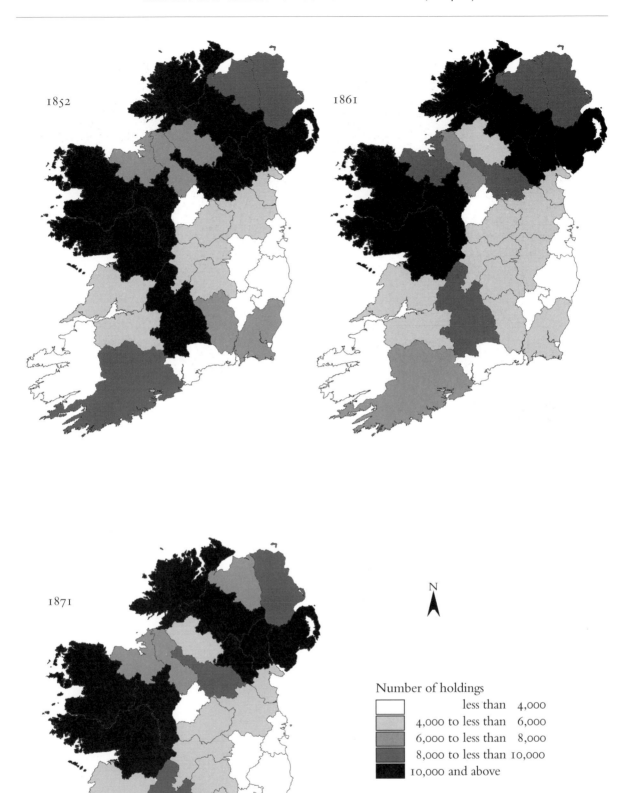

1852

1861

1871

N

Number of holdings

less than 4,000
4,000 to less than 6,000
6,000 to less than 8,000
8,000 to less than 10,000
10,000 and above

0   50 Miles

Map 78: Number of holdings above 1 and not exceeding 15 acres at county level

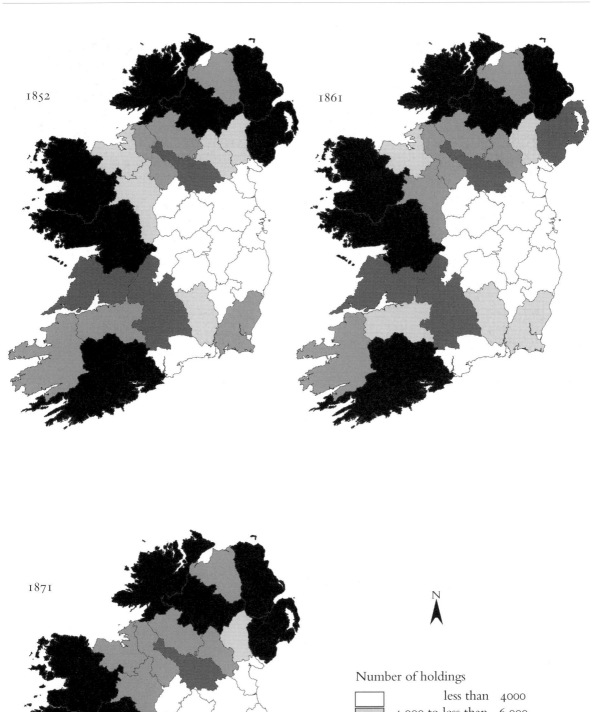

1852

1861

1871

N

Number of holdings

	less than 4000
	4,000 to less than 6,000
	6,000 to less than 8,000
	8,000 to less than 10,000
	10,000 and above

0　　　　　　50 Miles

Map 79: Number of holdings above 15 and not exceeding 50 acres at county level

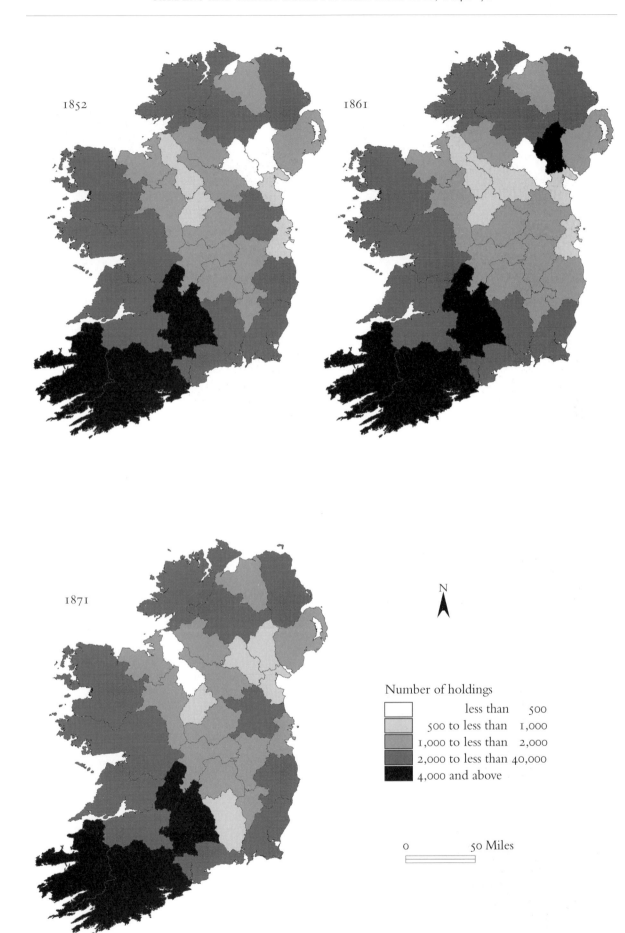

1852

1861

1871

N

Number of holdings

	less than	500
	500 to less than	1,000
	1,000 to less than	2,000
	2,000 to less than	40,000
	4,000 and above	

0   50 Miles

Map 80: Number of holdings above 50 and not exceeding 200 acres at county level

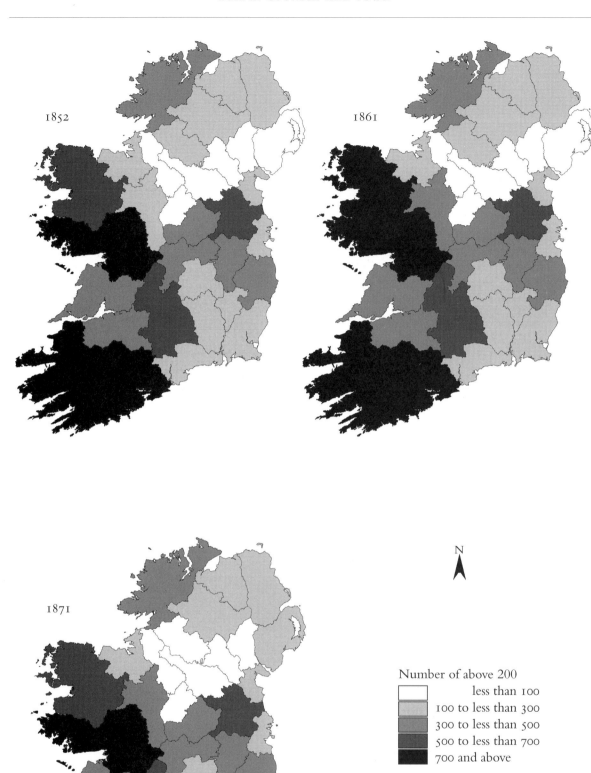

Map 81: Number of holdings above 200 acres at county level

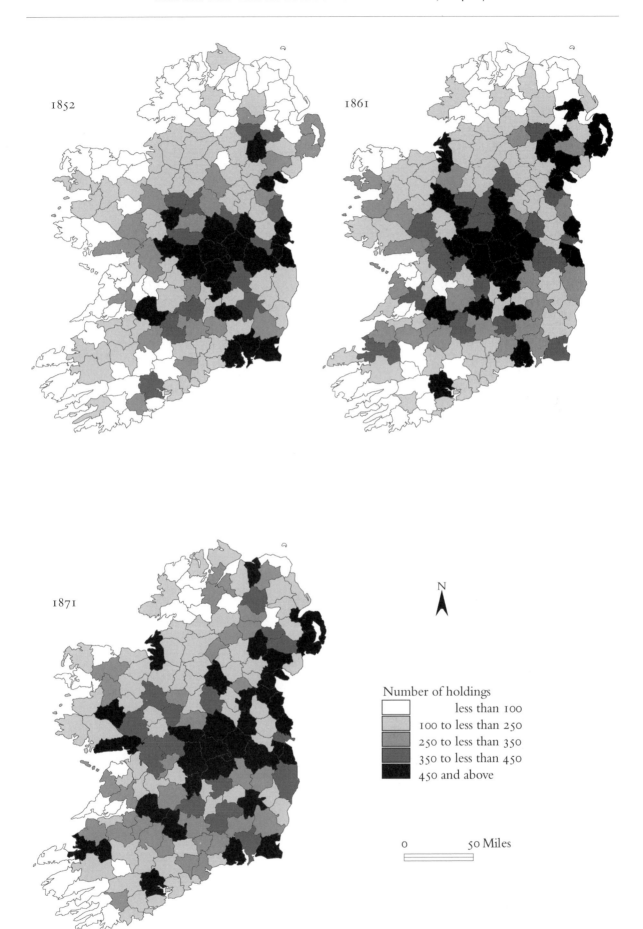

Map 82: Number of holdings not exceeding 1 acre at poor law union level

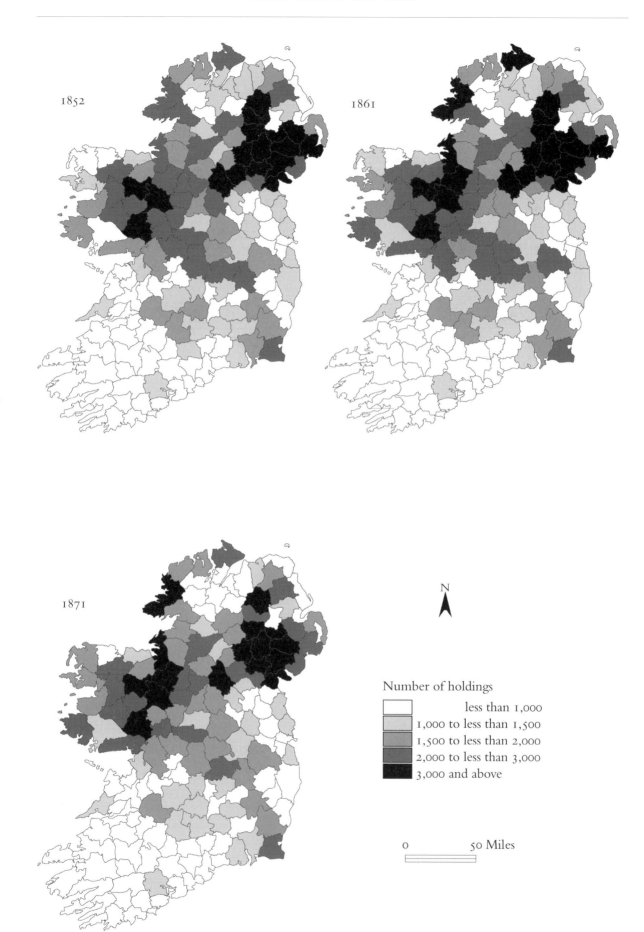

Map 83: Number of holdings above 1 and not exceeding 15 acres at poor law union level

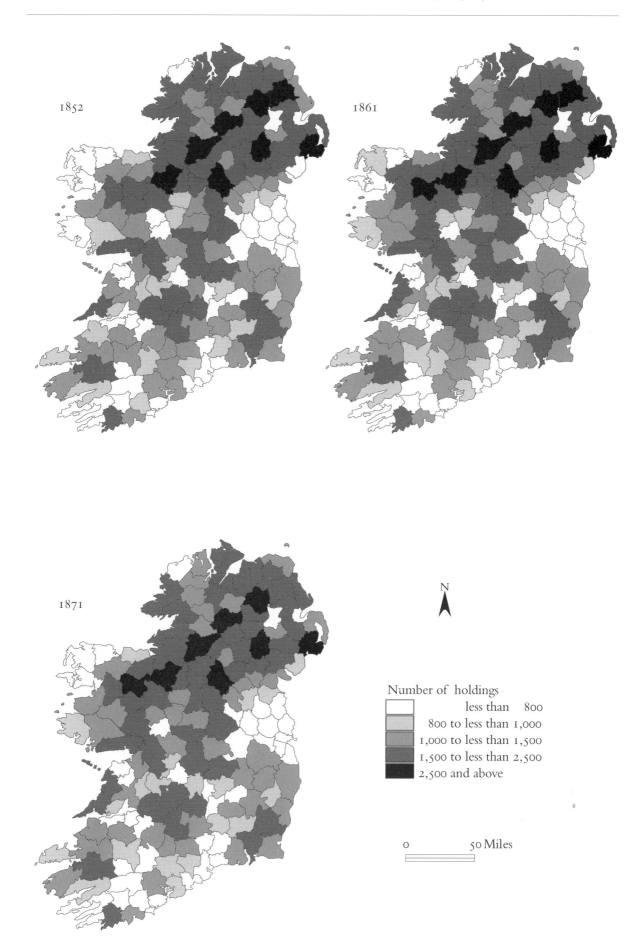

Map 84: Number of holdings above 15 and not exceeding 50 acres at poor law union level

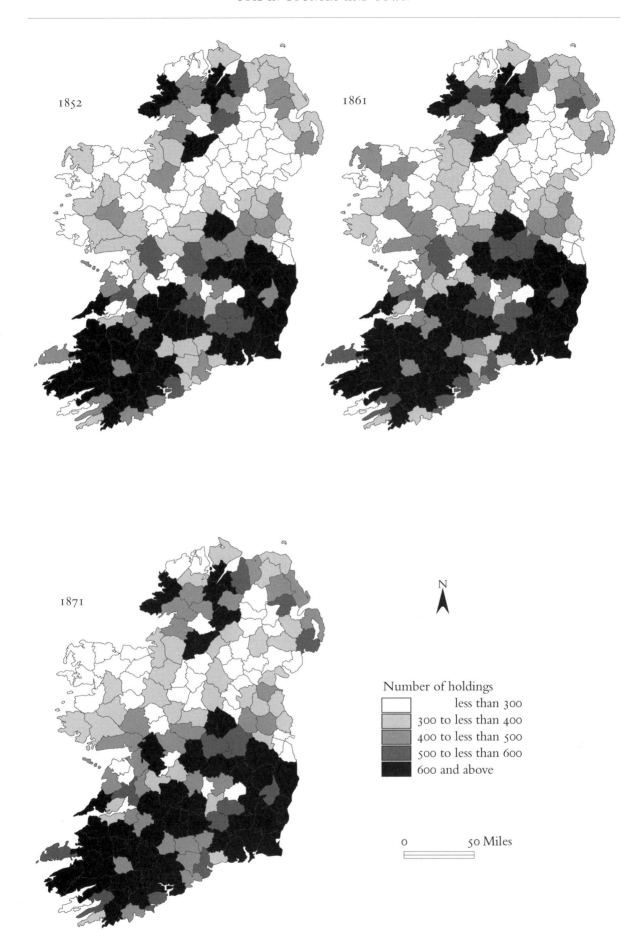

1852

1861

1871

N

Number of holdings

less than 300
300 to less than 400
400 to less than 500
500 to less than 600
600 and above

0   50 Miles

Map 85: Number of holdings above 50 and not exceeding 200 acres at poor law union level

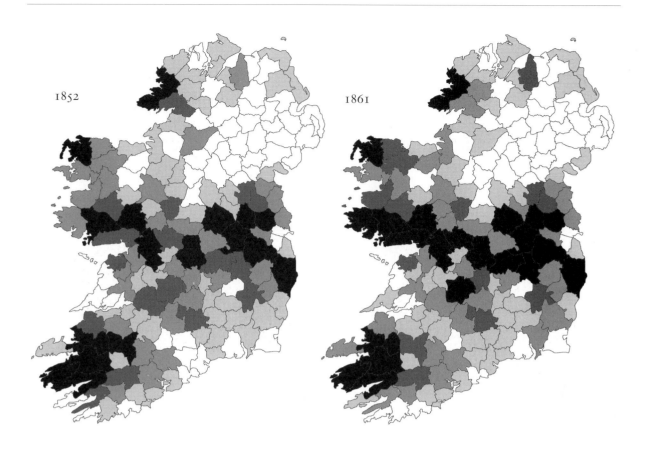

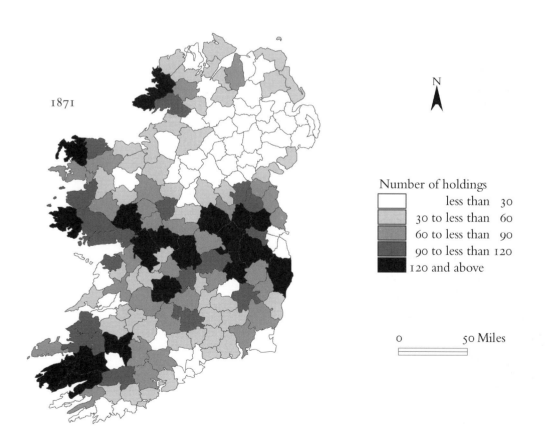

1852

1861

1871

Number of holdings

less than 30
30 to less than 60
60 to less than 90
90 to less than 120
120 and above

0   50 Miles

Map 86: Number of holdings above 200 acres at poor union level

The Great Famine is sometimes viewed as a catalyst accelerating changes in the composition of farm output that had been taking place slowly since the end of the Napoleonic wars. During the second half of the nineteenth century Irish agriculture came to specialise increasingly in animal husbandry. Nevertheless, the cultivation of the soil remained a significant component of Irish farming, although the balance swung away from corn and potatoes for humans and animals to the cultivation of fodder and forage crops for livestock. The diagrams and maps in this section illustrate changes in the extent of the acreage devoted to food – potatoes and grain – and to other roots, green crops, and hay (i.e. meadow and clover) in the two decades immediately after the Famine.

Figure 34 shows the acreage under food, fodder and forage crops. In total the acreage was little changed during the 1850s and 1860s, varying between about 5.5 million and 6 million acres. However, the distribution altered considerably. In 1850 the acreage under corn was 55% of total cultivated land, potatoes 15%, and hay 21%. Ten years later the proportions were 44%, 20%, and 27% respectively; and in 1870, 37%, 19%, and 32% respectively. The two big changes had been the decline in the percentage under corn and the rise in meadow and clover (see Figure 35).

It is clear that the metaphor of a catalyst has to be treated with caution. Potatoes offer the most interesting case of sluggish post-Famine adjustment since it was the destruction of the potato crop that was responsible for the disaster. The major changes in potato acreage occurred during the Great Famine. In the years immediately before the Famine the acreage planted had exceeded two million. In 1847 the planted area was only about 280,000 acres, very largely because so few seed potatoes were available. By 1852 the area had recovered to 857,000 acres and expanded further to 1,124,000 acres in 1861. It was still just over one million acres in 1871. This was less than 50% of the level in the early 1840s. Nevertheless, the area under potatoes had recovered some of its Famine losses. In short, once the blight had abated there was a limited return to pre-Famine agricultural patterns and dietary habits. Only after 1871 did potato acreage decline relentlessly until the end of the century.

The maps (maps 92, 99) illustrate both the partial recovery of potato cultivation and the regional distribution. With the passage of time potato cultivation recovered, more in the west than the east. There were exceptions to this pattern in counties Antrim and Armagh where the percentages of cultivated land under potatoes actually rose after the Famine. But these were increasing shares of a shrinking agricultural sector in two of Ireland's more industrial counties.

Figure 34: Acreage under various crops, 1847–71

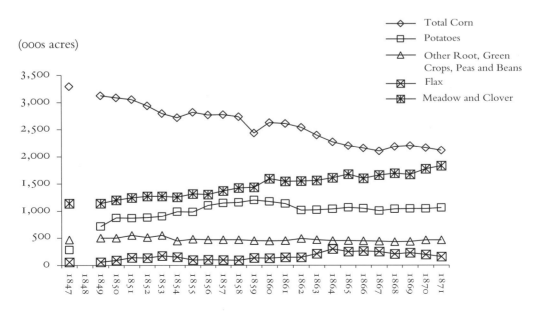

Figure 35: Percentage of cultivated land under various crops, 1847–71

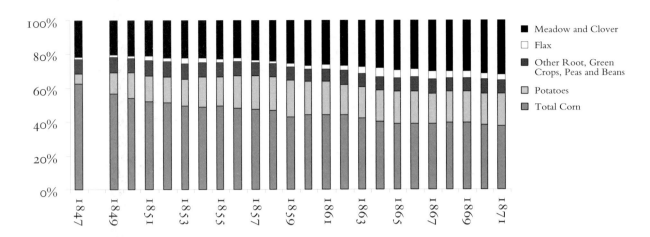

It is instructive to unscramble the total acreage under various grains. This is done in Figure 36. Unlike potatoes, the cultivation of corn did not collapse dramatically during the Famine. Traditionally, the most important grain had been oats, much of it grown for on-farm consumption. Oats continued to occupy this role throughout the 1850s and 1860s, notwithstanding a gradual decline of cultivation during the period. As can be seen from Figure 36, the area under oats fell from just over two million to just under two million acres during the 1850s. There was a continuing downward drift during the 1860s to around 1.6 million acres, and this trend persisted throughout the remaining three decades of the century. The maps show that oats were predominantly the grain of the north.

Wheat had long been grown in Ireland as a cash crop and before the Famine much of it had been exported. Around 750,000 acres were sown in 1847. Cultivation kept up reasonably well during the Famine, although it dipped sharply in the early 1850s. Thereafter there was a modest recovery until the end of the decade, followed by an inexorable decline through the 1860s. Unlike oats, the cultivation of wheat was geographically highly concentrated, location depending on soil, climate and proximity to markets. Wheat farming was very largely confined to the east and south of the country and in a few favoured locations elsewhere. The main message that emerges from the maps, however, is of the decline in wheat growing as a major activity for farmers during the 1850s and 1860s.

Figure 36: Acreage under various grains, 1847–71

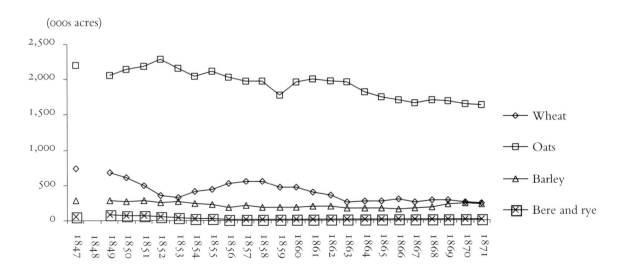

Barley was never an important crop in Ireland; in round terms it occupied less than one-tenth of the area under oats. Cultivation kept up reasonably well during the Famine at around 280,000 acres. It drifted down during the 1850s to less than 200,000 acres. It then settled down, generally a little below 200,000 acres, although there was considerable variation from year to year. Like wheat it was essentially a cash crop and, before the Famine, often grown for export. As the maps show, barley production was concentrated in the east and south of the country. Bere (winter barley) and rye were never important crops in nineteenth-century Ireland. For mapping purposes barley, bere and rye have been combined.

Turning to the main fodder crop, immediately after the Famine the area under meadow (i.e. hay and clover) was little more than one-third of that under corn. In 1860 it was 60%. By 1870 the proportion had risen to 82%. Four years later, in 1874, meadow acreage exceeded corn acreage for the first time in the nineteenth century. Although hay and clover were important everywhere, as the maps indicate, there was considerable regional variation, with some concentration in the south-west and the midland counties. The other animal fodder, roots and green crops, were also widely dispersed, although they were less important in north Connacht and south-west Ulster. Detailed local research is required to explain why in some localities more land was under hay than roots and vice versa.

Flax growing commands interest as the one important industrial crop grown in Ireland. In the country as a whole no more than about 2% of the cultivated land was under flax during the 1850s and '60s, although the acreage varied considerably over the years depending on the state of the linen industry. Figure 37, for example, reflects the effect of the American Civil War on the demand for linen and hence for flax. As the maps show, cultivation was confined almost entirely to the counties and Poor Law unions of Ulster.

Taking the long view, the cultivation of grain ceased to be a major activity in Ireland during the nineteenth century. The decline of population removed much of the local demand and also the labour required for its cultivation, while markets in other parts of the United Kingdom were supplied more efficiently from domestic or transatlantic sources. Similarly, potato growing declined because of the loss of labour and the re-organization of agrarian society. On the other hand resources flowed into the cultivation of fodder crops. These changes represent a shift away from labour-intensive agriculture to a land-intensive form. To that extent, the fall in population after 1845 – and hence of the labour force – encouraged the process. But the forces of comparative advantage and international trade were nudging Ireland in the same direction. The terrible famine removed two million men, women and children who had existed by growing and eating potatoes; a drag had been removed from the process of agricultural adjustment. Perhaps this is an alternative to viewing the Great Famine as a catalyst.

Figure 37: Acreage under flax, 1847–71

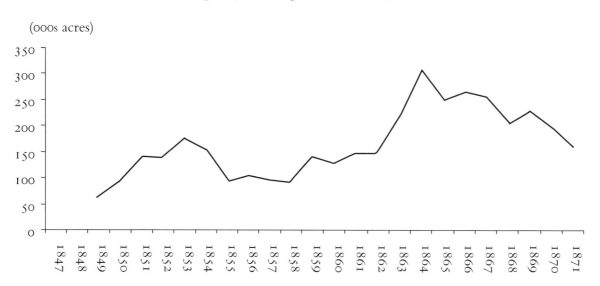

(000s acres)

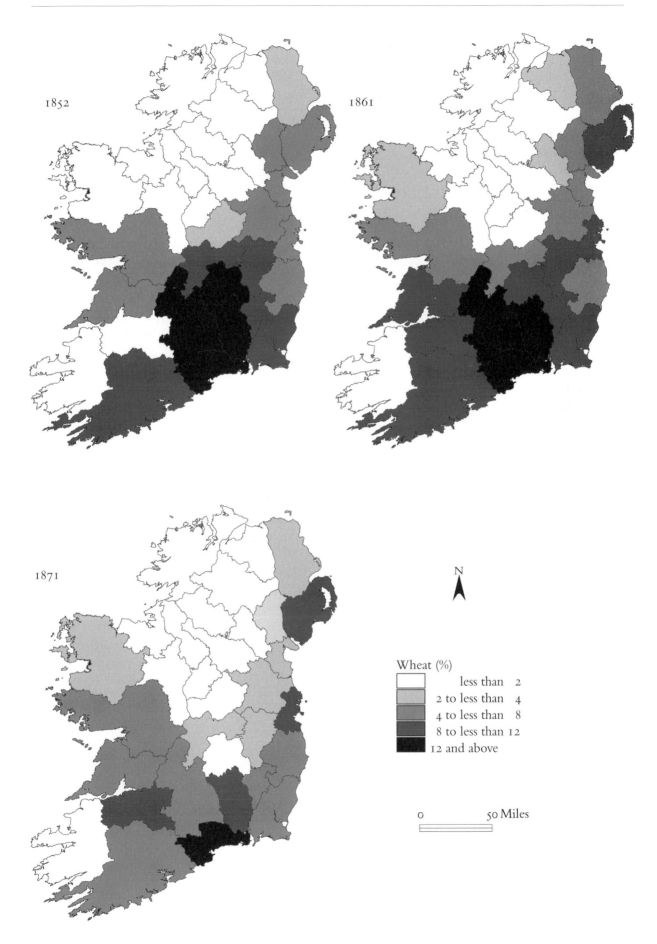

1852

1861

1871

N

Wheat (%)

less than 2

2 to less than 4

4 to less than 8

8 to less than 12

12 and above

0   50 Miles

Map 87: Wheat as a % of total acreage under cultivation at county level

Map 88: Oats as a % of total acreage under cultivation at county level

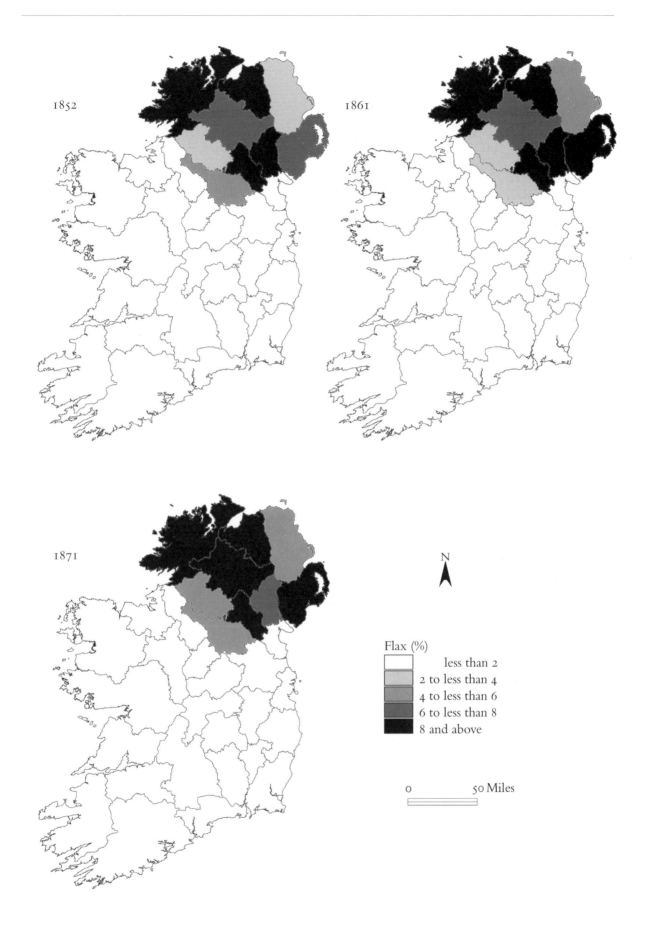

1852

1861

1871

N

Flax (%)

less than 2
2 to less than 4
4 to less than 6
6 to less than 8
8 and above

0   50 Miles

Map 89: Flax as a % of total acreage under cultivation at county level

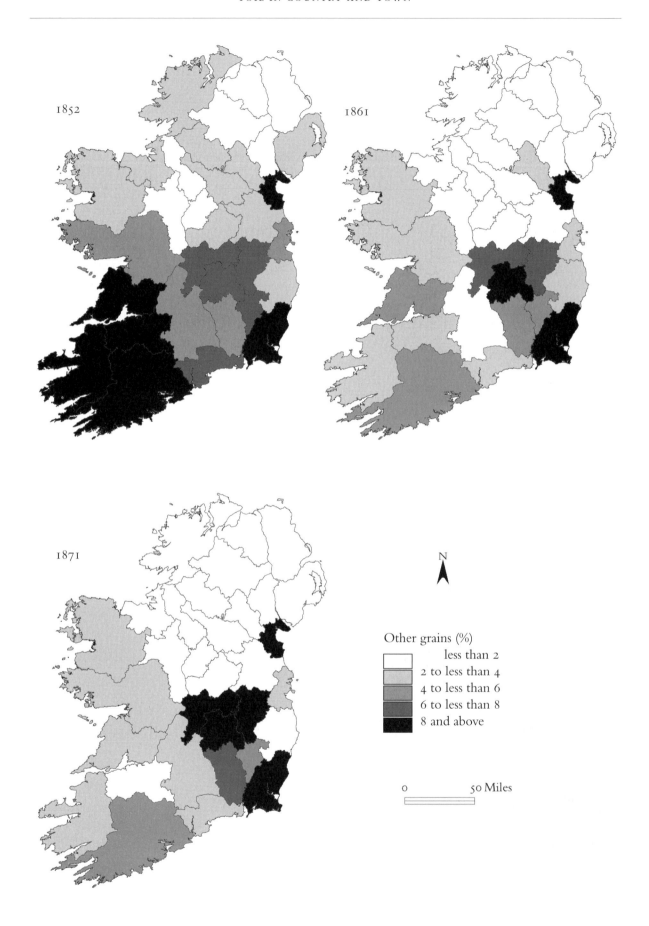

Map 90: Barley, bere and rye as a % of total acreage under cultivation at county level

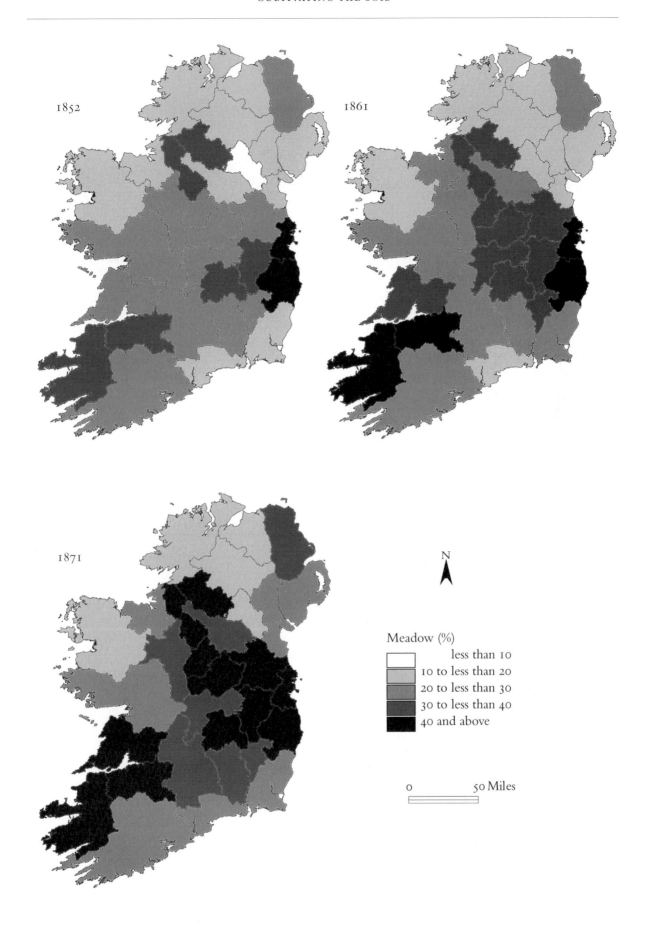

Map 91: Meadow as a % of total acreage under cultivation at county level

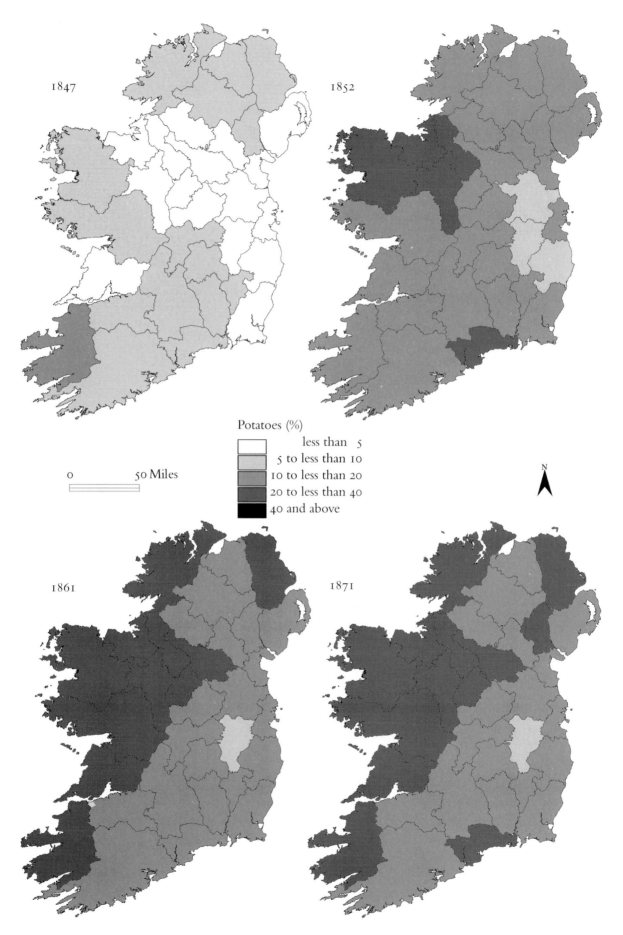

Potatoes (%)

less than 5
5 to less than 10
10 to less than 20
20 to less than 40
40 and above

0   50 Miles

1847

1852

1861

1871

N

Map 92: Potatoes as a % of total acreage under cultivation at county level

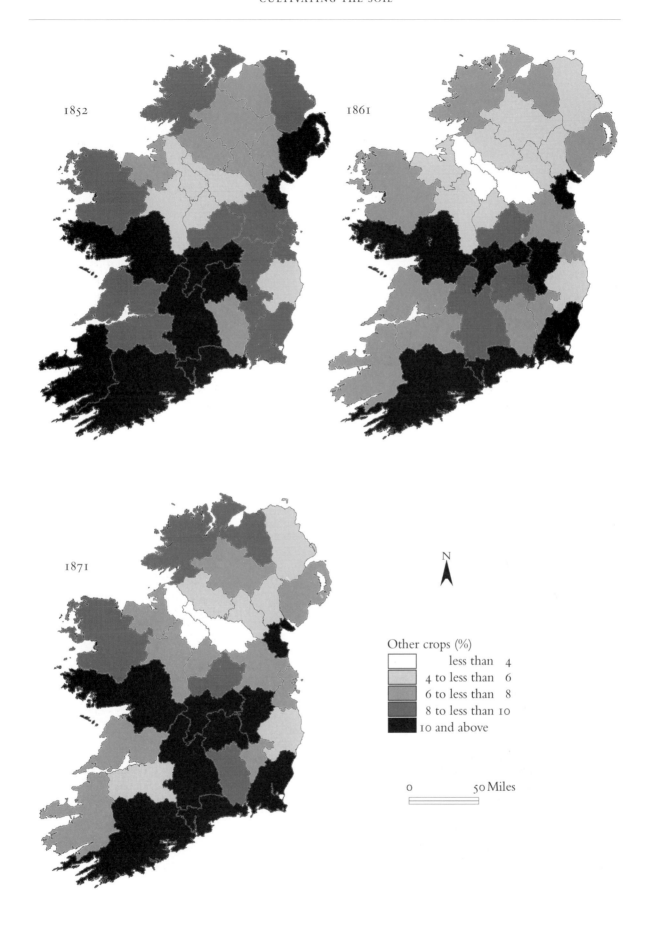

Map 93: Other root, green crops, peas and beans as a % of total acreage under cultivation at county level

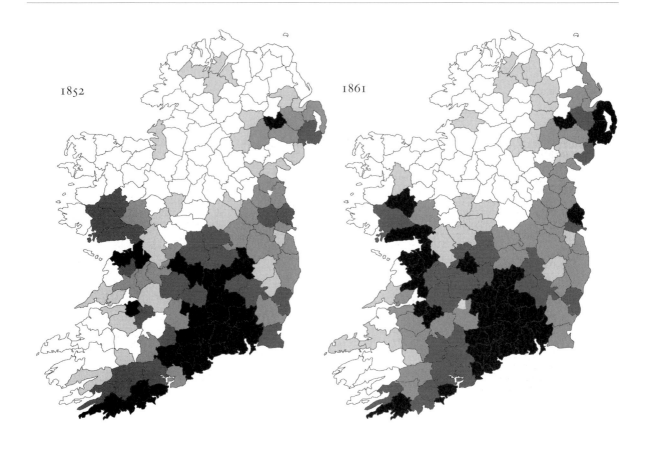

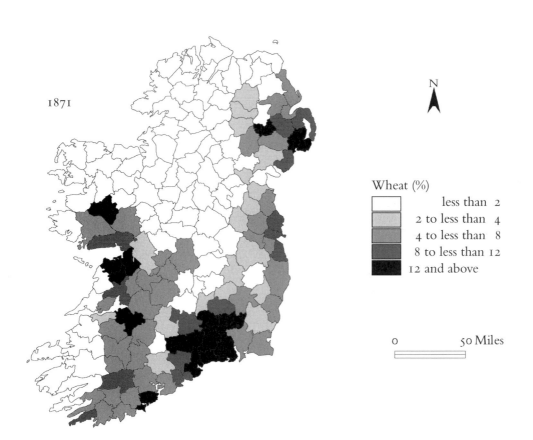

1852

1861

1871

N

Wheat (%)

less than 2
2 to less than 4
4 to less than 8
8 to less than 12
12 and above

0   50 Miles

Map 94: Wheat as a % of total acreage under cultivation at poor law union level

Map 95: Oats as a % of total acreage under cultivation at poor law union level

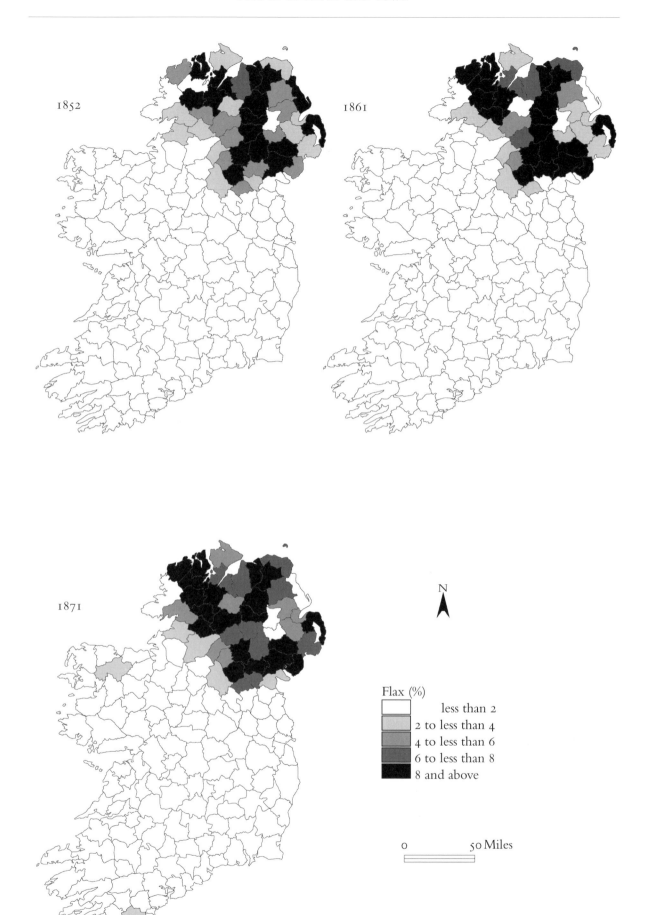

1852

1861

1871

N

Flax (%)

less than 2

2 to less than 4

4 to less than 6

6 to less than 8

8 and above

0   50 Miles

Map 96: Flax as a % of total acreage under cultivation at poor law union level

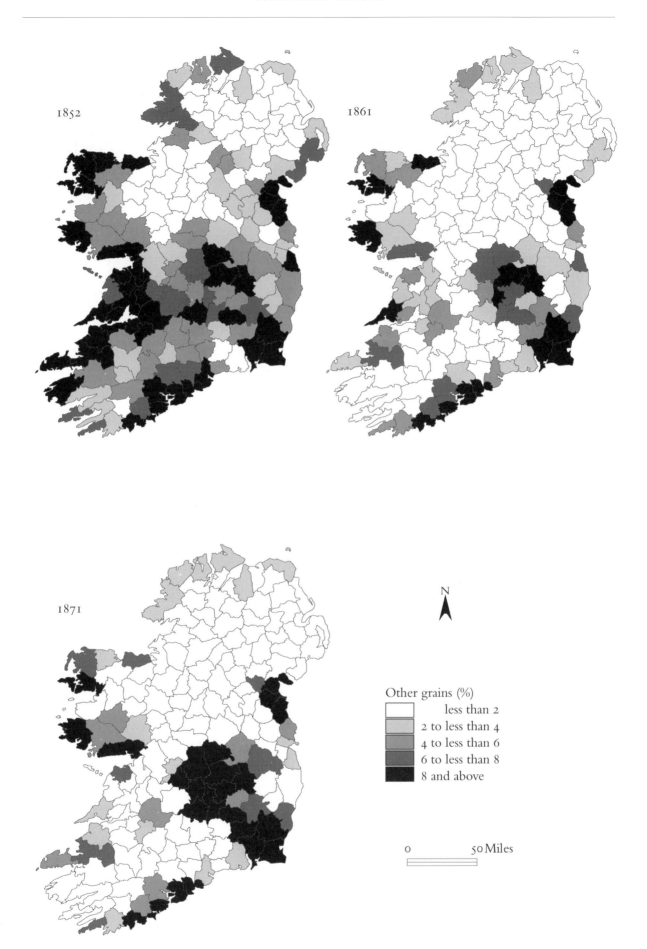

1852

1861

1871

N

Other grains (%)

less than 2

2 to less than 4

4 to less than 6

6 to less than 8

8 and above

0   50 Miles

Map 97: Barley, bere and rye as a % of total acreage under cultivation at poor law union level

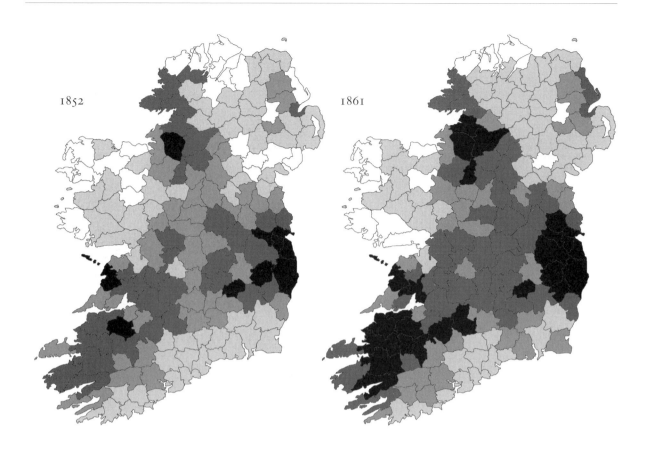

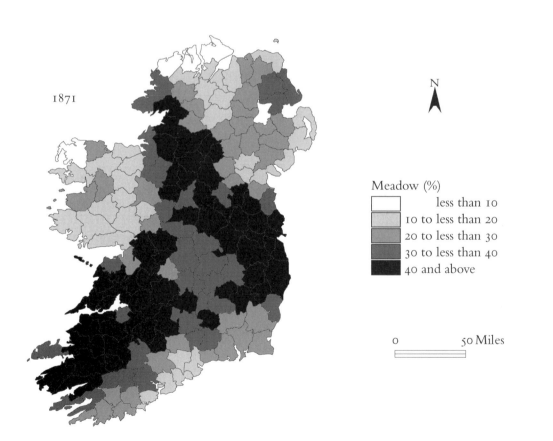

Meadow (%)

- less than 10
- 10 to less than 20
- 20 to less than 30
- 30 to less than 40
- 40 and above

0   50 Miles

Map 98: Meadow as a % of total acreage under cultivation at poor law union level

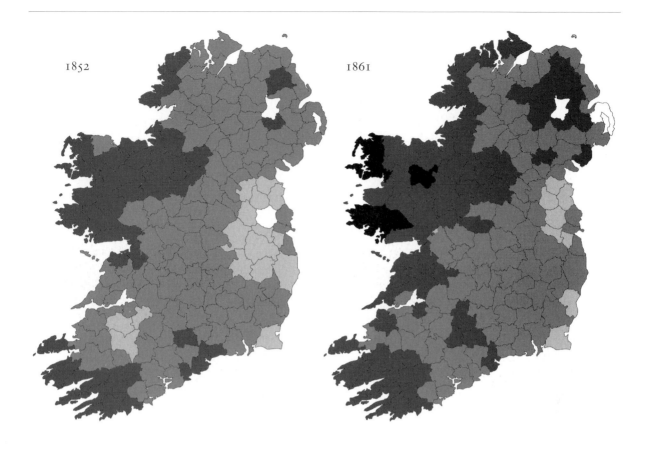

1852

1861

1871

N

Potatoes (%)

less than 5
5 to less than 10
10 to less than 20
20 to less than 40
40 and above

0   50 Miles

Map 99: Potatoes as a % of total acreage under cultivation at poor law union level

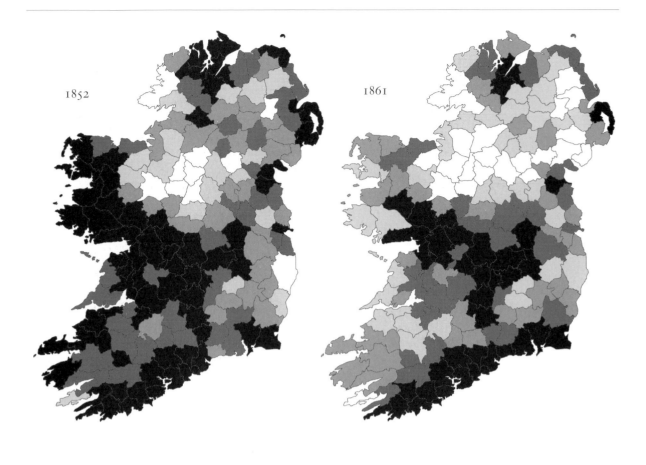

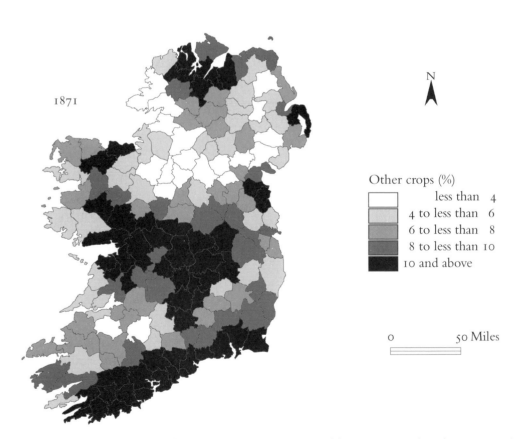

Map 100: Other root, green crops, peas and beans as a % of total acreage under cultivation at poor law union level

TAKING STOCK: HERDS, FLOCKS, PIGS AND POULTRY

During the second half of the nineteenth century Irish agriculture turned increasingly to pastoral production. The changes are summarised in Table 18, using Michael Turner's figures, which show the contribution of arable and pastoral farming to the value of total farm output. The share of the former in total output declined by two-thirds. The figures have to be treated with caution. They are derived by multiplying units of physical production by market prices and are therefore sensitive to the price series used. This is particularly true in the case of potatoes. As an example of the effects of using different price series we have Turner's own earlier estimates that valued crop output as 63% of total output in the early 1850s, 37% in 1869–71 and 23% in the early 1900s.[1] Nevertheless it is clear that there was a major realignment of agricultural production after the Famine. The domestic market for potatoes, oats and other basic foods was shrinking and the work force required to produce such labour-intensive arable crops was declining. On the other hand, the demand for the less labour-intensive products of pastoral farming was expanding throughout the United Kingdom.

The maps and diagrams in this chapter explore the changes in the livestock population. Figure 38 charts the rise in the numbers of cattle, sheep and pigs reared between 1841 and 1871 and the maps reflect their geographical distribution. The 1841 totals come from the census, except that the cattle total has been revised upward as suggested by Austin Bourke (pig numbers may also have been depressed in 1841).[2] The figures for 1847 onwards are taken from the annual Agricultural Returns (the figures for 1848 are incomplete). Cattle, sheep and pigs and their products generated the bulk of farm incomes in the post-Famine period. There were, in addition, half a million or more horses in Ireland; the great majority of them worked on farms or as cart horses in towns.[3]

As can be seen in Figure 38, the cattle population increased during the Famine decade and continued to grow until checked by the agricultural depression of the early 1860s. For the rest of the century the cattle population fluctuated between 3.5 and 4.0 million annually. Within these broad trends the numbers of dairy cows remained almost constant at about 1.5 million whilst the beef herds increased. Sheep numbers fell during the Famine, but then grew substantially up to the later 1850s when they declined. However, they recovered in the later 1860s and came to exceed cattle numbers. By contrast there was a sharp decline in pig numbers between 1841 and 1847, reflecting the crisis in the population; pigs and people shared a close affinity in pre-Famine Ireland. Thereafter there was a gradual but only partial recovery. Throughout the second half of the nineteenth century the pig population rarely

Table 18: The components of agricultural output

YEAR	1850	1871	1901
Value of crops	£16.5 million	£11.3 million	£7.7 million
Value of animals	£11.2 million	£28.9 million	£32.4 million
TOTAL	£27.7 million	£40.2 million	£40.1 million
Crops (%)	59.7	28.0	19.2
Animals (%)	40.3	72.0	80.8

SOURCE: Michael Turner, *After the Famine: Irish agriculture 1850–1914* (Cambridge, 1996) p. 108

1 Michael Turner, 'Output and productivity in Irish agriculture from the Famine to the Great War', *Irish Economic and Social History*, 17 (1990), 65–6. See also W.E. Vaughan, 'Potatoes and agricultural output', *Irish Economic and Social History*, 17 (1990), 79–92; and Peter Solar, 'The pitfalls of estimating Irish agricultural output in post-Famine Ireland', in *Irish Economic and Social History*, 25 (1998), 152–6. 2 P.M.A. Bourke, 'The Irish agricultural statistics of the 1841 census of Ireland. A critical review', *Economic History Review*, 2nd series XVIII (1965), 381–2. 3 Michael Turner, *After the Famine: Irish agriculture 1850–1914* (Cambridge, 1996), pp. 15–16.

Figure 38: Livestock numbers in Ireland, 1841–71

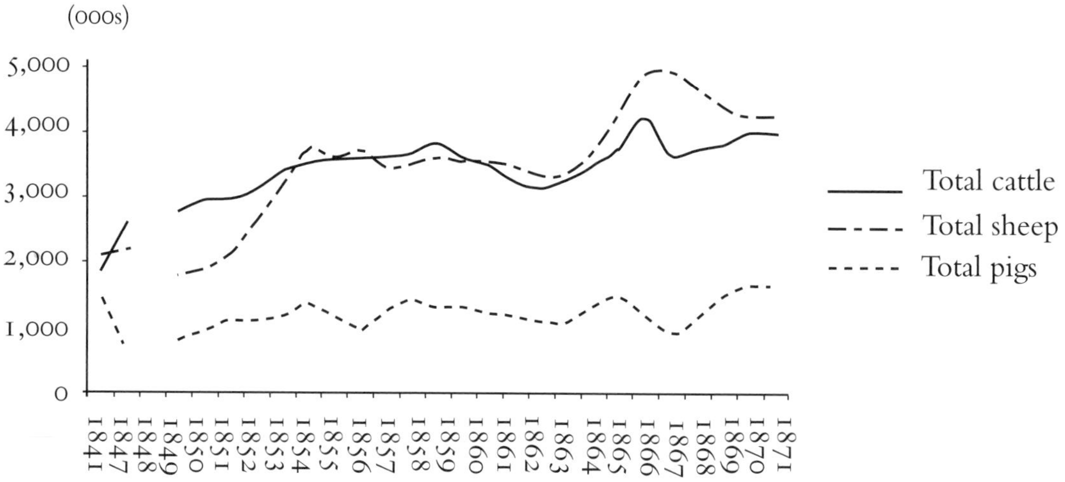

(000s)

Total cattle
Total sheep
Total pigs

regained the level of 1841, although the per capita number of pigs increased by around 50%.

The poultry population (not graphed) more than doubled in the second half of the century, from 8 million in the early 1850s to 18 million in the early 1900s. They were the source of an egg trade that, according to Turner, contributed 1.6% to the value of farm output in the early 1850s and 2.8% in the early 1870s (and over 6% by the end of the century)

Figures 39 to 42 arrange livestock populations according to the county ranking in 1841. Those for cattle show a generally stable geographical distribution, notwithstanding an increase in cattle numbers.

The populous cattle counties were Cork, Kerry, Tipperary and Meath. At the other extreme was a clutch of counties such as Dublin, Longford, Carlow and Louth with small cattle populations (Figure 39).

Figures 40, 41 and 42 deal similarly with sheep, pigs and poultry. Notwithstanding the substantial increase in the sheep population after the Famine, there was little change in the ordering of the counties. The most populous sheep counties were in the west and south-west, and Meath. The least populous were the counties of Ulster (except for Donegal), Leitrim and north Leinster see Figure 40.

Figure 39: County cattle numbers, arranged according to the ranking in 1841

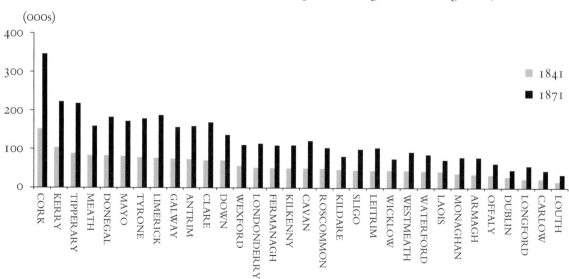

(000s)

1841
1871

194

Figure 40: County sheep numbers, arranged according to the ranking in 1841

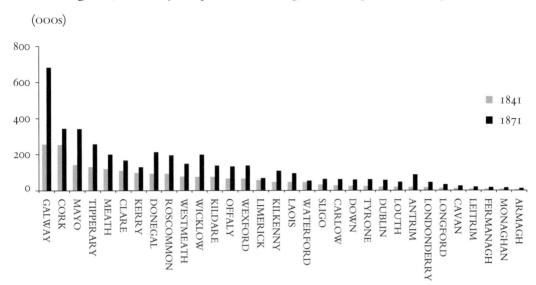

Pigs show a generally similar pattern of geographical stability, although a few counties (notably Galway, Antrim, Londonderry and Donegal), break rank as it were, and shift up the hierarchy between 1841 and 1871.

Figure 42, demonstrates a poultry ranking in 1841 not dissimilar to that for pigs. But there were considerable changes over time. We should, however, treat poultry numbers with considerable caution. It was no easy task to count one's chickens correctly when they numbered 100,000, or more, even in the smallest county.

Figure 41: County pig numbers, arranged according to the ranking in 1841

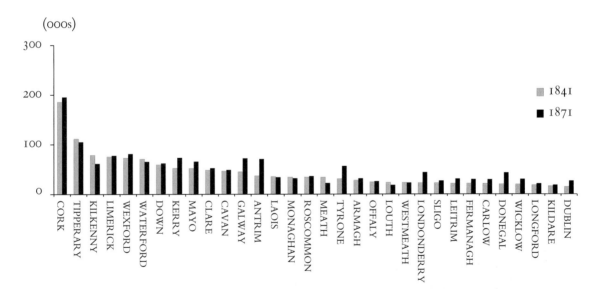

Figure 42: County poultry numbers, arranged according to the ranking in 1841

(000s)

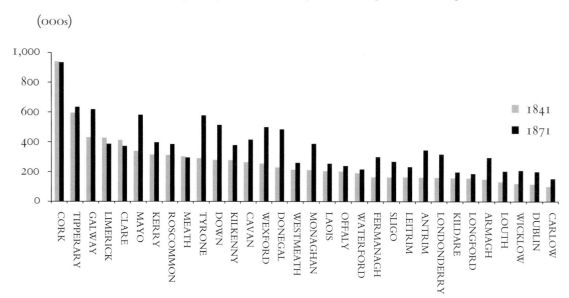

The numbers of livestock in a county were determined in part by the size of the county and it is instructive to present the figures per 100 acres. This is done in a series of maps and diagrams. Starting with cattle, the county maps reflect the increase in the density of the cattle population over the decades. They also reveal a tendency towards a concentration in the north and midlands as well as a southern belt of counties running from Carlow in the east to Clare in the west. As Figure 43 shows, the most important cattle counties on a per acre basis were considerably different from those indicated in Figure 39. Furthermore, the rankings shifted a good deal between 1841 and 1871.

The pattern of sheep farming judged on the basis of acreage diverged sharply from that of cattle map 105). By 1871 sheep were concentrated in a broad midlands belt running east-west from Louth and Wexford across to Mayo and Clare. This pattern can be seen in embryo in 1841 but it became much more pronounced after the Famine. Figure 43 ranks the counties according to the 1841 order of importance. There were some changes in rankings over time, particularly the growing importance of the eastern counties between Louth and Wexford.

Figure 43: County cattle numbers per 100 acres, arranged according to the ranking in 1841

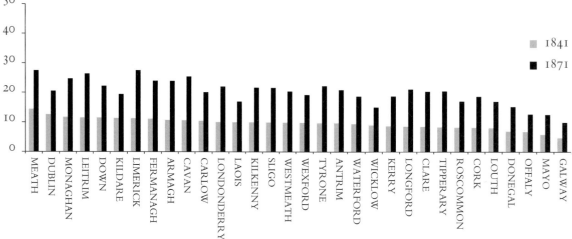

Figure 44: County sheep numbers per 100 acres, arranged according to the ranking in 1841

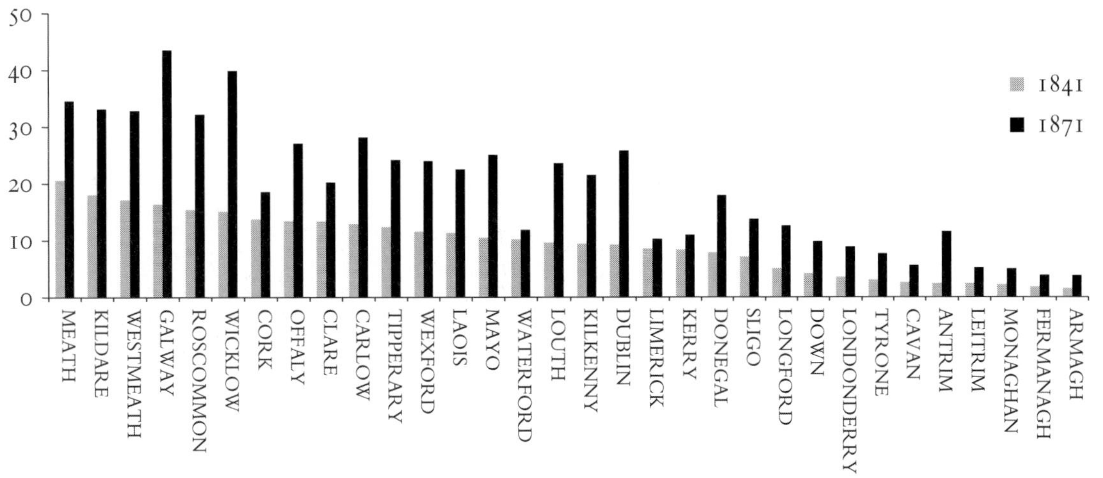

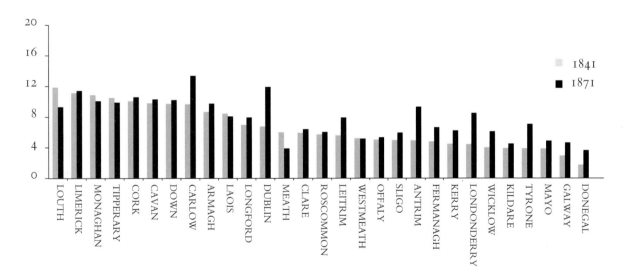

On an area basis, pig rearing was more pronounced on the south-eastern side of the country (excluding the east midlands) than in the north-west but, unlike cattle and sheep, there was a considerable change in the rankings of pig production over time. Counties such as Donegal, Galway, Mayo, Wicklow, Londonderry, Tyrone, Antrim, Leitrim and Dublin all became relatively more important as pig producing counties (Figure 45).

As we remarked earlier, the numbers of poultry in Ireland more than doubled after the Famine. During the Famine itself the flocks dwindled from 8.5 million to 5.7 million (or below), but soon recovered and exceeded 11 to 12 million by the early 1870s. We have not attempted to map the distribution of poultry, but generally counties with the greatest numbers of people were also those with the most poultry, hardly a surpising finding since poultry keeping was essentially a farmyard enterprise.

Figure 45: County pig numbers per 100 acres, arranged according to the ranking in 1841

Figure 46: County poultry numbers per 100 acres, arranged according to the ranking in 1841

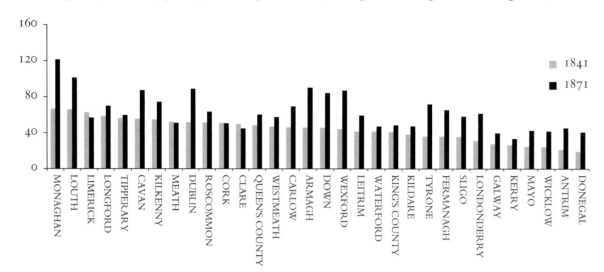

There is, finally, a series of maps showing the distribution of cattle, sheep and pigs throughout the poor law unions. They inevitably present a more complicated picture than the county maps. Starting with cattle, the PLU maps show a wide distribution of cattle numbers, although there was a tendency over time towards a concentration in Ulster, the North Midlands and the south. More striking, though, was a general darkening of the shading between 1841 and 1871. Since cattle densities really reflect two industries – dairying and beef – the wideranging spread is unsurprising as the two branches of the industry only partly overlapped.

The distribution of the sheep population, by contrast, was highly concentrated with a relatively narrow band running right across the south midlands. The pattern existed in embryo as early as 1847 but it had become very pronounced by 1871.

Pigs display a more varied regional distribution than sheep. There was some concentration of pigs in the unions in the south and south-east of the country and also in parts of Ulster.

Farming remained the basis of the Irish economy through the Famine and immediate post-Famine decades. The regional distribution of one type of farming as opposed to another was strongly influenced by market opportunities. Of course, farmers were generalists as well. Many farm inputs – oats, hay, potatoes, turnips for animal feed, farmyard dung for the fields and gardens – were produced on the farm. Farmers fed themselves and their families as well as supplying distant markets. Nevertheless, geographical specialisation was a marked feature of nineteenth century Irish agriculture.[4]

4 For further discussion see Líam Kennedy , 'Specialisation, the railways and Irish agriculture in the nineteenth century', in J.M. Goldstrom and L.A. Clarkson (eds), *Irish population, economy, and society* (Oxford 1981), pp. 185–93.

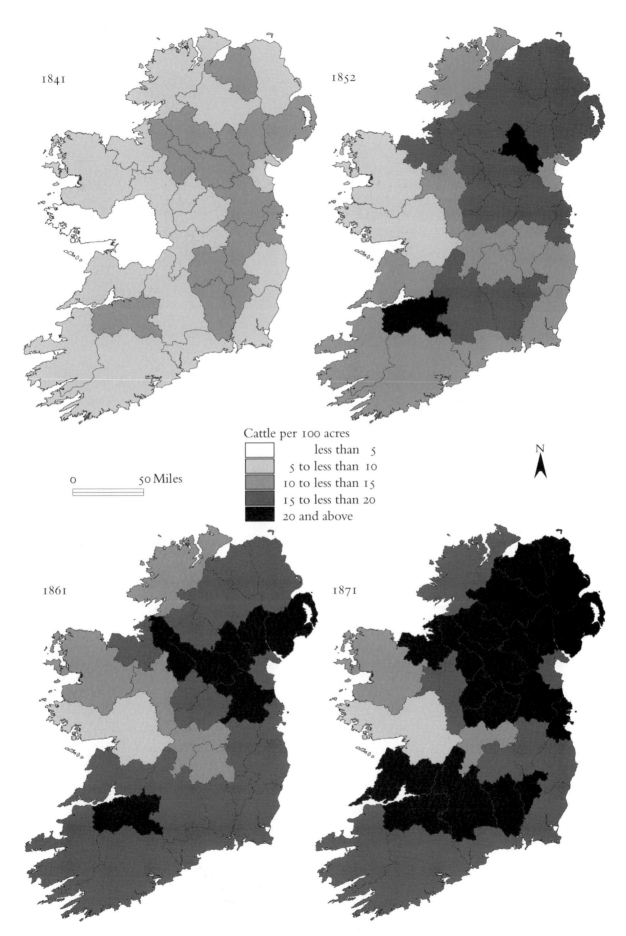

Map 101: Cattle population per 100 acres at county level

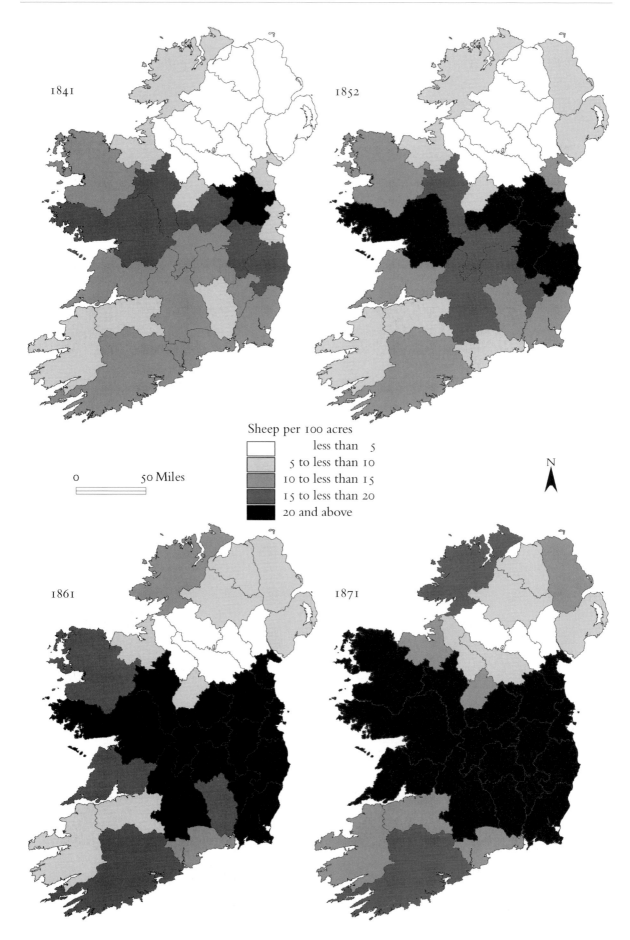

Map 102: Sheep population per 100 acres at county level

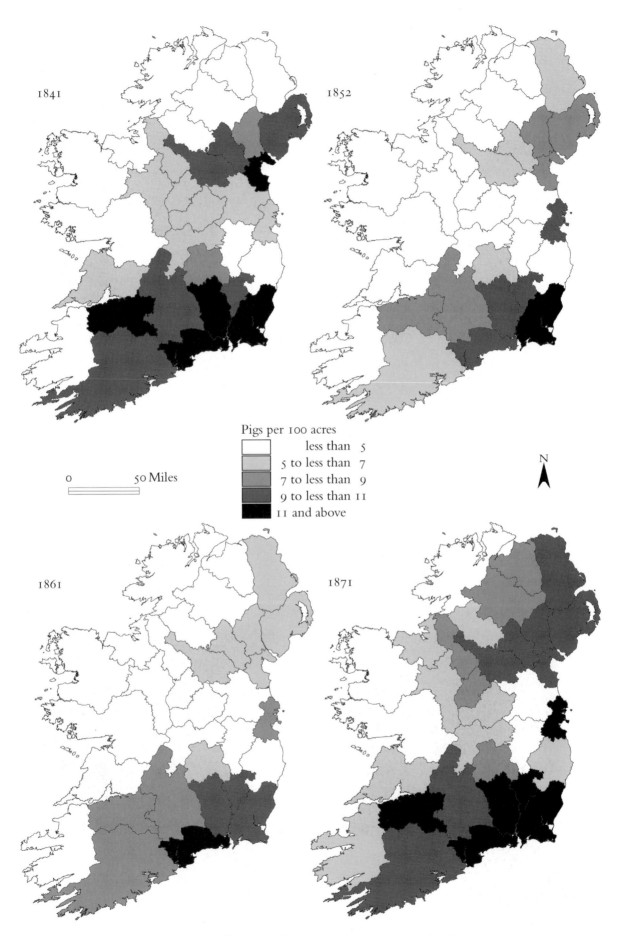

Map 103: Pig population per 100 acres at county level

1847

1852

Cattle per 100 acres

less than 5

5 to less than 10

10 to less than 15

15 to less than 20

20 and above

No information

0   50 Miles

N

1861

1871

Map 104: Cattle population per 100 acres at poor law union level

Sheep per 100 acres

less than 5

5 to less than 10

10 to less than 15

15 to less than 20

20 and above

No information

0   50 Miles

1847

1852

1861

1871

N

Map 105: Sheep population per 100 acres at poor law union level

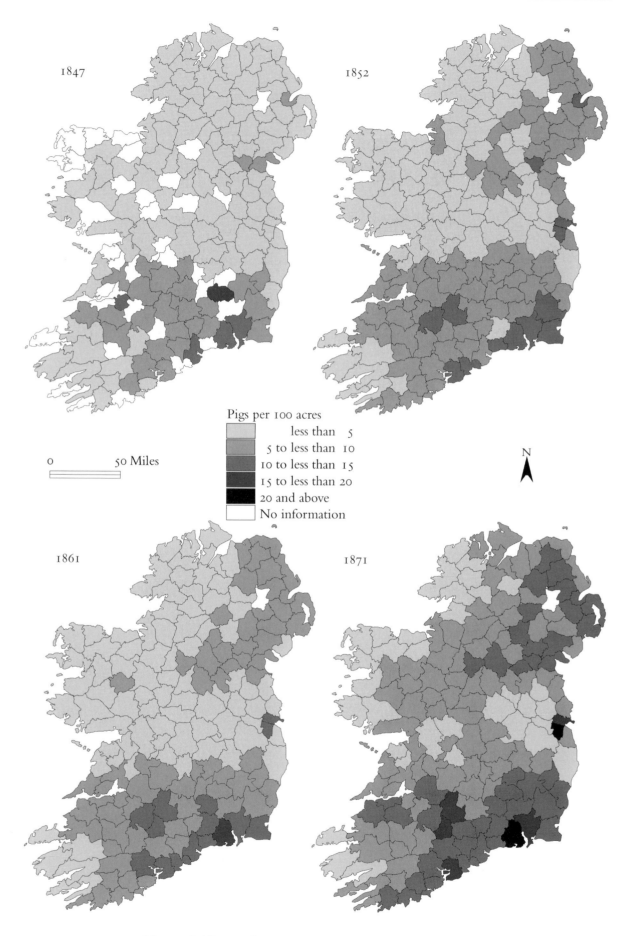

Map 106: Pig population per 100 acres at poor law union level

The Village of Tullig
Illustrated London News, 15 December 1849

CONCLUSION

There can be few more provocative titles in modern Irish history than Kevin O'Rourke's 'Did the Great Irish Famine Matter?'.[1] The essay is a cliometric rebuttal of Raymond Crotty's thesis, discussed in the introduction, that the Famine hardly affected the course of nineteenth-century economy and society. Crotty's view, in brief, was that forces exogenous to the Irish economy – changes in relative prices in the world economy and access to labour markets abroad – would in any case have brought about the changed patterns apparent in post-Famine society. O'Rourke's chosen battle ground is narrower than the title suggests, being confined to the impact of the Famine on employment in Irish agriculture, and the consequences for farming patterns and population change. Still, if the Famine was decisive in relation to these core issues, then the implications are profound. According to O'Rourke, without the Famine, potato output, far from contracting, would have expanded a little further by the 1870s. The tillage acreage, excluding potatoes, would have fallen, but by less than a fifth of the actual decline recorded between 1840–45 and 1876.[2] Most importantly of all, employment in agriculture, and ultimately the rural population, would have changed little in the absence of the mid-century crisis. This is a startling set of conclusions. In the words of O'Rourke, the Great Famine was indeed 'a major watershed'.

But what is a watershed in history? Attempts to establish the significance of the Great Famine, or otherwise, have commonly invoked images such as those of a 'turning point', a 'structural break', a 'watershed', a 'dividing line', an 'abyss', a 'gulf'. Such metaphors are productive, both of illumination and confusion. There are at least three senses in which the Famine might have 'mattered'.[3] Firstly, the crisis might have been the *fons et origo* of a series of important changes in Irish society. This seems to be the sense employed by some earlier writers on the Famine and its impact. Mapping the localities of Ireland before and after the Famine, as in this volume, is a useful way of detecting and dating changes, particularly incipient changes which might be missed in a more aggregated view of Ireland. Secondly, the Famine may have reversed the direction of pre-existing forces or trends in Irish society. Thirdly, while the Famine may not have reversed trends, it may have significantly accelerated or decelerated the course of social change.

Instances of the first – of novel developments, the origins and evolution of which may be traced unambiguously to the period of the Famine – are not easy to come by. But counting by numbers is to miss the point. Two in particular were among the most important consequences to flow from the Famine. The first, and purest example, is the permanent drop in the yield of the all-important potato crop, following the invasion of *Phytophthora infestans* in 1845. This deadly potato disease, hitherto unknown in western Europe, altered drastically the fragile ecological system of potato cultivation in Ireland, not just for the Famine years but for decades thereafter. Secondly, and relatedly, the pulverising of the bottom strata of Irish society, their smallholdings and their mud cabins, was the direct product of the crisis. These terrible social changes, which transformed population levels, the agrarian class structure and the housing stock, were enacted primarily within the Famine decade of 1845–55. The after-effects stretched forward in time, with diminished and diminishing intensity. So, if one is looking simply at population *levels*, there is no denying the Famine inaugurated a new era. In the century before the Famine the population had climbed

1 Kevin O'Rourke, 'Did the Great Irish Famine matter?', *Journal of Economic History*, 51 (1991), 1–22.   **2** This is on the assumption of a growth in the capital stock of post–Famine agriculture of 1.55 per cent per annum and a growth in wages of one per cent per annum.   **3** This conceptualisation, and the historical discussion which follows, draws heavily on Líam Kennedy 'Structural breaks in history: the case of the Great Irish Famine' (unpublished paper, Institute of Irish Studies, Belfast, 1998).

progressively upwards, reaching a peak close to 8.5 million people in 1845; in the century after, it tumbled to lower, and still lower levels. Similarly, the radical reshaping of the class structure was accomplished by forces intrinsic to the catastrophe itself: selective death, selective emigration, and brutal policies of land clearance stimulated by the crisis, and its financial burdens. Moreover, the fact that the effects were concentrated in a few harrowing years makes the experience of change qualitatively different from that of some extended process of adjustment. There is the world of a difference, not least for the millions of human beings who were directly affected, between the wasting away of communities through hunger and disease and the washing away of population through voluntary emigration, even though the effect on population levels may have been nominally the same.

Adopting a longer time perspective cannot alter this reality. Still, it is legitimate to enquire if, in the counterfactual world of Ireland without the Famine, other outcomes, such as the rate of population change, and ultimately population numbers, might have been different from those which materialised historically. Looking at the underlying dynamics, it is clear the rush of population was already losing momentum well before the mid-century crisis. Thus critics such as Crotty and Cullen would claim that severe adjustments were inevitable in any case, albeit at a slower and less painful pace.[4] The Irish economy, so the argument goes, could not have supported a huge population and a bloated rural proletariat at acceptable standards of living in the long run. The surprising point arising from O'Rourke's calculations, however, is that on the hypothetical assumption of no Famine, employment in agriculture would have remained virtually unchanged by 1876.[5] In other words, the huge eve-of-Famine population might well have been sustained, for at least several decades after 1845. This points to a preliminary conclusion. The Great Famine represented a watershed in the first (and strongest) sense in which the term has been defined: the Famine was the source of a collapse in population levels, along with the accompanying mass suffering and changes in class structure.

More typically, the Famine accelerated changes already in motion before the Famine: the third sense of the term watershed used above. In the case of emigration, for example, the rate greatly exceeded that of the pre-Famine decades, with the large stock of Famine emigrants in North America serving as a magnet for further intending migrants. There was also a shift in the regional origins of emigrants towards the West of Ireland. In relation to *rates* of population change, the Famine gave a further impetus to an existing trend towards lower and ultimately negative rates of population growth. The same may be true of the decline of Gaelic speaking, the rise of literacy, and the decline of general fertility in post-Famine society.[6]

In the religious sphere, while the 'devotional revolution' had it roots in earlier times, regular church attendance and the spread of piety seem to have moved onto a higher plane after the Famine. It is difficult not to attribute an independent role to the trauma of the Famine and the problems of meaning and identity that followed in its wake.[7] Moreover, the decimation of the lower orders through death and migration carved out a new social order in which orthodox religious beliefs and practices were more readily accepted.

On the eve of the Famine the rural poor subsisted on a range of foods which was limited by earlier standards. This narrowing of the dietary base of the cottiers and labourers intensified the vulnerability of large sections of the population to economic and ecological shocks. Then there is the irony: during the Famine years the dietary of the common people became more diversified, with the incorporation of yellow meal and soups of various kinds into the rations of the poor, but without the beneficial effect of averting mass starvation. The effect of this emergency shift in diet was not confined to the crisis alone. In the decades after 1850 yellow meal found its way into many household budgets, while the purchase of semi-luxuries like tea and tobacco, helped form part of the more diver-

4 Raymond Crotty, *Irish agricultural production: its volume and structure* (Cork, 1965), pp. 50–1; L.M. Cullen, *An economic history of Ireland since 1660* (London, 1972), p. 132. **5** This finding hinges crucially on the appropriateness of general equilibrium analysis as applied to the pre-Famine economy, on the model specification, and on the accuracy of the data employed. Each is open to challenge, hence the status of these conclusions must be deemed provisional. **6** Caution is necessary here because of the lack of time series data for the pre-Famine period which might be compared with the more extensive post-Famine data. **7** Emmett Larkin, "The devotional revolution in Ireland, 1850–75", *American Historical Review*, 77, 7 (1972; reprinted in *The Historical Dimensions of Irish Catholicism* [Dublin, 1996]).

sified consumption standards of the small farmers and labourers. In direct and indirect ways, the Famine changed the eating habits of the survivors of the Famine. This, in turn, accelerated changes in the structure of retailing, as production for home consumption gave way to foods purchased through the market. Or, looked at from a different angle, the Famine, by crushing the traditional economy of the potato eaters, hastened the commercialisation and monetisation of economic transactions in post-Famine society.

There may or may not have been a change in land-use patterns in favour of livestock farming between the peace of 1815 and the Famine. If there was, it can hardly have been great. The widening stream of grain exports after 1815 testifies to the resilience of the tillage economy, as also does its size on the eve of the great potato failure.[8] There is no doubt, however, that during the crisis years the rural economy was shifted bodily from labour-intensive tillage to labour-saving, land-intensive pastoral farming. This was due in part to the depressing effect of the Famine on potato yields, and in part also to rising wages (which may themselves be linked plausibly to the Famine). These forces were reinforced in the longer run by price trends in the British (and world) food markets which favoured a switch towards livestock production, though it is worth adding the subsidiary point that the drift away from tillage in the immediate post-Famine decades was muted.

A similar argument applies to changes in the size-distribution of farms. There is evidence of land consolidation in parts of the country before 1845 but there are also signs of continuing subdivision of holdings in other districts. Whether the apparent equipoise at the aggregate level was due to the restraining threats of secret agrarian societies or the ambiguity of market signals, or both, is not clear. The Famine took a heavy toll, breaking the tenuous grip on the land of multitudes of cottiers and labourers. Their dwarf holdings were swallowed up by neighbouring farmers. The secondary land market in con-acre land also shrank, adding to the distress of the rural poor. There is no doubt the catastrophic years of the late 1840s witnessed a radical restructuring of landholding, but once the immediate crisis had passed the pace of change in farm size was

gradual. The consolidation of middling-sized farms also meant that the plurality of inheritance regimes which characterised pre-Famine society now shifted in favour of impartible inheritance, that is, inheritance by a single son, and not necessarily the eldest.

The labour market is a picture of contrasting fortunes before and after the Famine. Money wage rates changed little between the 1820s and the 1840s.[9] However, from the 1850s onwards, a rising wage curve is discernible. The drastic depletion of an overstocked labour market by mortality and migration, and the continued salience of emigration – all with direct and indirect links to the Famine – helped create a new epoch in the wage history of nineteenth-century Irish society.

It is not possible to map changing political sentiments over time. But the story would be incomplete without some reference to politics and the Famine. The crisis does not appear to have translated into immediate and widespread disaffection with the union of Great Britain and Ireland. The skirmish between the Young Irelanders and the police at the Widow McCormack's cottage in 1848 was little more than a mock-heroic side-show to the tragic drama being enacted over much of Ireland in the later 1840s. There was, in time, a sequel. Its initial manifestation was on the other side of the Atlantic. Irish America, replenished and enlarged by the refugees of the Famine years and the economic migrants of the 1850s, created, first, the Fenian Brotherhood, and later contributed powerfully to revolutionary movements in Ireland during the later nineteenth and early twentieth centuries. 'Remember Skibereen' – a watchword which conjured up images of Famine and vengeance – animated many who sought, in their words, to break the link with England.

There are areas of Irish life where it is not easy to say if the Famine had a significant impact. The sphere of marriage and sexuality is a case in point. This may seem surprising, in view of dogmatic assertions of a link between the Great Hunger and the frustration of marriage expectations in post-Famine society. Certainly a trend towards later and less frequent marriage was apparent in some regions before 1845. These tendencies were even more apparent in post-Famine society. Still, closer statistical testing would be required to establish if the Famine

8 Cormac Ó Gráda, *Ireland: A new economic history, 1780–1939* (Oxford, 1994), p. 117.   9 Líam Kennedy & Martin Dowling,

'Prices and wages in Ireland, 1700–1850', *Irish Economic & Social History*, 29 (1997), 77–79.

had really accelerated or shifted the course of change. The implications of the Famine for illicit sexuality, as manifested in changes in illegitimacy rates over time, also await exploration. If one were being ambitious, one might add to this research agenda such diverse areas of human behaviour as gender relations, parent-child relationships, literary productions and the progress of 'civilising' processes in Irish society.

There are also areas of life where it seems reasonably clear that the Famine did not disturb, distort or deflect the course of change in the longer term. The course of prices, both domestic and export prices, is a case in point. It would be surprising had this not been the case. The agricultural and the industrial economies of Ireland were subject to market forces emanating from the international trading system, with the neighbouring island of Britain at its core.[10] As a small, open economy, Ireland was a price taker in relation to agricultural and industrial production. Typically, therefore, fluctuations and trends in prices were determined externally

Much the same can be said about disease patterns, though here one is talking more of the world of nature rather than political economy. The period of the Famine was marked by an explosion of epidemic diseases, related directly and indirectly to malnourishment, and against which medical technology was largely powerless. None were new to Irish society. Taking the longer view, there is no evidence that the Famine itself changed the pattern of diseases to which the common people were subject. Nor can one identify major epidemiological advances induced by the Irish Famine experience.

What of the children of the Famine? Perhaps these embodied, in a literal sense, the most profound effects of the Famine. It would be difficult, if not impossible, to reconstruct retrospectively the psychological implications for the survivors, though it seems unlikely that those who underwent personal tragedies were not haunted by the ghastly scenes of hunger and dying which attended their childhood. The nightmares of the poor, however, leave few traces, except in the archives of oral tradition. Some attempt may be made to gauge the physical effects in the longer run. Using evidence from comparative Famine studies, Ó Gráda concludes it is unlikely that the Famine gave rise to 'long-lasting cohort effects in post-Famine society'.[11] A reed in support of this contention might be the admittedly untypical case of Michael Davitt, a founder of the Land League and a leader of the agrarian struggle which broke out in 1879. Davitt, the son of an evicted tenant farmer, was born in 1846 in Famine-stricken Mayo, yet there is no sign of any diminution of his physical or intellectual capabilities as a result of a Famine birth.[12] A larger sample may be found within the thousands of local leaders and activists in the Land War (1879–82). This agitation, which significantly had its original base in the West of Ireland, has been described as 'the most remarkable mass movement in Irish history'.[13] This coming of political age of the generation of the Famine betokens neither broken spirits nor broken frames.

Still, material of this kind is indirect and suggestive rather than compelling. There are also some contrary signs in the nutritional literature. Lumey, who examined survivors of the Dutch Famine of 1944–5, concluded that a severe reduction in intrauterine nutrition did in fact produce long-term health effects, of an adverse kind, for both the mothers and their children.[14] Stunted growth and a degree of educational retardation seem real possibilities as well,[15] given the intensity and duration of the Irish Famine, though of course the worst affected would have been selected for death at an early age. Thus, while there can be little doubt that the Famine damaged the health of many who were conceived and born during the years of hunger and disease,

10 For example, on technical change in the linen industry, which badly affected female employment in rural Ulster and Connacht during the Famine decade, see Frank Geary, 'Regional industrial structure and labour force decline in Ireland between 1841 and 1851', *Irish Historical Studies*, 30 (1996), 167–94. 11 Cormac Ó Gráda, *Black '47 and beyond: the Great Irish Famine in history, economics and memory* (Princeton, N.J., 1999), p. 227. This is not to deny, as has been noted earlier in this volume, that children were especially vulnerable to particular nutritional problems, such as vitamin A deficiency, and hence xerophthalmia. Other diseases and deficiencies targeted the unborn and the newly-born. However, the likelihood is that those severely affected would not survive to adulthood. 12 The probability, though, is that Davitt suffered malnourishment as a child rather than within the womb, as he was born in the spring of 1846. 13 Joseph Lee, *The modernisation of Irish society, 1848–1918* (Dublin, 1973), p. 89. 14 L.H. Lumey, 'Reproductive outcomes in women prenatally exposed to undernutrition: a review of findings from the Dutch famine birth cohort', *Proceedings of the Nutrition Society*, 57 (1998), 129–35. 15 See, for example, S.M. Grantham-McGregor & George Cumper, 'Jamaican studies in nutrition and child development, and their implications for nutritional development', *Proceedings of the Nutrition Society*, 51 (1992), 71–9.

the numbers who survived to bear the marks of the ordeal must remain conjectural. In view of the class-specific nature of the crisis and the difficulties of surviving the first few years of life, their proportion within the cohort of Famine children was perhaps not all that noticeable a generation later. The issue requires further investigation.

Virtually all major divides in history are of a ragged kind. Continuities as well as discontinuities abound, even in the wake of catastrophic events which unleash new forces or effects. Among the apparent continuities, there may be significant mutation due to changes in the force or pace of change. In terms of the conceptual framework deployed earlier, the bulk of the evidence suggests that the Great Famine did mark a fundamental divide in modern Irish history. It was a dark chasm, partly bridged by stepping stones, between two epochs. Perhaps more so than the Glorious Revolution in England or the War of Independence in North America, the Great Irish Famine convulsed society at all levels, with consequences for virtually every sphere of life from the religious to the economic, and the cultural to the political. The nature and form of the relationships which connected the effects of the Famine to the phenomenon itself varied, as did the timing. Some of the relationships were indirect or worked with a time lag, but were no less potent for all that. Viewed in the mirror of late Victorian Irish society, pre-Famine Ireland must have appeared a strange, even foreign country.

Finally, it is important to acknowledge that one can be led astray by discussions of historical divides, of turning points and change, if in the process attention is deflected from the central reality of the Famine itself. The importance of the Great Hunger in modern Irish and European history derives, not from its perceived role in deflecting the course of historical change, but from the experience of suffering on such a vast scale. The primary historical reality remains the unnatural deaths of more than a million people under conditions of hunger, disease and indignity. This was in the context of a western world which presumed famines were a thing of the past. The Great Irish Famine confounded the optimistic assumptions of modernity.

LIST OF CONTRIBUTORS

L.A. CLARKSON is Professor Emeritus of Social History in the Queen's University of Belfast. He has published extensively in several areas of English and Irish economic and social history.

E.M. CRAWFORD is Senior Research Fellow in the School of Sociology at the Queen's University of Belfast. A nutritionist and historian, she has published on Irish dietary and medical history, and is editor of *Famine: the Irish experience 900–1900* (Edinburgh, 1989) and *The hungry stream* (Belfast, 1997).

PAUL S. ELL is Senior Research Fellow in the School of Sociology at the Queen's University of Belfast. He has an interest in data visualisation, quantitative approaches to data analysis, Geographical Information Systems and the dissemination of knowledge using the Internet. He is co-author of *Rival Jerusalems: the geography of Victorian religion* (Cambridge, forthcoming).

LÍAM KENNEDY is Professor of Economic and Social History at the Queen's University of Belfast and author of *Colonialism, religion and nationalism in Ireland* (Institute of Irish Studies, Belfast, 1996).

INDEX

Abbeyleix, Poor Law Union 20, 21

agricultural holdings size 162–75

agricultural returns 193

Antrim, County 18, 19, 26, 30, 40, 69, 74, 88, 89, 94, 95, 102, 108, 109, 113, 121, 124, 142, 195, 197

Antrim, Poor Law Union 20, 21, 135

Antrim Lower, Barony 22, 23

Antrim Upper, Barony 22, 23

Aran, Barony 22, 23, 78

Ardagh, Barony 22, 23

Ardee, Barony 22, 23

Ardee, Poor Law Union 20, 21

Ards, Barony 22, 23

Arklow, Barony 22, 23

Armagh, Barony 22, 23

Armagh, County 18, 19, 51, 69, 88, 89, 113, 116, 120, 121, 133, 163

Armagh, Poor Law Union 20, 21

Armagh, Town 28

Armstrong, W.A. 144

Athenry, Barony 22, 23

Athlone, Barony 22, 23

Athlone, Poor Law Union 20, 21, 126

Athy, Poor Law Union 20, 21

bacon see food

Bailieborough, Poor Law Union 20, 21

Ballaghkeen, Barony 22, 23

Ballina, Poor Law Union 20, 21, 126, 128

Ballinacor North, Barony 22, 23

Ballinacor South, Barony 22, 23

Ballinasloe, Poor Law Union 20, 21, 129

Ballinrobe, Poor Law Union 20, 21, 118, 126, 136, 137

Ballintober North, Barony 22, 23

Ballintober South, Barony 22, 23

Ballyadams, Barony 22, 23

Ballyboy, Barony 22, 23

Ballybritt, Barony 22, 23

Ballycastle, Poor Law Union 20, 21

Ballycowan, Barony 22, 23

Ballymahon, Poor Law Union 20, 21

Ballymena, Poor Law Union 20, 21, 136

Ballymena, Town 27, 28

Ballymoe (Co. Galway), Barony 22, 23

Ballymoe (Co. Roscommon), Barony 22, 23

Ballymoney, Poor Law Union 20, 21

Ballynahinch, (Co. Galway), Barony 22, 23, 95

Ballyshannon, Poor Law Union 20, 21

Ballyvaughan, Poor Law Union 20, 21

Balrothery, Poor Law Union 20, 21

Balrothery East, Barony 22, 23

Balrothery West, Barony 22, 23

Baltinglass, Poor Law Union 20, 21

Banagh, Barony 22, 23

Banbridge, Poor Law Union 20, 21

Banbridge, Town 27

Bandon, Poor Law Union 20, 21, 128

Bandon, Town 28

Bantry (Co. Cork), Barony 22, 23

Bantry (Co. Wexford), Barony 22, 23

Bantry, Poor Law Union 20, 21, 126, 128

Baptists 88–9, 93

Bargy, Barony 22, 23

barley see crops

Barretts, Barony 22, 23

Barrymore, Barony 22, 23

Bawnboy, Poor Law Union 20, 21

Bear, Barony 22, 23, 76

Belfast, Poor Law Union 20, 21, 135

Belfast, Town 22, 23, 26, 30, 41, 51, 55, 56, 67, 74, 76, 77, 78, 79, 89, 94, 95, 122, 124, 141, 144, 147, 148, 164

Belfast Lower, Barony 22, 23, 27, 77, 78

Belfast Upper, Barony 22, 23, 27, 77, 78

Belmullet, Poor Law Union 20, 21

Bennett, William 106, 129

Birr, Barony 22, 23

Board of Works 132, 134

Booth, Charles 144

Borrisokane, Poor Law Union 20, 21

Bourke, Austin 162, 193

Boylagh, Barony 22, 23

Boyle, Barony 22, 23

Boyle, Poor Law Union 20, 21, 126

Brawny, Barony 22, 23

bread see food

British Relief Association 126

Bunratty Lower, Barony 22, 23

Bunratty Upper, Barony 22, 23

Burren, Barony 22, 23

Burrishoole, Barony 22, 23

Caherciveen, Poor Law Union 20, 21, 126, 128, 129
Callan, Barony 22, 23
Callan, Poor Law Union 20, 21
Carberry East (East Division), Barony 22, 23
Carberry East (West Division), Barony 22, 23
Carberry West (East Division), Barony 22, 23
Carberry West (West Division), Barony 22, 23
Carbury (Co. Kildare), Barony 22, 23
Carbury (Co. Sligo), Barony 22, 23
Carleton, William 97
Carlow, Barony 22, 23
Carlow, County 18, 19, 50, 55, 73, 113, 116, 118, 194, 196
Carlow, Poor Law Union 20, 21
Carlow, Town 28
Carra, Barony, 22, 23
Carrick-on-Shannon, Town 106
Carrick-on-Shannon, Poor Law Union 20, 21, 104, 124
Carrick-on-Suir, Poor Law Union 20 21
Carrick-on-Suir, Town 28
Carrickfergus, Town 22, 23
Carrickmacross, Poor Law Union 20, 21
Carrigallen, Barony 22, 23
Cary, Barony 22, 23
Cashel, Poor Law Union 20, 21, 126
Cashel, Town 28
Castlebar, Barony 22, 23
Castlebar, Poor Law Union 20, 21, 120, 126, 136, 137
Castleblayney, Poor Law Union 20, 21
Castlecomer, Poor Law Union 20, 21
Castlederg, Poor Law Union 20, 21
Castleknock, Barony 22, 23
Castlerahan, Barony 22, 23
Castlereagh (Co. Roscommon), Barony 22, 23
Castlereagh Lower (Co. Down), Barony 22, 23, 95
Castlereagh Upper (Co. Down), Barony 22, 23, 95
Castletown, Poor Law Union 20, 21
Castletowndevlin, Poor Law Union 20, 21
cattle see livestock
Cavan, County 18, 19, 26, 69, 88, 115, 118, 124, 134
Cavan, Poor Law Union 20, 21, 126
Celbridge, Poor Law Union 20, 21
Central Board of Health 123, 124, 136
Central Relief Committee 129
celibacy 16, 54–9
cereals see crops
cholera see disease
Church of Ireland 88–93
Clanawley, Barony 22, 23
Clandonagh, Barony 22, 23
Clane, Barony 22, 23
Clankee Barony 22, 23
Clankelly, Barony 22, 23
Clanmahon, Barony 22, 23
Clanmaurice, Barony 22, 23

Clanmorris, Barony 22, 23
Clanwilliam (Co. Limerick), Barony 22, 23
Clanwilliam (Co. Tipperary), Barony 22, 23
Clare, Barony 22, 23
Clare, County 18, 19, 37, 38, 40, 45, 51, 61, 73, 78, 88, 89, 94, 113, 115, 118, 122, 124, 134, 135
Claremorris, Poor Law Union 20, 21
Clarmallagh, Barony 22, 23
Clifden, Poor Law Union 20, 21, 126, 128, 136, 137
Clogheen, Poor Law Union 20, 21
Clogher, Barony 22, 23
Clogher, Poor Law Union 20, 21
Clonakilty, Poor Law Union 20, 21
Clonderalaw, Barony 22, 23
Clones, Poor Law Union 20, 21, 129
Clonlisk, Barony 22, 23
Clonlonan, Barony 22, 23
Clonmacnowen, Barony 22, 23
Clonmel, Poor Law Union 20, 21
Clonmel, Town 28
Cobh 28
Coleraine, Barony 22. 23
Coleraine, County 18
Coleraine, Poor Law Union 20, 21
Coleraine, Town 28
Condons & Clangibbon, Barony 22, 23
Congested Districts Board 79
Connacht 18, 113, 130, 134, 136, 178
Connell, Barony 22, 23
Connell, K.H. 15, 56, 68
Connello Lower, Barony 22, 23
Connello Upper, Barony 22, 23
Cookstown, Poor Law Union 20, 21
Coolavin, Barony 22, 23
Coole, Barony 22, 23, 26
Coolestown, Barony 22, 23
Coolock, Barony 22, 23
Coonagh. Barony 22, 23
Cootehill, Poor Law Union 20, 21, 126, 130
Corcomroe, Barony 22, 23
Cork, Barony 22, 23, 78
Cork, City 22, 23, 28, 76, 89, 95, 124, 130, 144, 147
Cork, County 18, 19, 36, 61, 65, 69, 75, 77, 102, 108, 109, 113, 118, 120, 122, 130, 142, 194, 196
Cork, Poor Law Union 20, 21
Corkaguiny, Barony 22, 23
Corkaree, Barony 22, 23
Corran, Barony 22, 23
Corrigan, Dominic 124
Corrofin, Poor Law Union 20, 21
Coshbride, Barony 22, 23
Coshlea, Barony 22, 23
Coshma, Barony 22, 23
Coshmore, Barony 22, 23

Coshmore & Coshbride , Barony 22, 23
Costello, Barony 22, 23
cottiers (labourers) 16, 65, 102, 109
Courceys, Barony 22, 23, 76
Cousens, S.H. 37, 38
Crannagh, Barony 22, 23
Cremorne, Barony 22, 23
Croom, Poor Law Union 20, 21
crops 69, 176–92
    barley, bere 177, 178, 182, 189
    flax 176, 177, 178, 181, 188
    oats 177, 180, 187
    other root, green crops, peas and beans 185, 192
    potatoes 176, 177, 178, 184, 191
    rye 177, 178, 182
    wheat 177, 179, 186
Crosfield, Joseph 106
Crotty, Raymond 16, 207
Cullen, L.M. 208
Cullenagh, Barony 22, 23

Daly, Mary 16
Dartree, Barony 22, 23
Decies within Drum, Barony 22, 23
Decies without Drum, Barony 22, 23
Deece Lower, Barony 22, 23
Deece Upper, Barony 22, 23
Delvin, Barony 22, 23
Devon Commission 163
Devotional Revolution 208
diarrhoea see disease
diet (see also food) 68–75
Dillon Dr 120
Dingle, Poor Law Union 20, 21, 126
disease 90, 104–24, 128, 210
    cholera 104–5, 121–2, 126, 128
    diarrhoea 65, 104–5, 119–20, 128
    dropsy 104–5, 106–9
    dysentery 65, 104–5, 119–20, 128
    fever 65, 104–5, 117, 128
    infection 65, 104
    influenza 104
    kwashiorkor 106
    marasmus 104–5, 106–9
    measles 104–5, 112–15
    pellagra 120
    relapsing fever 65, 104, 105, 117, 118
    scarlatina 112–15
    scurvy 104, 110–11
    smallpox 104, 121–2
    tuberculosis 104–5, 112, 116
    typhoid 104
    typhus 65, 104, 110, 117, 118
    whooping cough 104
    xerophthalmia 104, 110–12
Donaghmore, Poor Law Union 20, 21
Donegal, County 18, 19, 40, 44, 69, 73, 75, 77, 78, 79, 88, 89, 102, 108, 112, 118, 124, 130, 134, 142, 194, 195, 197
Donegal, Poor Law Union 20, 21, 10
Donovan, Dr Daniel 107
Down, County 18, 19, 51, 55, 69, 74, 75, 88, 89, 94, 102, 113, 116, 133, 142
Downpatrick, Poor Law Union 20, 21, 128
Drogheda (Co. Louth), Barony 22, 23
Drogheda (Co. Meath), Barony 22, 23
Drogheda, Poor Law Union 20, 21
Drogheda, Town 28, 109
Dromore West, Poor Law Union 20, 21
dropsy see disease
Drumahaire, Barony 22, 23
Dublin, Barony 22, 23, 78
Dublin, City 16, 22, 23, 28, 30, 51, 55, 56, 74, 76, 78, 89, 95, 108, 109, 113, 115, 122, 124, 129, 144, 147, 148, 164
Dublin, County 18,19, 26, 36, 37, 40, 44, 55, 61, 69, 72, 73, 74, 88, 89, 94, 102, 108, 109, 113, 115, 116, 122, 124, 194, 197
Dublin North, Poor Law Union 20, 21
Dublin South, Poor Law Union 20, 21
Dufferin, Barony 22, 23, 95, 96
Duhallow, Barony 22, 23
Duleek Lower, Barony 22, 23
Duleek Upper, Barony 22, 23
Dunboyne, Barony 22, 23
Dundalk, Poor Law Union 20, 21, 128
Dundalk, Town 28, 109
Dundalk Lower, Barony 22, 23
Dundalk Upper, Barony 22, 23
Dunfanaghy, Poor Law Union 20, 21
Dungannon, Barony 22, 23
Dungannon, Poor Law Union 20, 21
Dungarvan, Poor Law Union 20, 21
Dungarvan, Town 28
Dunkellin, Barony 22, 23
Dunkerron, Barony 22, 23
Dun Laoghaire, Town 28
Dunluce Lower, Barony 22, 23
Dunluce Upper, Barony 22, 23
Dunmanway, Poor Law Union 20, 21
Dunmore, Barony 22, 23
Dunshaughlin, Poor Law Union 20, 21
dysentery see disease

Eagleton, Terry 15
East India Company 107

Edenderry, Poor Law Union 20, 21, 136
eggs *see* food
Eglish, Barony 22, 23
Eliogarty, Barony 22, 23
Emigration 16, 26, 40–1, 90, 97, 104, 105, 162, 209
Ennis, Poor Law Union 20, 21
Ennis, Town 28
Enniscorthy, Poor Law Union 20, 21
Enniscorthy, Town 28
Enniskillen, Poor Law Union 20, 21, 126, 128
Enniskillen, Town 28
Ennistimon, Poor Law Union 20, 21, 126, 128, 137
Erris, Barony 22, 23, 78

Farbill, Barony 22, 23
Farney, Barony 22, 23
Fartullagh, Barony 22, 23
Fassadinin, Barony 22, 23
Fermanagh, County 18, 19, 88, 89, 108, 113, 115, 118,
    124, 130, 133
Fermoy, Barony 22, 23
Fermoy, Poor Law Union 20, 21, 128
Fermoy, Town 28
Ferrard, Barony 22, 23
fertility 16, 26, 36
Fews Lower, Barony 22, 23
Fews Upper, Barony 22, 23
fish *see* food
flax *see* crops
food 65, 68–75
    bacon 68, 70, 74
    biscuit 130, 136
    bread 68, 72, 129, 136
    butter 68, 72
    cabbage 65, 68
    charlock 68
    eggs 68, 73–4, 194
    fish (including herrings) 65, 68, 69, 74–5
    flour 136
    Indian meal (maize) 66, 120, 130, 208
    meal 130, 136
    meat 68, 74, 130
    milk and milk products 65, 68, 72, 73–4, 111
    nettles 68
    oats/oatmeal 65, 66, 67, 68, 69, 71, 74, 177
    potatoes (*see also* crops) 65–7, 68–70, 72, 74, 107,
        109, 134, 208
        blight (*Phythophthora infestans*) 15, 67, 69, 207
        consumption of 15, 65, 66–70
        failure of 15, 65, 125
        production of 66, 69, 176–8
        prices of 66–7
        varieties of 69
    rice 130
    soup 129–30, 136
    tea 208
Fore (Co. Meath), Barony 22, 23
Fore (Co. Westmeath), Barony 22, 23
Forster, William, 106, 129
Forth (Co. Carlow), Barony 22, 23
Forth (Co. Wexford), Barony 22, 23
Frenchpark, Barony 22, 23

Gaelic language 16, 65, 95–6, 102–3
Gallen, Barony 22, 23
Galmoy, Barony 22, 23
Galway, Barony 22, 23
Galway, County 18, 19, 36, 40, 45, 65, 74, 78, 94, 95,
    102, 108, 109, 113, 115, 118, 120, 122, 124, 134,
    135, 143, 195, 197
Galway, Poor Law Union 20, 21, 126, 128
Galway, Town 22, 23, 28, 95, 124
Garrycastle, Barony 22, 23
Gaultiere, Barony 22, 23
Geashill, Barony 22, 23
gender 43, 44–9, 96
Glanarought, Barony 22, 23
Glenahiry, Barony 22, 23
Glenamaddy, Poor Law Union 20, 21
Glenarm Lower, Barony 22, 23
Glenarm Upper, Barony 22, 23
Glenquin, Barony 22, 23
Glenties, Poor Law Union 20, 21, 126
Glin, Poor Law Union 20, 21
Gorey, Barony 22, 23
Gorey, Poor Law Union 20, 21
Gort, Barony 22, 23
Gort, Poor Law Union 20, 21, 126, 128, 136
Gortin, Poor Law Union 20, 21
Gowran, Barony 22, 23
Granard, Barony 22, 23
Granard, Poor Law Union 20, 21, 126
Gregory Clause 126, 136

'half-grant' scheme 132–3
Hall, Revd Dr Robert Traill 106
herrings *see* food
houseful 60–3
housing 16, 65, 76–87, 207

Ibane & Barryroe, Barony 22, 23
Ibrickan, Barony 22, 23
Ida, Barony 22, 23
Idrone East, Barony 22, 23

Idrone West, Barony 22, 23
Iffa & Offa East, Barony 22, 23
Iffa & Offa West, Barony 22, 23
Ikeathy & Oughterany, Barony 22, 23
Ikerrin, Barony 22, 23
illiteracy 65, 94–101
Imokilly, Barony 22, 23
Inchquin, Barony 22, 23
Independents 88, 89, 93
Indian meal (maize) *see* food
industrialisation 16, 44, 57
Inishowen East, Barony 22, 23
Inishowen West, Barony 22, 23
Inishowen, Poor Law Union 20, 21
Iraghticonnor, Barony 22, 23
Irish language *see* Gaelic language
Islands, Barony 22, 23
Iveagh Lower, Barony 22, 23
Iveagh Upper, Barony 22, 23
Iveragh, Barony 22, 23
Iverk, Barony 22, 23

Jacob, Arthur 111
Jews 88, 93

Kanturk, Poor Law Union 20, 21, 126
Keenaght, Barony 22, 23
Kells, Barony 22, 23
Kells, Poor Law Union 20, 21
Kells Lower, Barony 22, 23
Kells Upper, Barony 22, 23
Kennedy, R.E. 56
Kenmare, Poor Law Union 20, 21, 126
Kenry, Barony 22, 23
Kerry, County 18, 19, 40, 50, 55, 61, 65, 73, 88, 89, 94,
    108, 113, 116, 120, 122, 124, 130, 133, 194
Kerrycurrihy, Barony 22, 23
Kilconnell, Barony 22, 23
Kilconway, Barony 22, 23
Kilcoursey, Barony 22, 23
Kilcullen, Barony 22, 23
Kilculliheen, Barony 22, 23
Kildare, County 18, 19, 38, 44, 51, 60, 72, 89, 108, 115,
    116, 118, 122
Kilkea & Moone, Barony 22, 23
Kilkeel, Poor Law Union 20, 21, 136
Kilkenny, City 22, 23, 27, 28, 124
Kilkenny, County 18, 19, 73, 115, 116, 124
Kilkenny, Poor Law Union 20, 21
Kilkenny West, Barony 22, 23
Killadysert, Poor Law Union 20, 21, 126
Killala, Poor Law Union 20, 21

Killarney, Poor Law Union 20, 21, 136
Killarney, Town 28
Killian, Barony 22, 23
Kilmacrenan, Barony 22, 23
Kilmacthomas, Poor Law Union 20, 21
Kilmaine, Barony 22, 23
Kilmallock Liberties, Barony 22, 23
Kilmallock, Poor Law Union 20, 21
Kilnamanagh Lower, Barony 22, 23
Kilnamanagh Upper, Barony 22, 23
Kilrush, Poor Law Union 20, 21, 126
Kiltartan, Barony 22, 23
Kinalea, Barony 22, 23
Kinalmeaky, Barony 22, 23
Kinelarty, Barony 22, 23
Kinnatalloon, Barony 22, 23
Kinsale, Barony 22, 23
Kinsale, Poor Law Union 20, 21
Kinsale, Town 28
Knockninny, Barony 22, 23
Knocktopher, Barony 22, 23

labouring classes (cottiers) 65, 69, 78, 79, 102, 109,
    144–8
Labour Rate Act 134
language (*see also* Gaelic language) 65, 95, 102–3
Laois (Queen's County) 18, 19, 28, 51, 54, 55, 73, 89,
    108, 113, 116, 124
Larne, Poor Law Union 20, 21, 135
Larne, Town 78
Law, Robert 115
Lecale, Barony 22, 23
Leinster 18, 108, 113
Leitrim (Co. Galway), Barony 22, 23
Leitrim (Co. Leitrim), Barony 22, 23
Leitrim, County 18, 19, 26, 73, 78, 108, 115, 118, 120,
    124, 135, 143, 194, 197
Letterkenny, Poor Law Union 20, 21, 129
Leyny, Barony 22, 23
lice 118
Limerick, City 22, 23, 27, 28, 78, 89, 124, 144, 147
Limerick, County 18, 19, 27, 44, 61, 65, 74, 108, 109,
    113, 116, 118, 122, 124, 143
Limerick, Poor Law Union 20, 21
linen 77, 169
Lisburn, Poor Law Union 20, 21
Lisburn, Town 27, 28, 79, 89, 113
Lismore, Poor Law Union 20, 21
Lisnaskea, Poor Law Union 20, 21
Listowel, Poor Law Union 20, 21
literacy 65, 94–101
livestock 193–204, 209
    cattle 194, 196, 198, 199, 202

livestock (*cont.*)
  pigs 194, 195, 197, 198, 201, 204
  poultry 195, 196, 197, 198
  sheep 194, 195, 196, 197, 198, 200, 203
Local Government Act (1898) 79
Londonderry, City 28, 79, 122
Londonderry, County 18, 19, 55, 75, 77, 88, 89, 108, 113, 118, 133, 195, 197
Londonderry, Poor Law Union 20, 21
Longford, County 18, 19, 26, 69, 94, 108, 113, 118, 121, 124
Longford (Co. Galway), Barony 22, 23
Longford (Co. Longford), Barony 22, 23
Longford, Poor Law Union 20, 21, 128
Lordship of Newry, Barony 22, 23
Loughinsholin, Barony 22, 23
Loughrea, Barony 22, 23
Loughrea, Poor Law Union 20, 21
Loughtee Lower, Barony 22, 23
Loughtee Upper, Barony 22, 23
Louth, Barony 22, 23
Louth, County 18, 19, 69, 94, 102, 108, 109, 113, 115, 116, 121, 124, 133, 194, 196
Lowtherstown, Poor Law Union 20, 21, 126
Lune, Barony 22, 23
Lurg, Barony 22, 23
Lurgan, Poor Law Union 20, 21
Lurgan, Town 27, 89

MacArthur, Sir William P. 118
Macroom, Poor Law Union 20, 21, 128
Magheraboy, Barony 22, 23
Magherafelt, Poor Law Union 20, 21
Magherastephana, Barony 22, 23
Magunihy, Barony 22, 23
Mallow, Poor Law Union 20, 21, 128
maize (Indian meal) *see* food
Manorhamilton, Poor Law Union 20, 21
marasmus *see* disease
marriage 16, 26, 36, 43, 50–3, 57, 209
Maryborough East, Barony 22, 23
Maryborough West, Barony 22, 23
Massereene Lower, Barony 22, 23
Massereene Upper, Barony 22, 23
Mayo, County 18, 19, 26, 36, 38, 44, 50, 51, 54, 55, 65, 73, 74, 78, 88, 94, 96, 102, 108, 113, 115, 116, 120, 122, 125, 130, 133, 134, 210
Meath, County 18, 19, 38, 40, 51, 116, 122, 124, 133, 194, 196
meadow and hay 176–7, 183, 190
Methodists 88–92
Micks, W.L. 79
Middlethird (Co. Tipperary), Barony 22, 23

Middlethird (Co. Waterford), Barony 22, 23
Middleton, Poor Law Union 20, 21, 128
Milford, Poor Law Union 20, 21
milk and milk products *see* food
Millstreet, Poor Law Union 20, 21
Mitchelstown, Poor Law Union 20, 21
Mohill, Barony 22, 23, 126
Mohill, Poor Law Union 20, 21
Mokyr, Joel 36, 37–8
Monaghan, County 18, 19, 26, 55, 88, 89, 113, 115, 121, 124, 134
Monaghan, Poor Law Union 20, 21
Morgallion, Barony 22, 23
mortality 16, 36–9, 65, 104, 105, 106, 108, 128, 129
Mountbellew, Poor Law Union 20, 21
Mountmellick, Poor Law Union 20, 21
Mourne, Barony 22, 23
Moyarta, Barony 22, 23
Moyashel & Magheradernon, Barony 22, 23
Moycarn, Barony 22, 23
Moycashel, Barony 22, 23
Moycullen, Barony 22, 23, 95
Moydow, Barony 22, 23
Moyfenrath Lower, Barony 22, 23
Moyfenrath Upper, Barony 22, 23
Moygoish, Barony 22, 23
Mullingar, Poor Law Union 20, 21, 126
Munster 18, 113, 130
Murrisk, Barony 22, 23
Muskerry East, Barony 22, 23
Muskerry West, Barony 22, 23

Naas, Poor Law Union 20, 21
Naas North, Barony 22, 23
Naas South, Barony 22, 23
Narragh & Reban East, Barony 22, 23
Narragh & Reban West, Barony 22, 23
Navan, Poor Law Union 20, 21
Navan Lower, Barony 22, 23
Navan Upper, Barony 22, 23
Nenagh, Poor Law Union 20, 21
Nenagh, Town 28
Nethercross, Barony 22, 23
Newcastle (Co. Dublin), Barony 22, 23
Newcastle (Co. Wicklow), Barony 22, 23
Newcastle, Poor Law Union 20, 21, 126
Newport, Poor Law Union 20, 21
New Ross, Poor Law Union 20, 21, 126
New Ross, Town 28
Newry, Poor Law Union 20, 21
Newry, Town 27, 28
Newtownards, Poor Law Union 20, 21
Newtownards, Town 27, 28

Newtownlimavady, Poor Law Union 20, 21, 135, 136
North East Liberties of Coleraine, Barony 18, 22, 23
North West Liberties of Londonderry, Barony 18, 22, 23
nutrition 107, 210
nutritional deficiency diseases 104, 106, 110–12

O'Brien, George 15
Ó Gráda, Cormac 15, 36, 40, 107
oats see crops
oatmeal see food
occupations 97, 141, 144–61
Offaly (King's County) 18, 19, 40, 50, 51, 89, 94, 108, 113, 116, 124, 130, 133
Offaly East, Barony 22, 23, 27, 60
Offaly West, Barony 22, 23
Oldcastle, Poor Law Union 20, 21
Omagh, Poor Law Union 20, 21
Omagh, Town 118
Oneilland East, Barony 22, 23
Oneilland West, Barony 22, 23
Orberry & Kilmore, Barony 22, 23
Orion Lower , Barony 22, 23
Orion Upper, Barony 22, 23
Ormond Lower, Barony 22, 23
Ormond Upper, Barony 22, 23
O'Rourke, Kevin 207, 208
Oughterard, Poor Law Union 20, 21
outdoor relief see relief
Owenybeg, Barony 22, 23
Owney & Arra, Barony 22, 23

Parsonstown, Poor Law Union 20, 21
Peel, Sir Robert 132, 134
Pemberton, Dr 118
Philipstown Lower, Barony 22, 23
Philipstown Upper, Barony 22, 23
pigs see livestock
Poor law 125–39
    acts 18, 126, 136
    unions 16, 18, 20, 21, 36, 109, 125, 178
population 16, 26–35, 40, 66, 78, 162, 208
Portadown 27
Portnahinch, Barony 22, 23
Portumna, Poor Law Union 20, 21
potatoes see crops, and food
'potato wage' 67
poultry see livestock
Presbyterians 88–92, 94, 95, 97
prices 66–7
Pubblebrien, Barony 22, 23

Quakers see Society of Friends

Raphoe, Barony 22, 23
rate-in-aid 126
Rathcline, Barony 22, 23
Rathconrath, Barony 22, 23
Rathdown (Co. Dublin), Barony 22, 23, 30
Rathdown (Co. Wicklow), Barony 22, 23
Rathdown, Poor Law Union 20, 21
Rathdrum, Poor Law Union 20, 21, 136
Rathkeale, Poor Law Union 20, 21
Rathvilly, Barony 22, 23
Ratoath, Barony 22, 23
relapsing fever see disease
relief
    food depots 104, 129
    out-door relief 109, 136–8
    public works 65, 126, 132–4
    soup kitchens 65, 104, 129, 135–7
    workhouses 65, 104, 105
religion 16, 88–93, 208
Richards, Edmund 129
Rogan, Joseph 118
Roman Catholics 57, 65, 88–92
Rosclogher, Barony 22, 23
Roscommon, Barony 22, 23, 55
Roscommon, County 18, 19, 26, 36, 40, 73, 88, 94, 108, 115, 118, 122, 124
Roscommon, Poor Law Union 20, 21, 126
Roscrea, Poor Law Union 20, 21
Ross, Barony 22, 23, 76, 78, 95, 96
Russell, Lord John 132

Salaman, Redcliffe 68
Salt North, Barony 22, 23
Salt South, Barony 22, 23
scarlatina see disease
Scarawalsh, Barony 22, 23
Scarriff, Poor Law Union 20, 21, 126
Schull 106
Shanid, Barony 22, 23
Sheep see livestock
Shelburne, Barony 22, 23
Shelmaliere East, Barony 22, 23
Shelmaliere West, Barony 22, 23
Shillelagh, Barony 22, 23
Shillelagh, Poor Law Union 20, 21
Shillelogher, Barony 22, 23
Skibbereen, Poor Law Union 20, 21
Skibbereen, Town 107, 208
Skreen, Barony 22, 23
Skull, Poor Law Union 20, 21

Slane Lower, Barony 22, 23
Slane Upper, Barony 22, 23
Slievardagh, Barony 22, 23
Slievemargy, Barony 22, 23
Sligo, County 18, 19, 26, 36, 51, 65, 94, 108, 113, 122,
    124, 133, 134
Sligo, Poor Law Union 20, 21, 126
Sligo, Town 28
Smallcounty, Barony 22, 23
Smallpox see disease
Society of Friends 88–9, 93, 106, 128–31
Solar, Peter 15
soup kitchens 65, 129, 135–7
St Mullin's Lower, Barony 22, 23
St Mullin's Upper, Barony 22, 23
starvation 65, 90 104–5, 106–9
Strabane, Barony 22, 23
Strabane, Poor Law Union 20, 21
Stradbally, Barony 22, 23
Stranorlar, Poor Law Union 20, 21
Strokestown, Poor Law Union 20, 21
Strule, Barony 22, 23
Swineford, Poor Law Union 20, 21, 126, 136

Talbotstown Lower, Barony 22, 23
Talbotstown Upper, Barony 22, 23
Temporary Relief Act 130, 136
Thomastown, Poor Law Union 20, 21, 128
Thurles, Poor Law Union 20, 21, 126
Thurles, Town 28
Tiaquin, Barony 22, 23
Tinnahinch, Barony 22, 23
Tipperary, County 18, 19, 45, 51, 61, 113, 116, 124,
    133, 194
Tipperary, Poor Law Union 20, 21, 112, 126
Tipperary, Town 28
Tiranny, Barony 22, 23
Tirawley, Barony 22, 23
Tireragh, Barony 22, 23
Tirerrill, Barony 22, 23
Tirhugh, Barony 22, 23
Tirkeeran, Barony 22, 23
Tirkennedy, Barony 22, 23
Tobercurry, Poor Law Union 20, 21
Toome Lower, Barony 22, 23
Toome Upper, Barony 22, 23
Tralee, Poor Law Union 20, 21
Tralee, Town 28, 105
Trevelyan, Sir Charles 134
Trim, Poor Law Union 20, 21, 126

Trough, Barony 22, 23
Trughanacmy, Barony 22, 23
Tuam, Poor Law Union 20, 21, 126
Tuke, James 129
Tulla, Poor Law Union 20, 21
Tulla Lower, Barony 22, 23
Tulla Upper, Barony 22, 23
Tullamore, Poor Law Union 20, 21, 126, 136
Tullamore, Town 28, 113
Tullygarvey, Barony 22, 23
Tullyhaw, Barony 22, 23
Tullyhunco, Barony 22, 23
Turner, Michael 193, 194
typhus see disease
Tyrone, County 18, 19, 55, 67, 88, 89, 118, 120, 124,
    133, 197

Ulster 16, 18, 27, 44, 108, 109, 113, 124, 126, 133, 136,
    137, 147, 163, 178, 194, 198
Uppercross, Barony 22, 23
Upperthird Barony 22, 23
Upperwoods, Barony 22, 23
urbanisation 16
Urlingford, Poor Law Union 20, 21

vaccination 122
Vitamin deficiencies 65, 110–12

'wage good' 67
wages 16, 133, 134, 141–3
Warrenstown, Barony 22, 23
Waterford, City 22, 23, 28, 76, 89, 95, 124, 130, 144, 147
Waterford, County 18, 19, 61, 74, 77, 96, 113, 124
Waterford, Poor Law Union 20, 21, 126, 130
Westmeath, County 18, 19, 40, 51, 94, 113, 120, 122, 133
Westport, Poor Law Union 20, 21, 126, 136, 137
Wexford, County 18, 19, 36, 50, 69, 75, 109, 113, 116
Wexford, Poor Law Union 20, 21, 136
Wexford, Town 28, 109
wheat see crops
Wicklow, County 18, 19, 73, 89, 113, 116, 120, 124, 197
Wilde, Sir William 15, 68, 104, 105, 106, 111, 112
Woodham-Smith, Cecil 15
workhouses 60, 65, 109

Youghal, Poor Law Union 20, 21
Youghal, Town 28